HEART OF ATLANTA

HEART OF ATLANTA

FIVE BLACK PASTORS AND THE SUPREME COURT VICTORY FOR INTEGRATION

RONNIE GREENE

Lawrence Hill Books

Chicago

Published by Lawrence Hill Books
An imprint of Chicago Review Press Incorporated
814 North Franklin Street
Chicago, Illinois 60610
ISBN 978-1-64160-527-4

Library of Congress Cataloging-in-Publication Data
Names: Greene, Ronnie, author.
Title: Heart of Atlanta : five Black pastors and the Supreme Court victory for integration /
    Ronnie Greene.
Description: Chicago : Lawrence Hill Books, [2022] | Includes bibliographical references and
    index. | Summary: "The Heart of Atlanta Supreme Court decision stands among the court's
    most significant civil rights rulings. In Atlanta, Georgia, two arch segregationists vowed to
    flout the Civil Rights Act of 1964, the sweeping slate of civil rights reforms just signed into
    law by President Lyndon B. Johnson. The Pickrick restaurant was run by Lester Maddox,
    soon to be governor of Georgia. The other, the Heart of Atlanta motel, was operated by
    lawyer Moreton Rolleston Jr. After the law was signed, a group of ministry students showed
    up for a plate of skillet-fried chicken at Maddox's diner. At the Heart of Atlanta, the
    ministers reserved rooms and walked to the front desk. Lester Maddox greeted them with
    a pistol, axe handles, and a mob of White supporters. Moreton Rolleston refused to accept
    the Black patrons. These confrontations became the centerpiece of the nation's first two
    legal challenges to the Civil Rights Act. In gripping detail built from exclusive interviews
    and original documents, Heart of Atlanta reveals the saga of the case's rise to the U.S.
    Supreme Court, which unanimously rejected the segregationists. Heart of Atlanta restores
    the legal cases and their heroes to their proper place in history."— Provided by publisher.
Identifiers: LCCN 2021036402 | ISBN 9781641605274 (cloth) | ISBN 9781641605298 (mobi) |
    ISBN 9781641605281 (pdf) | ISBN 9781641605304 (epub)
Subjects: LCSH: Heart of Atlanta Motel—Trials, litigation, etc. | Pickrick (Restaurant)—
    History. | Discrimination in public accommodations—Law and legislation—United
    States—Cases. | Civil rights—United States—Cases. | African Americans—Civil rights—
    History—20th century. | African Americans—Georgia—Atlanta—Biography. | Atlanta
    (Ga.)—Race relations—History—20th century. | BISAC: HISTORY / African American &
    Black | BIOGRAPHY & AUTOBIOGRAPHY / Political
Classification: LCC F295.N4 G74 2022 | DDC 305.896/0730758231—dc23
LC record available at https://lccn.loc.gov/2021036402

Typesetting: Nord Compo

Printed in the United States of America
5 4 3 2 1

To the civil rights pioneers,
Known and unknown,
Who risked their bodies,
To preserve our soul

and

To Brian, my brother, and Karen, my sister,
and in memory of Kelly.

When day comes we step out of the shade . . .
For there is always light,
if only we're brave enough to see it.
If only we're brave enough to be it.

—Amanda Gorman, "The Hill We Climb"

CONTENTS

PROLOGUE

A Presidential Plea, a Legal Fight Alighted

PRESIDENT JOHN F. KENNEDY PEERED into the television camera, youthful and solemn, prepared to address a nation charred by the blaze of racial discord. It was June 11, 1963, and the president was about to deliver his most significant civil rights speech. Earlier in the day, the Alabama National Guard, federalized by the commander in chief himself, had escorted two Black students through the doors of the white-columned University of Alabama, seven years after the school's first Black student departed amid death threats and riots. Alabama governor George Wallace had vowed to stand in the doorway to block any would-be Black students from rebreaking the color barrier, but that day a brigadier general delivered the president's orders to open the Tuscaloosa campus to all races. Wallace begrudgingly stepped aside. Five minutes later, James Hood, donning a dark suit and fedora, and Vivian Malone, wearing an elegant light-colored skirt and top, each twenty years old, strode peacefully through the doorway Wallace had just abandoned. Five months earlier, the southern governor's fevered inaugural speech had drawn full-throated support from his Alabama constituency: "I say segregation now! Segregation tomorrow! And segregation forever!" Today Wallace's searing rhetoric was cooled

1

by the power of federal law and the persuasion of the nation's highest elected official.

"I hope that every American, regardless of where he lives, will stop and examine his conscience about this and other related incidents," the president told the country on Tuesday evening.

The next week, Kennedy announced, he would present to Congress a package of civil rights reforms targeting discrimination in public education, public facilities, and voting rights. A significant new provision would bar private hotel and restaurant owners from turning away customers based on race. "Segregation forever!" had just been unwound at the state-operated University of Alabama. Kennedy would seek to unwind discrimination still rooted in private businesses across the country. No longer would the proprietors of local motels, diners, and movie houses be left to set their own standards regarding the customers permitted to walk through their doors.

The president described nothing less than a massive rewriting of the nation's civil rights laws, and the slate of proposals he sent forth the next week to Congress would represent, in their sweep of scope and their specific detail, the most exhaustive reshaping of the nation's rules on racial relations since the Emancipation Proclamation had been issued a full century earlier. For decades the US Congress had resisted meaningful civil rights reform, shooting down and shooing away nearly every call to enact laws requiring equality in housing, restaurants, and voting booths, and leaving protesters little choice but to take their demands for change directly to the nation's private businesses and public streets.

Nearly a year before Kennedy's first day in the Oval Office, a lunch counter sit-in movement had taken root nationwide. The protests began peacefully in Greensboro, North Carolina, on February 1, 1960, when four Black students from the North Carolina Agricultural and Technical College took seats at the lunch counter at the downtown Woolworth's, an establishment that served White people only. The sit-in movement, minister and activist Fred Shuttlesworth instantly realized, might very well "shake up the world." Within two months, the Greensboro Four movement swept to at least fifty-five cities in thirteen states, with formerly all-White lunch counters, libraries, hotels, and beaches paralyzed by protest.

This press for equality in public accommodations extended fully into the Kennedy presidency, with sit-ins and pickets fomenting discord and disrupting the status quo in the South and the North. Protesters often faced arrest, beating, and jailing on charges of violating segregation edicts, disturbing the peace, or trespassing. Many stayed imprisoned rather than bonding out, using their jailing to protest the nation's discriminatory ways. As Southern jails overflowed with Black protesters, sheriffs could hear the incarcerated masses singing freedom songs.

In Kennedy's first year in the White House, Black and White Freedom Riders had been beaten with baseball bats and tire irons as they tried to integrate buses in the Deep South. In Montgomery, Alabama, racists pummeled Freedom Riders and knocked unconscious a White Justice Department (DOJ) official who came to their aid, with violence so ruthless the segregationist governor John Patterson was forced to impose martial law. A year later riots tarred the University of Mississippi after the US Supreme Court directed the Oxford campus to open its doors to Black applicant James Meredith.

And then in May 1963, Birmingham public safety commissioner Bull Connor unleashed his police attack dogs and aimed powerful fire hoses at thousands of Black demonstrators marching for integration, targeting even hundreds of schoolchildren drafted into the protest. Connor's jails instantly overflowed with thousands of demonstrators, who were locked up for the crime of seeking to desegregate a city nicknamed "Bombingham" for all the Ku Klux Klan (KKK)–led bombings of Black churches and businesses. "You can never whip these birds, if you don't keep you and them separate," Connor charged in his whistling twang, with the word *birds* spewing from his mouth sounding like *boids*. "I found that out in Birmingham. You've got to keep your white and the black separate!" Empowered by their bigoted top cop, the city's segregating businesses posted signs saying, No Negro or Ape Allowed in Building.

Bull Connor's jowly scowl suddenly became the face of Southern resistance to the civil rights movement. Yet his racial rebellion backfired, with his barbarous methods finally spurring the federal government to action. "Police dogs tore into the march lines, and high-powered fire hoses knocked children along the pavement like tumbleweed. News photographs of the violence seized millions of distant eyes, shattering inner defenses," author Taylor Branch recounted in *Pillar of Fire: America in the King Years 1963–65.*

One month after Birmingham, President Kennedy would direct the federal government to put its might behind the protesters, who had long sought equal rights in Alabama and beyond, by enacting laws that would punish the offending hotels and diners and maybe even the sheriffs. "We are confronted primarily with a moral issue. It is as old as the scriptures and is as clear as the American Constitution," Kennedy said. The president never raised his voice nor stabbed fingers high in the air to drive home his message during the nearly fourteen-minute speech. He addressed a nation on edge, not with Wallace's fire-and-brimstone agitation, but with a stoicism decrying the "moral crisis" engulfing the country.

"It is a time to act in the Congress," he said. "I am, therefore, asking the Congress to enact legislation giving all Americans the right to be served in facilities which are open to the public—hotels, restaurants, theaters, retail stores, and similar establishments. This seems to me to be an elementary right. Its denial is an arbitrary indignity that no American in 1963 should have to endure, but many do."

Moments after the cameras dimmed, civil rights icon Martin Luther King Jr., who had privately pushed the president for two years to issue an executive order abolishing segregation, wired a telegram to the White House. The speech, the Reverend King told Kennedy, ranked among "the most eloquent, profound, and unequivocal pleas for justice and the freedom of all men ever made by any president."

Author Todd S. Purdum, who decades later chronicled the subsequent political battle in Congress over the president's civil rights agenda in *An Idea Whose Time Has Come: Two Presidents, Two Parties, and the Battle for the Civil Rights Act of 1964,* put the speech in its historical context: "Even from the distance of half a century, the words echo magnificently. On the night Kennedy first uttered them, they were lightning bolts in the summer sky."

Five months and eleven days later, on November 22, 1963, President Kennedy was assassinated in Dallas, Texas, at the age of forty-six.

When Kennedy beat incumbent vice president Richard Nixon to win the White House in 1960, he had vowed that new civil rights legislation "will be among the first orders of business when a new Congress meets in January" 1961, and he was swept into office with the support of more than 70 percent of the nation's Black vote. His signature address didn't arrive until twenty-nine months later, stirring civil rights organizations to question just how committed he was and emboldening critics who said the Massachusetts Democrat was more effective at winning the public's adoration than he was at securing actual change in Congress. As reformers waited for Kennedy to act, waves of protests, sit-ins, and violence consumed the country.

Not two months before Kennedy's national plea, Martin Luther King had been jailed in solitary confinement in Birmingham for the crime of demanding Black people receive the same rights as White people. Scribbling on scraps of newspaper and any other canvas he could find, the Atlanta minister penned a stirring call for action in his *Letter from Birmingham Jail*: "I cannot sit idly by in Atlanta and not be concerned about what happens in Birmingham. Injustice anywhere is a threat to justice everywhere," King wrote. "We know through painful experience that freedom is never voluntarily given by the oppressor; it must be demanded by the oppressed."

So on that June night, Kennedy was finally describing his White House blueprint for change. By the next morning the nation would awake to another reminder that continued inaction carried a lethal price.

In Jackson, Mississippi, National Association for the Advancement of Colored People (NAACP) field secretary Medgar Evers had returned home past midnight after meeting fellow activists who had launched voter registration drives and demanded school integration in the southern state. As Evers stepped from his car toward his house, carrying a stack of JIM CROW MUST GO T-shirts, a White supremacist's bullet punctured his back and sent him spiraling to the ground. His wife had watched Kennedy's address earlier that night. Now she awoke to the shattering of gunfire, and his family raced to him. "Please get up, Daddy!" his daughter pleaded. Moments later, Evers blurted out, "Turn me loose!" They were his last words.

The seeds of legislation John F. Kennedy planted just hours before would bloom into a lasting civil rights act approved by Congress after months of oft-bitter debate and delay and signed, finally, into law by his successor, President Lyndon B. Johnson, on July 2, 1964. "Its purpose is not to divide, but to end divisions," LBJ told the country upon signing the Civil Rights Act of 1964.

The act cast a multilayered net to trap racial bigotry, authorizing the attorney general to file lawsuits to enforce desegregation in public schools, approving the withdrawal of federal funds from programs practicing discrimination, and creating the Equal Employment Opportunity Commission to review cases of business inequality. In all, it included eleven separate segments—Title I through Title XI—under headings that ranged from Voting Rights to Desegregation of Public Facilities to Desegregation of Public Education to Nondiscrimination in Federally Assisted Programs.

Title VII, Equal Employment Opportunity, barred workplace discrimination based on sex, race, color, religion, and national origin and helped lay the groundwork two years later for the founding of the National Organization for Women. In 2020 the US Supreme Court issued a landmark ruling that gay and transgender people are protected under Title VII of the Civil Rights Act of 1964.

When the act was passed, its most groundbreaking and contentious provision was detailed under Title II, the section entitled Public Accommodations. That measure outlawed racial discrimination in hotels, restaurants, theaters, and other privately operated business hubs in cities and towns across the United States. The act would not apply to inns with five or fewer rooms in which the proprietor also resided, but it covered all other places of lodging. The Congress would employ the Commerce Clause as an ironclad defense against corporate racism: if you accepted customers and goods from across state lines, you fell under the act's Title II and could not, under law, turn away patrons because of their skin color.

"In short," the *New York Times* wrote in an editorial headlined A NATIONAL VICTORY after passage of the civil rights law, "the intention is to complete the task begun more than a century ago when Abraham Lincoln issued the Emancipation Proclamation. That act ended personal bondage for Negroes; the aim of this new historic measure is to end the second-class citizenship Negroes still occupy in the North as well as in the South."

Almost immediately—two hours and ten minutes after LBJ signed the law, to be precise—a segregationist Atlanta motel owner would legally challenge the president's right to dictate who could enter his business, the Heart of Atlanta motel. One evening later, a group of Atlanta ministry students would be repelled when they sought a seat at a city restaurant run by a future governor, a down-home establishment that for seventeen years refused to serve a single Black diner. In a flash, the battle over the Civil Rights Act of 1964 had alighted, with the courtroom saga playing out not in the courthouses of Montgomery or Selma or Oxford or Jackson, but in Atlanta, Georgia, marketed by its politicians as the "City Too Busy to Hate."

The Atlanta legal skirmishes would quickly find their way to federal court and then to the US Supreme Court, whose justices moved with dispatch to hear arguments and pass judgment on the Civil Rights Act of 1964 and its section on public accommodations. By year's end, the high court unanimously agreed the law passed constitutional muster, affirming the Kennedy blueprint.

The ruling further unraveled the Jim Crow system and cemented the power of Congress to regulate local businesses across the United States. The law's power remains in effect today, as unshakable as it was when issued more than five decades ago. It means any racial group can patronize any hotel or restaurant they want. The lunch counter sit-ins that lit a fire under Congress to act are now sixty years old and commemorated in the nation's museums.

The Supreme Court ruling's significance is now largely taken for granted, some legal experts contend, and *Heart of Atlanta v. USA* is only occasionally cited among the high court's most momentous decisions. The case goes unmentioned, or is barely noted, in several noteworthy books examining the 1964 law and civil rights struggles of the time. It is not featured in the nation's foremost museum devoted to civil rights and the Black community's quest for equality, the National Museum of African American History and Culture in Washington, DC.

"It is not a case that gets the level of attention of *Brown v. Board of Education*, but it is an important case because it transformed people's access to public accommodations," says civil rights scholar Rachel Moran, a distinguished professor of law at the University of California Irvine School of Law. "We now take for granted the ability for every person regardless of race to go to a restaurant or to a hotel. It really doesn't seem controversial anymore."

Also lost to history are a handful of Atlanta ministry students who sought a bed at the segregationist motel and a seat at the segregationist diner, only to be rejected from both establishments because of their skin color. The men were forced off the restaurant property by a pistol- and pickaxe handle–wielding Lester Maddox, who would rise to the Georgia governorship, and rebuffed in their bids to lodge at the Heart of Atlanta motel. The young ministers, devotees of Martin Luther King Jr.'s movement of nonviolent social justice, kept returning, putting their lives at risk in an unyielding quest for equal access. Their efforts proved instrumental to the government's courtroom victories in Atlanta and Washington. Yet these pastors, like the twin legal cases built in good measure from their testimony, are mere footnotes to the nation's civil rights story.

When I connected with the two surviving ministers, and the widow of a third, each was deeply moved by the prospect of restoring this seminal story to its proper place in history.

"You brought tears to my eyes," said Albert Sampson, one of the ministers, who now preaches in Chicago. "I've been waiting for this call all my life."

1

AN AWAKENING
IN ATLANTA

IN THE ATLANTA SUMMER OF 1964, a handful of ministry students huddled in their dorm rooms and absorbed President Lyndon Johnson's message that the country's new laws targeting hate and discrimination would heal, not divide. Some of the students would soon read every word of the Civil Rights Act of 1964, keeping a copy among their cherished readings, and their classroom and cafeteria conversations often turned to the question of race relations in their city and country.

The students had descended upon the tree-shrouded Atlanta campus of the Interdenominational Theological Center (ITC) to attain master of divinity degrees, studying under scholars and preachers and presaging future careers as pastors who would fan out and lead congregations from such varied places as South Carolina, Texas, Illinois, Georgia, Ohio, and beyond. Now, as the US government pressed to ban private industry discrimination at the very moment KKK killings haunted southern cities, the ministry students absorbed the civil rights lessons encircling them, in Atlanta and beyond. Compelled to action, the activist ministers decided to test the law themselves at local businesses long known for holding the line against integration.

They eyed two businesses in particular. One, the Pickrick restaurant, had been run for seventeen years by Lester Maddox, a tenth-grade dropout, die-hard segregationist, and soon-to-be governor of Georgia. Maddox treated his customers like kin in his bustling cafeteria, renowned for its skillet-fried chicken, small-town decor, and dirt-cheap prices. The other business in the ministry students' sights, the Heart of Atlanta motel, had operated for eight years under the stewardship of Moreton Rolleston Jr., an Emory University–trained lawyer who, like Maddox, barred Black customers from entry. His motel featured 216 rooms, two picturesque swimming pools, and an advertising slogan as the finest lodging from New York to Miami.

The businesses stood some three miles apart, the motel erected in the hub of bustling downtown two blocks from Peachtree Street, and the restaurant standing five blocks north of the Georgia Tech campus. Its proprietors shared a united segregationist vision. They would serve whoever they damn well chose. Black Americans could labor in the kitchen or tidy unkempt rooms, but they couldn't sit at one of the Pickrick's cozy four-top tables or jump off the Olympic-height diving board from the Heart of Atlanta, an eight-minute drive away.

Maddox's was a spreading and divisive voice in Atlanta. Twice defeated in his bids to become the city's mayor, primarily because Atlanta's expanding Black vote had turned unconditionally against him, Maddox each Saturday took out ads in the Atlanta newspapers entitled "Pickrick Says." Far more than a listing of his food specials for that week, the "Pickrick Says" ads shared the proprietor's sharp-tongued meditations as his city and nation underwent a civil rights reckoning, and they became required reading for like-minded Atlantans. "BECAUSE OF THE COMMUNIST inspired racial agitators and the unGodly and unConstitutional [sic] legislation that they helped to get through my United States Congress, my business and I are threatened with the loss of our liberty and freedom," he charged in one ad.

The previous June, shortly after President Kennedy's call for laws to punish segregating businesses, fifty Atlanta eateries had voluntarily agreed to drop their racial roadblocks. That pact followed a contentious two months in the city, with one hundred college students, representing a group called the Committee on Appeal for Human Rights, detained by police on trespassing charges amid sit-in demonstrations of downtown restaurants. Lester Maddox responded to his peers' move to integrate by resigning from the local restaurant association and saying its representatives should have instead "been protecting the members from desegregating." Earlier that year, during the January inauguration ceremonies for Georgia governor Carl Sanders, Maddox had flown a banner plane overhead. EAT SEGREGATED, it said. GO PICKRICK.

Moreton Rolleston didn't book weekly ads or fly banner planes to address society's ills, and he never sought the mayor's perch, but he spoke his mind with his own brand of assertiveness and intractability. As the wave of congressional mandates began flowing down from Washington, DC, to local businesses like his, Rolleston offered a firm line of defense. "This is the end of the line," he told reporters. Rolleston exuded an air of professionalism, for himself and his resort motel, standing for photos in his razor-sharp suit and tie, his gleaming swimming pools framed in the background.

Maddox and Rolleston braced for integrators in Atlanta as the nation's local news pages filled with stories of racial hatred, fighting, and fatalities. In Liberty, Mississippi, a Black small-timber business owner was shot in the face after witnessing a segregationist state official kill a local NAACP director and deciding to tell the truth of what he had seen. In Jacksonville, Florida, White supremacists shot a mother of ten in the stomach because they wanted to, in their own words, "get a nigger" amid race riots in the city. In Meadville, Mississippi, the KKK beat two Black teens nearly to their deaths, then tossed their still-breathing bodies into the waters to suffocate. In Saint Augustine, Florida, a motel owner raced to splash acid into the swimming pool after both Black and White people jumped in. In Cleveland, Ohio, a young White reverend was crushed to death by a bulldozer as he lay in its path to block construction of a segregated school.

The Atlanta of the early 1960s could boast that it never experienced the bloody racial violence of southern cities in its neighboring states of Alabama and Mississippi. Yet this southern stronghold seethed with its own instances of racial friction in the 1960s.

By 1971 *Ebony* magazine would dub Atlanta the "Black Mecca of the South," writing that "black folks have more, live better, accomplish more and deal with whites more effectively than they do anywhere else in the South—or North." And indeed, forceful civil rights activism had sprouted in the city by the 1960s, no more visible than through the visage of Atlanta-born Martin Luther King Jr., who returned to the Ebenezer Baptist Church as copastor with his father in 1960. Another anchor of racial activism, the Southern Christian Leadership Conference (SCLC), planted its roots in Atlanta in 1957 when five dozen ministers and civil rights pioneers huddled in the city and vowed to redeem "the soul of America" through nonviolent protest throughout the South. King was elected the first president of the SCLC, which began with minimal funds or success but by the early 1960s had become engaged in student sit-ins and the Freedom Rides for integration.

The city had long been an anchor for Black colleges, with the hallowed names of Morehouse and Spelman and Clark all moored there, helping Atlanta build and sustain a thriving Black middle class. Many of its members turned out to the bustling Auburn Avenue commercial district, which was so filled with industry and entertainment it was once described as "the richest Negro street in the world." Martin Luther King Jr. was born on Auburn Avenue and would open the SCLC headquarters on the same street three decades later. In the 1960s the avenue hummed with commerce and music, with sharply dressed men and women in their finest dancing dresses turning out to the Royal Peacock club to hear crooner Sam Cooke, the King of Soul, perform.

Progress had been achieved in Atlanta, but it had come haltingly, coursed with casualties and racial indignities. In 1960 Black citizens couldn't ride in White taxicabs as city schools, lunch counters, and shops remained segregated. Paula Young Shelton, the daughter of future Atlanta mayor Andrew Young, wept as a child when her family was turned away from a just-opened Holiday Inn restaurant in the city. "We stepped into the fancy lobby with chandeliers hanging from the ceiling, and we asked for a table," she wrote. "But they wouldn't let us in."

Shelton later said her parents tried to shield their children from the most blatant racism in the city by avoiding clearly segregated stores, movie houses, and public transportation. But even as a child she experienced the racial dividing line in Atlanta. In elementary school, one White teacher refused to call her by her name but instead referred to her as "the little girl with the natural," a reference to her Afro hairstyle. The Youngs moved into the Cascade Heights neighborhood in

Southwest Atlanta, becoming the second Black family in the community, and the child paid witness as White flight began to take off. "White folks started leaving, and Black folks started moving in, and the demographics changed drastically," she recalls. Her father's social justice activism would attract brothers and sisters in the movement to converge in Atlanta, and Shelton says many visitors lodged with the family because Whites-only hotels would not accept them. "There were always people sleeping on our living room floor, but I really felt like this was our extended family, and I think that was one of the things that allowed us to thrive in Atlanta," says Shelton, now an educator and writer. "You did have that community of activists."

Those activists began pushing back, demanding equal footing with White residents. In March 1960, one month after the Greensboro Four sit-in movement, a collection of college students placed an ad in the Atlanta newspaper under the heading "An Appeal for Human Rights," saying they refused to "wait placidly" for equal rights. "We want to state clearly and unequivocally that we cannot tolerate, in a nation professing democracy and among people professing Christianity, the discriminatory conditions under which the Negro is living today in Atlanta, Georgia— supposedly one of the most progressive cities in the South," they wrote.

That year dozens of Black university students went away to jail for ten days after trying to integrate the restaurant at the city's Terminal Station amid citywide demonstrations against all-White eating establishments. As Black residents pressed for lunch sit-ins, White patrons sometimes fought back, once spraying protesters with a mysterious mist as activists tried to order lunch at Woolworth's and Newberry's in the city.

Another prime target was the Rich's department store, which served Black customers but on less equal terms than its White clientele. Black patrons could not try on a pair of shoes before buying them. Those who needed to use the restroom had to go down to the basement to find the grimy facilities there, and Black customers were not welcome in the store's exclusive Magnolia Room restaurant. Outraged by the double standard, in the summer of 1960, the Student Nonviolent Coordinating Committee (SNCC), led by Julian Bond, held sit-ins and told Black customers to destroy their Rich's charge cards. Martin Luther King Jr. was among those arrested in a sit-in that October after he sought service at the Magnolia Room, bringing media attention to the movement in Atlanta. "If by chance, your honor, we are guilty of violating the law please be assured that we did it to bring the whole issue of racial injustice under the scrutiny of the conscience of Atlanta," King wrote in a wire-bound notebook, preparing his statement before the judge after his arrest. "I must honestly say that we firmly believe that segregation is evil, and that our southland will never reach its full economic, political and moral maturity until this cancerous disease is removed."

The city earned notoriety for peacefully integrating its public schools in 1961, when nine Black students entered all-White schools without a single catcall or fisticuff, though the groundwork for that moment had been laid by an NAACP lawsuit that had forced the city's hand and by a federal court order in 1959 that had declared the Atlanta schools segregated and unlawful and ordered the system to enact an integration plan. Even as Atlanta's image glowed with a school desegregation that drew only scattered dissent in the city, less attention was focused on the racial slurs White students hurled at their new Black classmates once the cameras went away. Years before the school fight, Black residents had been forced to go to court to demand equal play on golf courses in the city. Atlanta's Black population rose up in protest in 1962, when Mayor Ivan Allen Jr., otherwise viewed as a staunch supporter of civil rights, tried to cool racial tensions by ordering a three-foot barricade be built to discourage Black homeowners from expanding into an affluent White community; three months later, a judge ordered the barrier, nicknamed Atlanta's Berlin Wall, torn down.

By the early 1960s, influential figures in Atlanta's White business establishment, in a nod to the Black community's growing influence and demands, agreed to open the doors of some of the city's busiest hotels and eateries to all races. "Most of the business community, because they are about making profits, came to the conclusion that 'we're going to have to work with this, or our businesses aren't going to be viable anymore,'" says Deirdre Oakley, a professor of sociology at Georgia State University who studies urban social issues. "You had some holdouts and racial violence."

Paula Shelton shares that assessment. "Because there was a Black middle class and a Black activism, my dad always said it was economics that really drove the White community in Atlanta to be more cooperative," she says. "And it really came down to the White business community realizing this wasn't a moral issue or a social issue. It was an economic issue."

Activists sought deeper change. By November 1963 a coalition of nine civil rights groups demanded Atlanta move at a brisker pace to desegregate all of the city's businesses and improve housing, employment, and education for Black residents. "Atlanta's race relations image needs considerable improvement," the coalition wrote.

The most volatile events arrived two months later, as more than three hundred demonstrators were arrested as they waged a citywide campaign to integrate restaurants and hotels. In January 1964, KKK supporters clashed in a confrontation with members of the Student Nonviolent Coordinating Committee and the Committee on Appeal for Human Rights during a sit-in at Leb's Restaurant, a downtown eatery continuing to serve only White customers. The melee was so disruptive the Atlanta Restaurant Association took out full-page ads saying the city had placed too much pressure on local restaurants to integrate, and the mayor pleaded for a monthlong cooling-off period from demonstrations. His call went unheeded.

The Reverend Jesse Jackson, the South Carolina–born Baptist minister and civil rights activist who rose to stand side by side with Martin Luther King Jr., said it was no surprise Atlanta had become a hotbed for activism, with its stout supply of Black colleges, bustling transportation thoroughfare, and thriving working class. "The middle class tend to lead a revolution because they are upwardly mobile aspiring people," Jackson said in an interview. "Atlanta was a natural place of activism."

"All roads met in Atlanta," Jackson continues. "Atlanta was the place where you could have a cover for your struggle."

The city's inhabitants, Jackson explains, carried with them a "pent-up quest for dignity." Even as the Black community could point to gleaming lights of success, from its university graduates to its expanding stock of homeownership, it also for decades lived a life of second-class status, barred from Whites-only eateries, hotels, and shops.

"Atlanta," Jackson says, "was the centerpiece of joy and pain."

Atlanta has long been viewed as racially progressive, but in the 1960s, tension escalated. In 1962 an NAACP activist pressed for equality amid a KKK rally. *AP*

As the pastors in training set out to integrate the restaurant and motel that summer of 1964, the headlines in the Black-focused *Atlanta Inquirer* newspaper spoke to the discord still darkening the city's path to racial harmony:

PARENTS OF HANGED NEGRO YOUTH THREATENED; SUSPECT RACIAL MURDER

FUTURE LOOKS BLEAK FOR WIDOW OF POLICE-SLAIN NEGRO

FIVE LITHONIA, DEKALB POLICEMEN STOMP; DRAG WOMAN THEY FORCE FROM HOME

NEGRO MAN ATTACKED, KNIFED BY FOUR WHITES IN N. ATLANTA

$75,300 TO BEAUTIFY WHITE PARK; NO MONEY AVAILABLE FOR NEGROES

The newspaper, founded four years earlier, spoke to a growing body of readers fed up by injustices at the city's schools, businesses, and courts. Atop its front page, beside the *Atlanta Inquirer* nameplate, the newspaper declared, ON GUARD FOR HUMAN RIGHTS 24 HOURS A DAY with the words framed in a black box. Atop the other side of page 1, a similar box reminded subscribers, READ YOUR BIBLE DAILY AND GO TO CHURCH

SUNDAY. The *New York Times* soon dubbed the newspaper "the loud voice in Atlanta." Its followers embraced its call to disrupt the status quo.

In fewer than three decades, this Southern city of nearly half a million residents had turned from predominantly White to majority Black. In 1940, White residents comprised 65 percent of Atlanta's populace. By 1970 Black residents had nudged just ahead in the population count, comprising 51 percent of citizens in a racial majority that would continue to hold for decades.

Atlanta's population diversified, in part, through an influx of Southern families residing in rural enclaves in Georgia and other states who saw opportunity in one of the region's most commercially active hubs. As Black people shifted from Deep South agrarian labor to manufacturing and industrial jobs in Atlanta's urban core, their financial means expanded—and they became more likely to send their children to college and more engaged in their churches, two crucial centers of activism in Black communities. "If we look at the seeds of civil rights activism in the city of Atlanta, the Great Migration is also something that is very important," says Andra Gillespie, an Emory University associate professor of political science specializing in African American politics. "That actually creates the type of social environment that is conducive to social movement organizing. They are going to get infused with new volunteers and new energy. So, you now have a cadre of Blacks who are better off socioeconomically."

Atlanta's Black population also swelled as a number of northern businesses decided to relocate south to take advantage of a state with little organized labor, says Georgia State sociologist Oakley. "So you have factories leaving the big northern cities like Chicago and Detroit moving south, which created work opportunities down South," she explains. "So people from rural Georgia could move to the Atlanta area and make a lot more money."

This growing population was clustered more densely in Atlanta than it had been in sparsely populated rural pockets, with closer connections to schools, churches, and jobsites. Atlanta's Black neighborhoods were largely, though not exclusively, concentrated in the center of the city, surrounded by swaths of White to the north, west, and south. The Black middle class and upper class did expand its reach beyond the city core, as families such as the Youngs moved into formerly all-White strong-holds. But by 1965, Black people comprised nearly 44 percent of the city's residents yet occupied 22 percent of its landmass, author Ronald H. Bayor noted in *Race and the Shaping of Twentieth-Century Atlanta*.

"Everybody is in community and proximity together," Emory's Gillespie observes. "It really does create a special environment that allows for movements to happen."

Atlanta's emerging Black voice was hungry to quell discrimination that festered even as White residents slipped in the population count. Yet White people, everyone knew, continued to control the government, police, and municipal purse strings, operating from a seat of power that wouldn't fully change its racial dynamics until years later. In the early 1960s, the vast majority of Atlanta's parks, recreation centers, football fields, swimming pools, baseball diamonds, and tennis courts were situated in White communities. White tennis patrons could serve and volley on 119 courts set aside in predominantly Anglo communities. Black players had just eight such courts to turn to in their own neighborhoods. White residents had forty-one major parks from which to choose. Black communities had three. Most police officers were White, and not one of the twenty city of Atlanta department heads were Black later that decade, when the *Atlanta Constitution* conducted an assessment. "Although some blacks held jobs, by and large, they had no real power in policymaking and hiring, which in turn yielded no avenue to change policy," wrote author Maurice J. Hobson in *The Legend of the Black Mecca: Politics and Class in the Making of Modern Atlanta*.

One area where Black residents could make a difference was at the polls, and the percentage of the city's minority voting bloc rose astronomically. In 1945 Black voters comprised just 4 percent of the city's voting rolls. That figure shot up to 29 percent in 1961 and 36 percent five years later. For years advocates had launched voter registration drives targeting Atlanta's Black community, plastering flyers throughout neighborhoods with the message REGISTRATION DOES NOT COST A PENNY! The handbills distanced Atlanta from those Southern cities where first-time voters faced absurd questioning from registrars and even physical attacks from sheriffs bitterly opposed to giving Black citizens an election-day voice. Atlanta's handbills informed residents they would only have to answer straightforward questions about their name, age, and address, for instance, and would face no intimidation. YOU WILL RECEIVE COURTEOUS TREATMENT FROM THE REGISTRAR, the notices announced. REGISTER YOURSELF! TAKE ANOTHER TO REGISTER!

The campaign worked, in a massive way, with voter registration lines filled with Black laborers running into the hundreds outside the Fulton County Courthouse, the line snaking around a city block. Lester Maddox would experience the power of the Black vote when he twice ran for mayor, losing each time because the community was entirely against him. In 1965, Atlanta elected the first Black member to its Board of Aldermen since Reconstruction, the beginning of a larger tide that would eventually arrive.

But not until 1973 did the city elect its first Black mayor, Maynard Jackson, the son of a Baptist minister, in a vote viewed as a turning point not just for Atlanta but the entire New South. "Jackson's ascension embodied the rise of the city's black educational elite to new heights of political power. The legend of Atlanta as a 'Black Mecca' had gained new meaning. After waiting in the wings and biding their time for decades, now the black educated elite would rule," Hobson wrote.

Nine years earlier, in the summer of 1964, the fight for racial equality was fully engaged in the city's streets, churches, and schools. Dozens of Black parents and their children hoisted placards to protest a "fire trap" junior high school undergoing renovation, a school serving some 1,200 eighth graders residing in largely Black neighborhoods. Several of the men donned short-sleeved white shirts in the July sun, and many of the women wore summer dresses, their hair neatly coiffed in modest buns. Lining side by side in front of the Smith-Hughes Vocational School downtown, they decried the building as second-rate and unsafe, not up to par compared to schools filled primarily with White children. SEGREGATED SCHOOLS MUST GO! their handmade signs of protest declared. Midday, the protesters paused for prayer.

That same month, a fourteen-year-old Black boy named Jerry Maxey was found hanging from the limb of a large oak tree in a wooded section of northwest Atlanta that had been cleared to make way for a city Urban Renewal Program. The teen had been to the dentist that day, but never came home. By month's end, the medical examiner would rule his death a suicide. His parents believed he had been murdered. Their child, smiling broadly, with his dress shirt buttoned to the top button for his school photograph, worked at a hamburger stand after school and during summers. "Jerry wouldn't have killed himself," his dad said. "I don't believe it."

In another part of the city, a twenty-three-year-old Black father of three was knifed by four White men outside a package store on a late Friday evening. They attacked him, he said, for no reason beyond the color of his skin.

At the Interdenominational Theological Center dormitory, the ministers knew well they could be proselytizing their way into a physical confrontation of their own, even as they adhered to their friend and colleague Martin Luther King Jr.'s practice of nonviolent protest. The ministers had been visitors to the Reverend King's home, and regulars at his sermons inside the stout redbrick Ebenezer Baptist Church. King's message was that nonviolence was itself an act of courage, a refrain he shared most eloquently in 1968, the year of his death:

> On some positions, cowardice asks the question, is it expedient? And then expedience comes along and asks the question, is it politic? Vanity asks the question, is it popular? Conscience asks the question, is it right? There comes a time when one must take the position that is neither safe nor politic nor popular, but he must do it because conscience tells him it is right.

Following their consciences as they planned to integrate businesses staunchly opposed to their patronage, the preachers were convinced they were on the right path, backed by their faith and the law, the one just signed by the US president.

On the same evening Lyndon B. Johnson signed the act into law, Moreton Rolleston filed a lawsuit, *Heart of Atlanta Motel Inc. v. United States of America and Robert F. Kennedy*. He sought $11 million in damages. In a twisted irony, Rolleston later cited the Thirteenth Amendment, which abolished slavery in the United States, as part of his defense. The lawyer said Congress and the president were enslaving him by forcing him to take customers not of his choosing. Lester Maddox would invoke the same amendment in his own defense against the preachers' quest to integrate his diner. After Rolleston filed suit, two of the ministers sought rooms at his motel, telling the proprietor the Civil Rights Act of 1964 granted them access to his inn's accommodations. He turned both away.

On July 3, 1964, one day after Rolleston filed his lawsuit against the US government, three ministry students sought to order chicken from the Pickrick restaurant and Maddox. The proprietor stood ready for them. After the new civil rights law had advanced in Congress, Maddox had bought his first-ever handgun, and he had begun selling axe handles to his clientele.

As their car pulled into the restaurant parking lot that Friday evening, Maddox confronted the ministry students. When the driver went to open the door, Maddox aggressively tried to force it shut, then placed his pistol in the young minister's face. As the students began to leave, Maddox bashed their car with an axe handle. "I'll use axe handles, I'll use guns, I'll use paint, I'll use my fists, I'll use my customers, I'll use my employees," he shouted.

The students then huddled with lawyers accustomed to integration battles in a city that had grindingly fought public school desegregation before finally embracing it and had suddenly become the face of White opposition to the landmark 1964 civil rights legislation.

Six days after the Pickrick encounter, the ministers filed suit against Maddox and his restaurant. So, within one week of Lyndon Johnson's historic signing and plea for calm, the city of Atlanta had become the epicenter of the legal battles over the Civil Rights Act of 1964.

By year's end, both cases would turn against the businesses and in favor of congressional power, Kennedy's civil rights platform, and the ministers and other activists who had pushed to ensure it applied in their city. Rolleston, losing at every turn, would press his case all the way to a US Supreme Court led by Chief Justice Earl Warren. For a decade, the Warren court had ushered in a wave of social change for the country, issuing rulings ranging from *Brown v. Board of Education of Topeka et al.*, ordering the nation's public schools to desegregate, to

Gideon v. Wainwright, requiring localities to appoint legal counsel to defendants too poor to hire their own attorneys.

The Supreme Court quickly scheduled *Heart of Atlanta v. USA,* setting it for oral arguments just three months after Rolleston's lawsuit had gone to court, a rapid turnaround that showed how seriously the nation's highest court viewed the legal and social questions posed by the case. That December 14, 1964, the US Supreme Court unanimously ruled against Rolleston, affirming Title II of the Civil Rights Act of 1964 as legally sound in a 9–0 vote.

The ministry students who stood face-to-face with Lester Maddox and tried to spend a night at Moreton Rolleston's Heart of Atlanta motel are unheralded among the civil rights pioneers who risked bloodshed to ensure equality. As the Civil Rights Act of 1964 was framed by some of the most famous figures in American history, from John Kennedy to Lyndon Johnson to Martin Luther King Jr. to Earl Warren and Robert Kennedy, these activists stepped directly into the center of the strife. Yet their roles have been left outside the story's legacy. They're not in the picture.

They include the Reverend Albert Dunn, a Texan who had been arrested in the Freedom Rides of 1961 and was arrested again that year when, as a student, he joined a group of ministers seeking breakfast at the Atlanta Terminal Station restaurant. Among those agitating to integrate the Pickrick, Dunn was among the most passionate. He ignored Martin Luther King Jr.'s father's urging that the group not try to confront Lester Maddox, with Martin Luther King Sr. fearing the fracas would only draw more attention to the ardent segregationist. Dunn pressed ahead, only to have Maddox escort him off his property at gunpoint. At the ITC, Dunn kept his own copy of the Civil Rights Act of 1964.

And they include the Reverend Woodrow T. Lewis, the group peacemaker, who nonetheless turned out to order lunch from Lester Maddox, axe handles and all. As a younger ITC student, Lewis had been arrested in a downtown march for progress and, after leaving Atlanta, led protest marches urging more jobs for minorities and fought the closing of schools for Black children. Lewis was set in his career path since he stood atop his mother's living room stool at age twelve and began preaching sermons. He would go on to lead churches in his native South Carolina.

Also among them is the Reverend Albert Sampson, who overcame a childhood stutter to find a rich oratory voice and who, while in high school in Massachusetts, found himself in the library drawn to a "little yellow book" stressing nonviolent demonstration, written by Mohandas Gandhi. Martin Luther King personally ordained Sampson, who had studied at Shaw University in North Carolina, where he staged sit-ins, pushed to open doors of the state's White-serving hotels, and plotted strategy with another college student, his close friend the Reverend Jesse Jackson of North Carolina A&T College.

Another is the Reverend Charles Wells Sr., whose pastor father worked in the coal mines and who got into school scuffles while staring down prejudice in his hometown in Pennsylvania. As a teenager, Wells drew glares when he began dating a White girl, the daughter of the president of a city bank. He ignored the stares and kept on dating her. Wells later went on to lead boycotts from the pulpit of his Georgia churches, moving with the assured manner of a military man, as you'd expect of a former US Army first lieutenant.

And they include the Reverend George Willis III, who joined the army as a teenager to become a paratrooper and made a name for himself in the boxing ring, once upsetting the crowd in Yokohama, Japan, after securing a split-decision victory over his Japanese amateur opponent. It was Willis, nicknamed "Yellow Socks" in his boxing days, who faced the barrel of Lester Maddox's pistol while pulling up to the restaurant. Known to keep his voice measured even when angered, Willis would pastor at ten churches over fifty-two years, mostly in Texas. He kept a pen and paper in his pocket at all times, ready to jot down the messages when he felt the Lord speaking to him.

The ministers received counsel from a group of attorneys that included Constance Baker Motley, then a lawyer with the NAACP Legal Defense and Educational Fund in New York. As White males dominated the nation's courtrooms and judicial chambers, Motley was the rare Black female handling cases of significance, realizing a dream she had at age fifteen while growing up in New Haven, Connecticut. When the ministers sued the Pickrick and Lester Maddox, Motley sat before reporters to explain the meaning of the case, a regal figure exuding a command of the legal facts. She helped craft a courtroom strategy documenting how the Pickrick restaurant engaged in interstate commerce and unquestionably fell under the act, easily outmaneuvering the lawyers representing Maddox.

Motley broke barriers, time and again. She represented James Meredith in his successful quest to become the first Black student at Ole Miss, walking aside Meredith as they left federal court hearings surrounded by picketers decrying the effort to mix the races at the Old South university.

"I think Mrs. Motley is the most significant thing to happen in my lifetime, because without her I don't think there would have ever been a James Meredith going to Ole Miss," Meredith recently said.

Motley helped prepare the landmark *Brown v. Board of Education* Supreme Court case and would go on to become the first Black female elected to the senate in New York State and the first Black female appointed a federal judge. Her career path had launched at the NAACP Legal Defense Fund, where she met Thurgood Marshall, the civil rights groundbreaker and future US Supreme Court justice. The Pickrick lawsuit was among her last cases as an NAACP lawyer.

Like the students she represented, Motley was calm on the surface and fiercely determined below it. "She didn't seem to have any fear in her," the Reverend Lewis recalls. "I would admit her being a woman lawyer in that time was surprising to me. She mannered herself in such a way that she got us through this. She was a Black woman in this position up against primarily all White men."

Motley died in 2005. Like others, her role in the Atlanta case is little known.

Today just two of the ministers are alive, the Reverends Lewis and Sampson.

When I reached him in South Carolina, Lewis was stunned by my phone call and deeply moved when I later sat down with him in his home and shared video archives and documents from a legal saga sometimes relegated as a footnote to the civil rights movement. One piece of video footage, kept as part of the Walter J. Brown Media Archives & Peabody Awards Collection of the University of Georgia

Special Collections Library, shows Lester Maddox violently repelling four sharply dressed Black men from his restaurant early in 1965. The archives identify just one of the four men, Charles Wells. When I sat down with Lewis in South Carolina in 2019, he identified the other men: himself, Albert Dunn, and George Willis.

Lewis was viewing the footage for the first time. "Lester had vowed he would not serve Negroes," Lewis said to me. "We were adamant we were going to integrate his restaurant and make his words a lie."

I reached Sampson in the summer of 2019, tracking him down in Chicago, where he has been a neighborhood pastor and community organizer for decades. He wore an "I Have a Dream" wristwatch with Martin Luther King's image displayed in the center. Coretta Scott King gave him the watch a year after her husband's death, he says. In Chicago he exuded the air of a neighborhood politician, greeting comers and goers as he ate lunch one afternoon downtown in 2019. At age eighty, he was nattily dressed in a monogrammed yellow shirt.

The Reverend Albert Sampson, who pushed to integrate Atlanta businesses in the 1960s, became an activist pastor in Chicago. *Photo by Sara Stathas*

During our first chat, when I told Sampson I was an author retracing the events in Atlanta of fifty-five years earlier, he took a moment to collect his thoughts. Like others who risked personal harm to shatter the nation's color divide, he worried the legal fight was dissipating from the public's memory. Sampson believes the quest to open Atlanta's doors to all races had an impact that stretches beyond the Supreme Court's ruling that places of public accommodations cannot discriminate. In a larger sense, he said, the rulings signaled to minorities that they have a legal right to fully partake in the world of commerce.

"This is the most important story in Black history because it opened the door to commerce," Sampson says. "Commerce says you can go and participate in the economy. And can't nobody bother you."

2

LESTER MADDOX:
"STAND UP FOR AMERICA"

LESTER GARFIELD MADDOX WAS BORN in Atlanta in 1915 and raised on "the other side of the tracks," he would write decades later, "in the shadow of the steel mill where my father worked in Atlanta, and our family never quite got out from under that shadow—literally and figuratively—throughout the years my brothers and sisters and I were growing up. We lived in a section of the city known as Tech Flats, where Mom and Dad raised chickens and had milk cows and a vegetable garden to supplement the income from the mill."

He was born the second son to Flonnie and Dean Maddox, and his family would grow to nine: Mom, Dad, four boys, and three girls. "Mouths to feed, though, meant hands to work, and there was little time for idleness. When the mill whistle blew my brothers and I were waiting at home to help Dad as soon as he arrived, and Dad never believed a child with good hearing had to be told twice what was expected of him. If a reminder was needed, it came in the form of an ever present bundle of hickory switches and a trip with Dad to the barn," Maddox recounted in *Speaking Out*, his autobiography.

His family lived on State Street and, around the corner, eight to ten Black families resided on Crawford Place. Black and White children mingled in the community without fanfare or fisticuffs, Maddox said, "perhaps because we did so by choice and not by decree."

Tensions were more likely to surface inside the home, with his father returning from work late most paydays and weaving under the weight of whiskey. "I think I sensed, even as a child, that Dad's alcoholism was rooted in the deep frustrations he must have felt. He had no formal schooling. His reading and writing were painful and laborious and he knew full well that he had reached the peak of his earning power as a roll-turner in the mill, and that even with all his moonlighting efforts, he would never be able to provide for his family as he would have liked. I suppose he had the misfortune of being a perfectionist without the means to carry it out."

His mother preached abstinence to her husband and took the children every Sunday to services at the North Atlanta Baptist Church on Tenth Street, dressing the brood in their nicest garments. Dad rarely showed up, but young Lester felt a pull to the Almighty. From an early age, he adopted his mother's fundamentalist worldview, absorbing lessons from a woman who closely studied biblical prophecy. Like his mother, he developed a distaste for alcohol and as an adult would never drink or smoke.

As a child Lester Maddox encountered challenges in school from the first grade, barely passing onto the second. Then one day he tripped over his raincoat and severely banged his forehead on an iron object on the ground, requiring stitches. His grades continued to plummet. An eye exam revealed he was acutely nearsighted, and the school suggested putting him in a special program for children with learning disabilities. When Lester visited the school and saw the books with giant print, he recoiled, begging his parents for another chance to stay in his school and ultimately securing his wish. When he was finally fitted with new glasses, the world opened to him in full color. "Never having had normal vision before, I had no reason to think the blurred images I saw were not as they should be. Now the buildings, lights, signs, people, everything up and down the street, stood out with startling clarity."

He continued his studies in his own school but never excelled in the classroom. Then his mother became seriously ill with goiter, forcing him to quit school for several weeks to help at the home until she recovered.

He finally went to high school, but Lester Maddox had already developed an entrepreneurial spirit.

By then his family's home was populated with cows, vegetables, hogs, and chickens, operating as a small family farm, and the teenager would string together a half-dozen broiled chickens, sling them over his shoulder, and knock door-to-door. "Yes ma'am," he'd declare. "I've got six of the finest fryers that were ever grown, and I'm gonna sell all six of 'em to you for one dollar and twenty cents!" Many housewives would shoo away the skinny teen, but a few bought. He set up a soft-drink stand outside his house and tried his hand as a caddie. But Lester, feeling like a "sissy," didn't wear his glasses except when required to for classes, so he kept them off even as he caddied for golfers forcefully whacking the hard, little balls. One day a ball he didn't see coming plunked him right on the head, sending him tumbling to the ground and onto the hospital for more stitches. The youth retired from the caddie business.

He developed a knack for turning a dollar. As a boy, he got a job bagging peanuts whenever the circus came to town, earning three cents an hour. The peanuts sold in abundance, but Lester had little bounty to show for his labors. But then a brainstorm came over him. He would buy giant bags of raw peanuts at a produce market downtown, walk two and a half miles home and, with his mother's help, cook them on a woodstove, then walk the two and a half miles again back downtown to sell them by the bushel. "The extra effort netted me a dollar and a half for a fifty-cent investment, provided I did not burn or eat my stock," he observed. A career was taking shape.

Then the Great Depression hit, and his father took more deeply to the bottle, nursing grudges as younger, less experienced laborers were handed better mill work assignments than he secured. Soon Dean Maddox got into a fistfight with the mill boss. A pink slip followed, forcing the parents to scrounge for ways to feed a family of nine. His father hauled bricks for a while, and then his parents bought used washing machines for a few dollars apiece and opened their own community business doing laundry. They landed just a few customers. Many days, Lester said, he traipsed to high school with no lunch and shoes worn with holes.

He soon started playing hooky, looking to pocket a few cents sweeping out stores, until one day his father caught him downtown when school was in session. Back home they went, and Lester braced once more for the whacks of the hickory switch. His dad grabbed the makeshift weapon, which bears a resemblance to a whip but can punish with greater force. Dean Maddox stood still, unmoving, until he finally dropped the switch and walked away. His dad never said a word, but Lester surmised what was happening. How could the father punish the son for trying to make a buck?

Lester dropped out of high school in the tenth grade and launched a series of jobs, first as a delivery boy for a downtown jeweler, then as a worker at the Sixth Street pharmacy, and then as an apprentice dental technician. At every turn, he knew he didn't want to end up like his father. "America was *the* land of opportunity," he wrote. "I had my goal, I had initiative, and hard work never scared me. Now, with God's help, I was on my way."

His poverty-stricken, God-fearing formative years in Atlanta would forever shape Maddox's worldview. He saw the purpose and consequence of hard labor and by-your-wits ingenuity, experiencing how someone with nearly nothing could strive to make something. He believed that no one should tell a man how to live his life, particularly not the federal government, which had no business meddling into the affairs of private enterprise. When Lester Maddox stunningly rose to the Georgia governor's mansion decades later, a high school dropout who managed to outfox the political establishment with an equal portion of close friends and visceral enemies, he kept his door open for regular visits from the "little people." Through those doors entered laborers and ex-cons committed to God and redemption, men and women whose hardscrabble upbringing mirrored his own.

———————

Not long after dropping out of high school, Maddox was walking down the street in 1933 when he spotted a girl with dark brown hair and blue eyes sitting on her bicycle outside an ice cream parlor. "She's the one!" he said to himself, without having met her. Maddox asked around and learned the girl was named Virginia Cox and that her family had just moved into the neighborhood. They met and courted, but Virginia would not accept her suitor's hand for marriage, at least not just yet. They needed to be more financially stable before stepping through the threshold of marriage, the young couple agreed. Lester landed work as an assistant plant foreman, earning $16 a week, and worked his way up to $19.75. Three years after his first glance at Virginia Cox, he married her in the spring of 1936 inside a preacher's home in Marietta, Georgia.

In one of his many jobs, Maddox for a while ran Lester's Grill, selling sandwiches and ice cream to neighborhood customers. Business began to grow, so much so that, years later, Maddox set out to run a restaurant on a much larger scale. On Hemphill Avenue near the campus of Georgia Tech, he eyed an unused plot of land and was surprised to learn he could secure a bank loan for the property.

Maddox knew he needed a new name, believing "Lester's Grill" was too pedestrian for the more expansive restaurant he envisioned. "Picnic at Pickwick," he told Virginia. "How does that sound?" Lester himself loved it and began dreaming of the Pickwick restaurant's grand opening.

But then he found the name Pickwick was already taken. He couldn't shake the first syllable, "pick," even looking it up in the dictionary to see it meant to select, to eat fastidiously. Thumbing through his dictionary, he ran across the word "rick," to pile up or to heap, to amass. The Pickrick was born, and a slogan with it. "You pick it out, we'll rick it up."

On December 7, 1947, the Pickrick doors swung open. Within a decade, Maddox reported, he would be serving nearly half a million customers a year. He boasted that his was the first restaurant in the city to offer free refills on coffee and tea, and he devised games to draw in customers and keep them returning. One time he offered fifty dollars to the family bringing in the youngest child for a meal. A young couple, on their way home from the hospital after giving birth, stopped by with their three-day-old girl to collect the bounty and sit for supper.

Maddox, a balding, bespectacled restaurateur once described as presenting the look of the neighborhood pharmacist and another time said to resemble "an angry chicken," greeted his regular customers like a family patriarch. During bustling lunch hours, he'd walk the one-story brick and timber restaurant in suit and tie, waving at tables filled with ladies in dresses on lunch break, young men stopping in for a hearty meal, or businessmen hitting their favorite daily spot. He worked the room as a folksy politician, extending his hand to thank customers for sitting down for a meal, saluting others who kept coming back, and leaning down to confide that these visitors, his faithful, were keeping him in business. "Is everything Pickrick?" he'd ask in his whistling high pitch. His Pickrick restaurant was home, the place he and his own family took most of their meals, and anyone he allowed in was family too. "Hi, boys! It's people like you who keep me going," he said.

His diner sold souvenir copies of the Declaration of Independence for thirty-five cents, with the items promoted for sale to "American Patriots." Customers could also pick up American flags, Confederate flags, and "Pickrick drumsticks," wooden axe handles Maddox began making available for sale when the Civil Rights Act of 1964 was passed. Maddox would sometimes step back into the kitchen himself, baking biscuits, preparing salads, frying chicken, and grilling steaks. He'd walk the length of his restaurant with a coffeepot in one hand and a water pitcher in the other, ready for refills.

Customers lined up at the food counter en masse, picking out their favorite pies, sweet teas, skillet chicken, chicken gizzards, and other mainstays, then paid at a cash register with an American flag draped nearby. Maddox's son would work the cash register, collecting one dollar and six cents from one customer and then ninety-eight cents from the next, and the assembly line of diners would make their way to cozy tables in a restaurant with a black parrot in a cage overhead whistling tunes, whistling at ladies, and mimicking words. As his faithful sat for their repast, Black workers, donning Pickrick white caps and work shirts, cleared the empty tables so the next round of diners could sit.

The tables were always full.

The customers were always White.

"I am a segregationist and I chose to operate my restaurant on a segregated basis," Maddox would explain later in life. "Because of this I was called a racist, although the words are far from synonymous. A segregationist is an individual—black, white, or any other color—who has enough racial pride and racial integrity and love for his fellow human beings to want to see *all* races protected and preserved."

His restaurant featured a segregation wishing well, where customers could toss coins and make a wish for segregation. The fountain glistened with nickels, dimes, and quarters, a heartening sight to a native enraged by the "race mixers" in Atlanta.

Maddox would repel any Black visitors trying to enter his restaurant, but he'd kick out White guests, too—if he somehow learned they were integrationists or "agitators" working for the American Civil Liberties Union or some other civil rights group. "My fight that I'm waging," he once testified, "is not against Negroes but for Negroes. If we were all Negroes and I was one of them, I would wage the fight I am waging today."

His back got up at the notion of the federal government or anyone else in politics telling him how to run his own business in Atlanta, Georgia. He'd fight those efforts with his fists and, if need be, firearms. He'd bristle at anyone telling him he couldn't follow his own path to liberty.

The Pickrick was known for its skillet-fried chicken. While Maddox allowed only White customers, he hired both Black and White employees to work his kitchen. *Kenan Research Center at the Atlanta History Center*

As his business expanded, he used the platform to espouse his political views through the weekly ads he booked every Saturday in the local *Atlanta Journal* and *Constitution*. The "Pickrick Says" ads featured a photograph of Maddox in suit and tie, and they ran thirteen and a half inches down the page and four inches across, a prodigious soapbox for the proprietor. For some in Atlanta, his ruminations were must-reads, the first newspaper column they'd turn to as they began their weekends. "Most people would get the Saturday paper, then go straight to the 'Pickrick Says' ad to see who Lester was lambasting in his column," one local political operative observed.

Again and again, he came back to the laws emanating from Congress dictating new rules to local businesses. "A GREAT TRAGEDY of our time is that public officials seeking votes, and business leaders seeking dollars, would use and misuse our negro citizens for their own selfish gains. They are nothing but renegades and scalawags," Maddox declared in "Pickrick Says." "BUSINESSMEN surrendering to the unconstitutional and socialistic 'directives' out of Washington, don't deserve to be in business."

In another "Pickrick Says" ad, placed in the Atlanta papers as the federal courts told him he was legally obligated to open his doors to all races, Maddox spread his message like a torch. He regularly filled his sentences with all-caps sentiments, the intensity and rage flowing through his fingers as he crafted his newest message to his faithful readers.

"AND IT IS A SAD DAY for Atlantans, Georgians and all Americans, that there is no top elected public official in the City of Atlanta, State of Georgia, or the U.S. Government man enough and American enough to fight back at the hoodlums, criminals, mobs and Communist-inspired racial agitators who are subjecting the lives and properties of law abiding citizens to robbery, violence, rape, destruction and death," he wrote. "GOD GIVE US MEN AND WOMEN IN HIGH PLACES WHO WILL STAND FOR GOD AND COUNTRY AND STAND AGAINST UNGODLY COMMUNISM."

The ad then noted that day's specials: roast young turkey with dressing, giblet gravy, and cranberry sauce for fifty-five cents; breaded veal cutlet and braised short ribs for the same price; the house special, skillet-fried chicken, for half a dollar.

"WE RESERVE, and will defend, our God-given American rights to accept or reject any customer," Maddox reminded his readers.

Another time, Maddox distributed a leaflet at his restaurant with a grave warning: "One drop of Negro blood in your family could push it backward 3,000 years in history," he told his patrons. Another leaflet featured a crudely drawn cartoon mocking interracial marriage, with the grandparents in the picture aghast to learn one grandchild was White and the other was Black.

At the Pickrick, he found a supportive audience for his bitter brand of race relations, with his clientele fully at home in the welcoming confines of his restaurant. "I know that in eating there I could enjoy my food, and I would be eating in a place where all of the customers were of my type and class and so forth," said an Alabaman who would stop by the Pickrick whenever he was in town. "It is a white restaurant so far as I know, and that is why I ate there."

Maddox led a firebrand Atlanta group opposing sit-ins and integration, called Georgians Unwilling to Surrender. The group's acronym, Maddox believed, captured the fortitude required to keep the races separate: GUTS. He would later form another group, People's Association for Selective Shopping, or PASS, which urged White people to boycott integrated businesses.

Not long before he married, Maddox had become interested in local politics, heading out to political rallies at the urging of his mill plant boss. With his "Pickrick Says" ads serving as his own political platform, and his income steady from his busy restaurant, he put his name in the hat for Atlanta mayor, seeking a formal pulpit from which to deliver his message.

Maddox based his political operations from inside the Pickrick, running for office initially as an independent and later as a conservative Democrat, seeking the mayor's seat in 1957 and again in 1961.

Along the way, he stepped into the scrutiny of the same Atlanta newspaper chain that had been running his weekly ads. "The real issues of the campaign were obscured in the Atlanta media. The Cox newspaper monopoly of the *Journal* and *Constitution* never let up in characterizing me as a racist and demagogue. They made no effort to distinguish between a segregationist—which I was then and am today—and a racist—which I was not then and never will be," he argued.

Maddox blanched at the media coverage. "They chose to look upon my conservative stand as a danger to the community rather than an effort to stand up for and protect the rights of the people I intended to represent—meaning *all* Atlantans," he wrote.

Lester Maddox engaged his media enemies at times with a vigor reminiscent of a future incendiary voice in American politics, dethroned President Donald Trump. The men were raised in worlds so disparate that, had they been born in the same era instead of three decades apart, they surely would have never crossed paths. While Maddox spent his youthful years laboring for dollars in southern poverty and dropped out of high school, Trump was born in the media capital of New York City, attended a private boarding school, and was, according to a *New York Times* analysis, a millionaire by age eight. Trump, brimming with braggadocio, exudes a domineering dismissiveness in his public appearances that contrasts with the mannered "Yes, sir" and "No, sir" Maddox employed in his most civil exchanges when fielding questions from reporters. Yet each espoused rigid, line-in-the-sand political views, and their respective rhetoric on race drove deep divisions among their constituencies.

"Southerners like me know the game Trump is playing. We have seen it, sadly, time and again. Trump is the rightful heir to Lester Maddox's ax handles and George Wallace standing in the schoolhouse door," Stuart Stevens, a writer and Republican political consultant, opined in the *Washington Post* in 2019.

Kay Willis, the widow of George Willis, one of the ministry students who was physically rebuffed from entering Maddox's restaurant, is among those who say the racial unrest triggered by a Trump presidency had resurrected painful memories. "It was a very sad time," Willis says of the struggles of the 1960s. "All this stuff is rearing its ugly head again. It's been hidden, but since he's been in office it's coming full circle."

The current discord was exemplified in 2017 in Charlottesville, Virginia, when a "Unite the Right" rally turned deadly, with a twenty-year-old

White supremacist plowing into a crowd of peaceful counterprotesters, killing thirty-two-year-old paralegal Heather Heyer and injuring dozens of others. Days later, the president enraged peaceful protesters when he said, "I think there's blame on both sides." And then in 2020 the fervor of the Black Lives Matter movement was stoked with the police killing of an unarmed Black man, George Floyd, in Minneapolis. "I can't breathe," Floyd said as a White officer kept his knee upon his neck for nine-and-a-half minutes. As protesters took to the streets, Trump employed the nation's military might to shut them down.

Long before Donald Trump, Lester Maddox viewed his opponents— the news media, agitators, activists, and politicians with views contrary to his own—as "the enemies of freedom, and the enemies of the American way of life." He hoisted handcrafted signs calling out foes and embracing friends, waging, when need be, a one-person free-enterprise demonstration. DOWN WITH JOHNSON, SOCIALISM, COMMUNISM, one of his signs said. UP WITH WALLACE, FREE ENTERPRISE, CAPITALISM, LIBERTY, PRIVATE PROPERTY RIGHTS, AMERICA.

Wallace and Maddox stood in political lockstep. The Alabama governor would heartily support his Georgia friend's subsequent bids for statewide office, and he and his first wife, Lurleen, posed for pictures with Lester and Virginia Maddox. When Lyndon Johnson visited Atlanta in May 1964, Maddox helped bankroll a banner plane carrying a WALLACE FOR PRESIDENT sign overhead as the president addressed the city. The same month, when sitting Georgia governor Carl Sanders opposed a visit to the state by Wallace, Maddox called a press conference to tell reporters Sanders had "slapped the faces of all patriotic citizens of Alabama and Georgia."

One of Lester Maddox's book chapters had echoes of Donald Trump decades before the then presidential candidate made "Make America Great Again" his mantra in 2016. Maddox titled his autobiography's chapter 13 "Stand Up for America" upon its publication in 1975.

Like Trump, Maddox punched back at his media critics. For years, one steady target was Ralph McGill, the Pulitzer Prize–winning publisher of the *Atlanta Constitution* newspaper, whose writings Martin Luther King Jr. had praised for their eloquence in his letter from the Birmingham jail.

Lester Maddox could count on hearty political support from Alabama governor George Wallace. Lester and Virginia Maddox, at right, pose with George and Lurleen Wallace. *Kenan Research Center at the Atlanta History Center*

"The ultra-liberal Atlanta *Constitution*, with McGill as publisher and his protégé Eugene Patterson as editor, never let up attacking Lester Maddox. To them I was a bigot, racist, and just about anything else they could think of to make me out as some kind of devil," Maddox wrote.

To call out the legendary journalists, he made his way down to the newspaper offices one day to see just how many Black employees he could find. Not many, he said, compared with the forty-five Black laborers he had on his own restaurant's staff of sixty-five at the time. "Everywhere I looked there were white faces, with only an occasional black pushing a broom," he wrote, relishing his findings. Maddox always sought the last word.

Maddox's son, Lester Maddox Jr., says his father pushed back against the press for good reason. "I think they treated him like they're treating President Trump now," the son told me one morning in August 2020 outside his Georgia home. "The liberal people."

His father's biggest fight was not with Black customers seeking a seat at his restaurant, he said, but at the notion of the government telling him what to do. "He didn't think the government should run the private businesses," Maddox Jr. says. "He was a strong Christian and he treated everybody fair."

Were he alive today, Lester Maddox would likely recoil at any comparison to Donald Trump or nearly any other leader in the modern American political world and would rail, in his relentless manner, against any effort to portray him as a one-note figure. His friends believe Maddox was unfairly pigeonholed by the racial fracas at his restaurant in 1964 and 1965. Those episodes, they say, revealed just a piece of his persona. To them, Maddox was a brutally honest businessman and, later, political office holder who never sugarcoated his views to please anyone and who spoke, as one colleague remarked, with a "childlike honesty" and "home-spun humor." Starting as a teen, Maddox would hop on a bike, sitting in the wrong direction, and pedal going backward, a signature move he would continue even as Georgia governor. When he rose to the governor's mansion, Maddox would surprise critics by hiring Black Georgians for state posts and ordering investigations to improve the state prison system. While visiting prisons across Georgia, he sang gospel hymns with inmates. "Serve your time," he told them, "then never come back."

"Few have accused Lester Maddox of being a suave, sophisticated man of culture. Yet, despite his lack of education, his poverty-stricken childhood and his unpolished personal style, he rose higher than most of his contemporaries who had those qualities," Bob Short, once a staff member on Maddox's gubernatorial campaign, wrote in a biography, *Everything Is Pickrick: The Life of Lester Maddox*. "He was the most honest politician I have ever known. Most political creatures weigh the consequences of every statement before they make it. Maddox didn't. He told the truth, as he saw it, regardless of the consequences."

In Atlanta, Maddox would pay the price for his hard-line stance against integrators, first in his bids for local office and then in the affairs of his restaurant. Even Short, in a complimentary assessment of Maddox's life and political tenure, conceded the pistol and pick handle episodes at the Pickrick would prove to be "an albatross around his neck for the rest of his life."

Though he helped him win the governor's seat, Short told me he disagreed with Maddox's fierce stance against integration. A former Atlanta journalist who worked for multiple Georgia governors and later the administration of Lyndon Johnson, Short says he was close with renowned civil rights leaders from Julian Bond to John Lewis. "I was on the other side of that issue, frankly," Short said recently, recalling the Pickrick altercations.

Yet he found Maddox to be a fascinating figure, a man who, in many respects, seemed as if he were two people melded into one: the Lester Maddox who fought with his own hands to block Black people from his restaurant and the Lester Maddox who would open the doors of state government to the downtrodden and God-fearing inmates. "He could be the nicest, most polite, helpful, caring person that you would ever meet, and on the other hand he could be just mean as hell," Short says. "You never know what you get. I found him to be very bright and inquisitive and intuitive and educated far beyond his tenth grade."

Short believes the origins of Maddox's racial views were likely more personal than those for Trump, a man born into a world of elitism, class, and racial distinctions. For Maddox, the government decree that he integrate his business struck deeply against his core belief of personal liberty, and it targeted a home away from home he built essentially with his own two hands. "Maddox based his thoughts on race at the Pickrick because he saw that as an invasion to his property rights," Short says. "He violently defends his position, that position being that he had the right to his own property."

Maddox lost both of his bids for city mayor, in 1957 to William B. Hartsfield, the namesake of the Atlanta airport, and in 1961 to Ivan Allen Jr., who earlier that year as president of the Chamber of Commerce had pushed White business leaders to desegregate city lunch counters.

In his first race, Maddox went head-to-head with Hartsfield among White voters, but still lost 41,000 to 24,000 because the city's Black voters went entirely against him. Hartsfield won 98 percent of the vote in thirteen mainly Black precincts. Four years later, Maddox and Allen both curried support among White voters, but Allen garnered nearly every Black vote, outgunning Maddox among that constituency by a stunning margin of 31,000 to 125, helping him cruise to a decisive win with 64 percent of the votes. "If blacks had not voted, Maddox would have won 35,919 to Allen's 33,089," author Ronald Bayor observed in *Race and the Shaping of Twentieth-Century Atlanta*. The 1961 election came amid a racial awakening in the city, with schools integrating and the local Chamber of Commerce and Black church leaders coming together to urge an end to segregation of downtown businesses. The Atlanta tide was clearly against a restaurateur who refused to join this civil rights movement. Maddox summed up his loss by saying he had "beaten everybody but Martin Luther King." Allen, in a striking contrast, would hold a dinner honoring King three years later after the spiritual leader was awarded the Nobel Peace Prize.

Maddox also ran for state lieutenant governor in 1962 and lost once more, though the run helped expand his name statewide beyond just the city of Atlanta. Never forgetting his political enemies, Maddox vowed to block members of the White establishment in his crosshairs from dining at his restaurant. "If I should see somebody like Ivan Allen or Ralph McGill or somebody like that come into my door, I would rush out there faster than I did" when Black activists tried to enter, he once said.

In a diversifying Atlanta, Lester Maddox's political reach was limited by race and his undying segregationist beliefs. As in his restaurant, his political support was essentially Whites-only. His soapbox, he saw, would have to continue to blare from his restaurant, not from City Hall or through any local ordinances he could usher through via the perch of public office.

In short order, a handful of Atlanta ministry students would try to puncture the racial divide and challenge the notion that Lester Maddox could choose who stood in line for a plate of food at his popular cafeteria.

The men had never met Maddox, nor had they made the acquaintance of Moreton Rolleston, proprietor of the Atlanta motel that also shut its doors to Black customers. Disciples of Martin Luther King Jr., the students would endeavor to become the first Black customers to walk through the Pickrick's doors and sit down for plates of ribs, turkey, chicken, and peach pie, and the first Black patrons to lay their heads upon the beds of the Heart of Atlanta and jump into the soothing waters of its shimmering pools.

3

KING'S LESSONS, AND BLOODSHED IN THE SOUTH

THE SEMINARY STUDENTS PREPARED TO CHALLENGE the Atlanta segregationists after having paid witness as their brothers and sisters in the movement had been beaten, burned, arrested, kicked, and killed for the offenses of being Black and demanding equal rights under law with White people. And they proceeded by carrying on the wisdom of their mentor, King, and his preaching of nonviolence. Even as your oppressors punch, pummel, and bludgeon, King urged, do not strike back. Let your nonviolence speak to the righteousness of your cause. Across the country his supporters underwent nonviolence training, practicing how to maneuver their bodies when the fists began to fly. Not everyone adhered to King's methods, with some in the movement saying pacifism served as a meek reply to bullies. The Atlanta preachers saw meaning in the method. Several of them were among the masses who had descended upon the nation's capital on August 28, 1963, for the March on Washington for Jobs and Freedom, and there they embraced King's dream of racial equality.

Two months after President Kennedy's national address, and one hundred years following President Lincoln's Emancipation Proclamation freeing slaves from bondage, the justice march drew more than two hundred thousand souls preaching, singing, and agitating to end the slavery still shrouding the nation. As the crowd filled seemingly every patch of ground from the Lincoln Memorial to the Washington Monument, they locked arms as they walked and hoisted placards demanding change in a nation still waged in a bloody race war. "We shall overcome someday," sang Joan Baez.

From the steps of the Lincoln Memorial rose "the moral leader of our nation" and the final speaker of the day, King, copastor of Atlanta's Ebenezer Baptist Church. As King took to the lectern, he looked out upon a throng of Black and White and of young and old blanketing the National Mall, marchers who traveled by bus, train, plane, car, and foot to form an army of racial resistance on this eighty-three-degree day filled with open skies.

Albert Sampson, the former ministry school student then leading the Atlanta chapter of the NAACP, listened intently to King's words, commiserating that afternoon with Andrew Young, the future mayor of Atlanta, and John Lewis, the Freedom Rider who would become a Georgia congressman. Lewis, then just twenty-three and chairman of the Student Nonviolent Coordinating Committee, rose to the stage with a forceful call for justice. "To those who have said, 'Be patient and wait,' we have long said that we cannot be patient. We do not want our freedom gradually, but we want to be free now! We are tired. We are tired of being beaten by policemen. We are tired of seeing our people locked up in jail over and over again," he demanded.

Ministry student Woodrow Lewis was there, too, having taken a charter bus down from New York, where he worked a summer job in a restaurant, to join the marchers. Lewis could only get so close to hear the speakers among the assembled throng, and he had to strain to catch a glimpse of King. Yet Lewis found the Atlanta reverend's "eloquent, profound, spiritually fulfilling" words so moving he could barely sleep on the charter bus back to New York, and he felt a renewed enthusiasm to engage in civil rights activism.

"But one hundred years later," King preached, "the Negro still is not free. One hundred years later, the life of the Negro is still sadly crippled by the manacles of segregation and the chains of discrimination. One hundred years later, the Negro lives on a lonely island of poverty in the midst of a vast ocean of material prosperity."

King's speech from the DC mountaintop, rhythmic and impassioned, moved his masses like a church sermon. *All right*, the people responded. *My Lord*. As the civil rights leader's cadence rolled forth in lyrical, rising waves, his audience sat in rapt attention, like parishioners inside his Atlanta church.

"This is no time to engage in the luxury of cooling off or to take the tranquilizing drug of gradualism," he implored. "Again and again, we must rise to the majestic heights of meeting physical force with soul force." *My Lord. Yes*. "We will not be satisfied until justice rolls down like waters and righteousness like a mighty stream." *Tell it. Amen!*

His crescendo building, King put aside his text and rode his spirit to his delivery's highest peak.

> I have a dream that one day on the red hills of Georgia, the sons of former slaves and the sons of former slave owners will be able to sit down together at the table of brotherhood. I have a dream that one day even the state of Mississippi, a state sweltering with the heat of injustice, sweltering with the heat of oppression, will be transformed into an oasis of freedom and justice. I have a dream that my four little children will one day live in a nation where they will not be judged by the color of their skin but by the content of their character. I have a dream today! I have a dream that one day down in Alabama, with its vicious racists, with its governor having his lips dripping with the words of "interposition" and "nullification," one day right there in Alabama little black boys and black girls will be able to join hands with little white boys and white girls as sisters and brothers.

Let freedom ring! King implored. *Let freedom ring!*

Through its thunderous support for change, the Washington march provided a seal of approval for the slate of civil rights laws President Kennedy had proposed to Congress. The marchers on Washington were pressing for a revolution, demanding, with their posters and chants and prayers, that the government's leaders finally frame that revolution with laws that would serve as a blunt-force instrument against supremacists and segregationists.

The proposed laws, then beginning a tortuous travel through the politicking halls of Congress, would target discrimination in schools, voting booths, and workplaces. A crucial new prong envisioned by Kennedy would grant Congress the power to tell local restaurants and hotels they had to swing their doors open to all customers. So long as those businesses accepted customers from out of state, they would lose the right to pick their clientele based on skin color.

Across the United States, the path to racial harmony remained pockmarked by lynching and bombing. Less than one month after King's speech imploring an end to hatred in Alabama, four young Black girls, eleven-year-old Denise McNair and fourteen-year-olds Addie Mae Collins, Carole Robertson, and Cynthia Wesley, were killed in a bomb blast at Birmingham's Sixteenth Street Baptist Church. The attack was conceived and executed by four members of the Ku Klux Klan, Robert E. "Dynamite Bob" Chambliss, Bobby Frank Cherry, Herman Frank Cash, and Thomas E. Blanton Jr. The bombing was an act of racial terrorism, targeting a church that had long been a meeting place for civil rights sermons and strategy sessions. The killers planted sticks of dynamite under the building's stairs, and their bomb detonated that Sunday morning, taking the young girls' lives on September 15, 1963. "This tragic event," King said, "may cause the white South to come to terms with its conscience."

On January 31, 1964, a Black man named Louis Allen was found sprawled upon his driveway in Liberty, Mississippi, with the left side of his face nearly blown off from shotgun blasts. Allen had run a small timber business in town and had scant involvement in the civil rights movement. Three years earlier, however, he had witnessed Eugene Hurst, a segregationist state legislator, fire his pistol at local NAACP leader Herbert Lee, killing him at the Westbrook's Cotton Gin. Local police pressured Allen to say the NAACP leader was armed with a tire iron and that Hurst had acted in self-defense. "You saw that piece of iron, didn't you?" a deputy sheriff pressed him.

Allen initially succumbed to the pressure, telling the Federal Bureau of Investigation (FBI) he "decided it was best for his welfare to lie and state that he had seen a tire iron," Justice Department records say. Later, he agreed to tell the truth to the FBI and a grand jury. When he learned he would be granted no protection, he opted against taking the witness seat. But word of his talks to federal authorities spread, and even though Hurst, who had professed self-defense in the shooting, was never prosecuted, Allen suddenly found himself losing business and harassed by police. A deputy sheriff, the son of a local KKK leader, later broke Allen's jaw in 1962. The night before he planned to flee town, Allen was gunned down, with his son discovering his body in the family's driveway. The deputy sheriff who had led the arrest campaign against Allen was assigned to investigate his death. No charges came.

Two months later in northern Florida, the city of Jacksonville had exploded into a race war. Black protesters picketed at hotels and restaurants in an emphatic push for equality, with their demonstrations choking the city's streets. On March 22, 1964, the city mayor deputized nearly five hundred firefighters to quell these "hit and run" groups, and the race war was instantly more fully lit, with ten Black churches bombed overnight. More than 140 people, all of them Black, were arrested for protesting in Jacksonville's streets.

As the fires burned, four young White Jacksonville men the next day drove to a Black neighborhood. "Let's get a nigger," one of the men said. On the evening of March 23, a thirty-five-year-old Black mother of ten, Johnnie Mae Chappell, had walked to a local store to get ice cream for her children. When she got home, she realized she lost her wallet along the way and began retracing her steps, joined by two neighbors. As they searched for the wallet, they heard a loud pop as a dark sedan sped by. "I've been shot," Chappell cried out, clutching her abdomen and falling to the ground on the shoulder of US 1. At the hospital, she was pronounced dead on arrival.

Only one man, J. W. Rich, twenty-one years old, went to trial. Rich admitted firing the fatal shot but told police "the gun was fired by accident." In December 1964, Rich was convicted of manslaughter and sentenced to ten years in prison. He ended up serving three years for killing Johnnie Mae Chappell, who was buried in an unnamed cemetery choked with weeds.

In May 1964 in Meadville, Mississippi, two nineteen-year-olds, Henry Hezekiah Dee and Charles Eddie Moore, were abducted by members of the Ku Klux Klan as they hitchhiked. The KKK drove the teens to a national forest, taped their mouths shut, and began beating them with sticks as another member trained his shotgun at them. The KKK members then stuffed Dee and Moore in the trunk of the car, drove to an offshoot of the Mississippi River, and tossed their still-alive bodies into the waters, weighted down by items including the engine block of an army jeep.

Authorities had only found the lifeless bodies of Dee and Moore because they were searching for three civil rights workers who had gone missing in Philadelphia, Mississippi, named James Earl Chaney, Andrew Goodman, and Michael Henry Schwerner.

Schwerner, who was White, and Chaney, who was Black, worked for the Congress of Racial Equality, or CORE, a civil rights organization in Meridian, Mississippi, committed to adding Black voters to the rolls. Goodman, also White, was among hundreds of college students who descended on Mississippi that "Freedom Summer" to support voter registration, education, and civil rights drives. The KKK "reviled" Schwerner, Justice Department records say. "Indeed, the killing of Schwerner was a routine topic discussed at Klan meetings attended by both Meridian and Philadelphia Klansmen, but Klan orthodoxy prevented such action unless authorized by the state Klan leader," the Justice Department report said. Finally, "state Klan leader Sam Bowers gave that authorization."

On June 21, 1964, Schwerner, Chaney, and Goodman visited the charred remains of a church burned out by the KKK. As they drove back to the CORE offices in the organization station wagon, Neshoba County deputy Cecil Ray Price pulled them over at about 3:00 PM for allegedly speeding. Price, himself a KKK member, escorted them to the Philadelphia jail, booking Chaney for speeding and the other two men for investigation, "ostensibly in connection with the church arson." He then informed Edgar Ray Killen, a Klan leader, that the three young men were in custody.

Finally, about 10:30 PM, Price told Chaney to pay a twenty-dollar fine and released the young men, telling them to "see how quickly they could get out of Neshoba County." As the activists headed south on Highway 19 for the forty-mile drive toward Meridian, two carloads of

Klansmen followed them, one in a 1958 Chevrolet and the other in a Ford. Deputy Price, driving his official patrol car, joined the pursuit and, after a high-speed chase, caught up with Chaney, Schwerner, and Goodman as they turned off Highway 19. He forced them into his patrol car as another Klansman took the wheel of the CORE station wagon.

The mob drove to a darkened side street. There, they shot each man, then drove their lifeless bodies to a farm, where they deployed a bulldozer to bury Chaney, Goodman, and Schwerner in an earthen dam. A massive FBI manhunt found the bodies on August 4, the ghosts of Mississippi resurrected with them.

As he and his seminary school brothers watched as even children became casualties of the nation's racial venom, Woodrow Lewis says the pain was so profound it took a physical toll. "The killings were very, very, very sad and disheartening. Hurting. But at the same time, it gave us that drive to keep on going and to keep on trying to strive to do more," he says. "It didn't knock us down," he adds, but inspired them to push more forcefully for equal rights. "We had that drive and that nerve and that impetus to keep on going."

The ministers were further driven to action as business owners answered integration attempts by poisoning the waters of racial togetherness.

On June 18, 1964, forty miles south of Jacksonville in Saint Augustine, Florida, Black and White protesters heeded Martin Luther King's call to integrate local businesses by gleefully jumping into the Whites-only pool at the Monson Motor Lodge. As they splashed in the water, the motor lodge proprietor poured a jug of acid into the swimming pool. That spring, King and his Southern Christian Leadership Conference had targeted the North Florida hamlet in a concerted drive to disarm color barriers in the nation's oldest city. White supremacists responded by spraying gunfire on the house the SCLC had rented for King. Then the civil rights icon and another activist Baptist minister, Ralph Abernathy, were among those arrested for trying to dine at the Monson Motor Lodge on June 11. Now, one week later, the acid flowed in a caustic attempt to contaminate the Saint Augustine movement for equality.

One day later, on June 19, a full year after the late president's plea for new legislation, the US Congress finally passed the Civil Rights Act of 1964. In that fateful year, evidence of the law's need had been etched all season in blood.

4

A REVOLT HATCHED
IN A SEMINARY

At the Interdenominational Theological Center in Atlanta, the ministry students had been left numb by the assassination of John F. Kennedy, with their campus closed for several days of introspection after the president was gunned down by a sniper's rifle while driving in a motorcade in Dallas.

The students likewise had been haunted by the murder of Medgar Evers, the Mississippi NAACP field leader who had been shot down in his driveway by White supremacist Byron De La Beckwith in the early morning after JFK's nationwide civil rights address. Then the ministers watched as two all-White juries were unable to convict Beckwith, despite considerable evidence of his guilt. At one trial, Mississippi governor Ross Barnett, who had just left office, shook hands with Beckwith, leaving the unmistakable impression the weight of state government stood with the killer. Three decades later, with Evers's widow Myrlie pushing for justice, and with Jackson, Mississippi, *Clarion-Ledger* journalist Jerry Mitchell reporting how a state agency had helped Beckwith screen jurors at his earlier trials, local authorities and the FBI reopened the inquiry. Beckwith was convicted of Evers's murder and sentenced to life in prison, where he would die. Thirty-one years after Evers collapsed in a pool of blood in his driveway, in a killing that shifted the arc of the nation's civil rights movement, a conviction had arrived.

The Atlanta students' school, the ITC, had been founded in 1958 as a joint initiative of four different seminaries that were subsequently brought together under one campus that included a chapel, cafeteria, dorm rooms, and classrooms. The theological center merged the Baptist-affiliated Morehouse School of Religion, the United Methodist–affiliated Gammon Theological Seminary, the Christian Methodist Episcopal Phillips School of Theology, and the Turner Theological Seminary of the African Methodist Episcopal church. John D. Rockefeller Jr., son of the nation's first billionaire and himself a wealthy philanthropist, provided crucial funding for the school to open its doors in September 1959, shortly before his death. In its maiden class, the theological center counted twenty-one faculty and ninety-seven students.

That summer of 1964, amid course offerings including the Psychology of Religion, Contemporary Theology, and Pastoral Counseling, a cluster of students studying under the Turner AME wing of the master's program huddled over their cafeteria lunches and in their dorm rooms to discuss what steps they should take to ensure the nation's new civil rights laws were evenly applied.

"It was a sad time," says one of the men, Woodrow T. Lewis. "As students there, we were very adamant about making changes. We were kind of militant. We were young, we were strong, we were abrasive, and we wanted to get out and do something and fight for the right of our own Black citizens. We could hardly believe what was going on, the atmosphere of the people, the White Ku Klux Klan."

Lewis was compelled to act after passage of the national civil rights bill. "I felt we should do something to break the ice," he says.

Two of his ITC brethren, Albert Dunn and George Willis, pushed the group to patronize an establishment long known for holding the line on integration: the Pickrick restaurant owned by Lester Maddox. Dunn pressed ahead even as Martin Luther King Sr. urged him to stay away from Maddox and his contentious core of supporters.

"He didn't want to give Lester the publicity," Dunn would recall years later, in an interview with the *Atlanta Journal-Constitution* on the three-decade anniversary of the civil rights law's passage. "But we

Woodrow T. Lewis pushed for racial equality while an Atlanta seminary student in the 1960s. *Courtesy Interdenominational Theological Center*

thought Daddy King was just being an Uncle Tom. We were young and unafraid, and we wanted to take on that beast."

In many respects, the young ministers personified Lester Maddox's deepest fears. Disciples of the Reverend King Jr., they, like their mentor, dressed formally when they conducted the affairs of civil rights, donning suits and sports jackets. And like King, they viewed the fight for equality in a religious framework. Black voters had single-handedly destroyed Maddox's two bids to become mayor, and the failed candidate blamed King and his followers for those losses. The ministry students, then, represented King's flock to Maddox, and they readied to press against the one principle he held most dear: his right to operate his private affairs any way he wanted. Maddox would never serve Black people in his restaurant. He'd fight like hell before he'd allow civil rights agitators close to Martin Luther King to integrate his business.

Lewis and another schoolmate, Charles Wells, immediately agreed to join Dunn and Willis. They would take on the beast. "Dunn, Willis,

Wells, and I were all classmates. We flocked together closely," Lewis says. "We could relate because we were from the same denomination."

Albert Dunn, short, stocky, and prone to bouts of sweating, was a veteran civil rights demonstrator who had been arrested in Jackson, Mississippi, during the Freedom Ride protests of 1961. In Atlanta he emerged as a forceful voice. He was a religious man who was not shy to confront others, including his schoolmates. "He was always grounded in challenging us to live up to our faith. And don't play preacher," says Albert Sampson, a onetime seminary student at the ITC. "His thing was you can't play preacher."

Willis was equally adamant but preached a nonviolent strategy in the fight for racial harmony, though he had stood toe to toe with opponents in the ring. "He always made us try to understand, the color of your skin had nothing to do with how the Lord created you. We have to be forceful in our rights, but we don't have to be brutal," says his widow, Kay Willis.

Ever studious, George Willis stood ready to jot down sermon ideas whenever they came to him. "He always kept a pen and pencil in his pocket," Kay Willis says. "Whenever the Lord gave him a message, he wrote it down." When someone did George Willis a kindness, he'd often respond with three successive thank-yous. "Thank you, thank you, thank you," he'd say. Kay Willis has found herself at times repeating the same six-word appreciation.

Soon Dunn and his three schoolmates would invite Al Sampson, their former ITC classmate, to join them knocking on Lester Maddox's door. Sampson, in turn, would join Wells in seeking to spend an evening at the Whites-only Heart of Atlanta motel operated by Moreton Rolleston Jr.

The students were filled with vigor, but as they cast plans to eat food and rent rooms at White-only establishments, they reminded themselves of King's preaching. They would set out to integrate the businesses, even ignoring King Sr.'s urging against confronting Maddox, but would do so in the nonviolent manner the civil rights leader had espoused.

Lewis moved forth with inspiration from King's sermon in Washington, where he absorbed one of the reverend's core pleas. "We must rise to the majestic heights of meeting physical force with soul force."

Classmate Willis would "sit at the feet of Dr. King" at Friday night sermons and consume his message, says his widow. "You learned from the master. That's where he got his stability. He said he was a servant," she says.

Challenging segregationists now with nonviolence promised to be a daunting task. Dunn, a veteran of Atlanta lunch sit-ins, was hungry to push back. Willis, likewise, felt an urge to stand up to his new opponents, and Wells, the tallest of the men and a veteran US Army first lieutenant, stood as an imposing presence in any setting. If we're going to do this, the group decided, we need to do it Martin's way.

"The emotions of our feelings were high, very, very high," Lewis says. "But at the same time, we were somehow kind of able to maintain our cool and calmness in the form of nonviolence, because we so often thought of his teachings."

Sampson shared his brothers' hunger to catapult the color barricade in Atlanta establishments and says King's vision guided them. According to Sampson, "he was a thinker. Dr. King said it's either nonviolence or nonexistence. Nonviolence is another chemical that puts out the fire."

The Atlanta ministers felt emboldened by the civil rights law passed by Congress and signed by President Johnson. Sampson believed the law presented itself as a shield, protecting the men as they designed plans to visit the Pickrick restaurant and the Heart of Atlanta motel.

"I'm in a situation where I have the law on my side," Sampson said recently. "It's comfortable for me. We had to make sure we were in a strong moral position, because if we were to die or live, we would do it with no fear."

An adopted son raised in Massachusetts, Sampson stuttered as a child but worked so hard to surmount his speech impairment he would go on to win an oratory contest in high school. While a high school student north of Boston, he was drawn to the idea of nonviolent protest, and he then put his views into action as a student activist at historically Black Shaw University in Raleigh, North Carolina. At Shaw, he took part in lunch counter sit-ins while serving as president of the NAACP Youth & College chapter. Sampson was also among a group of college students who shadowed state legislators for one week in North Carolina, studying bills and attending hearings alongside, among others, Jesse Jackson, the student body president and quarterback at North Carolina A&T.

Yet even as the students acted as legislators in the state capital, many hotels would not allow them to stay in Whites-only establishments, forcing the Black students to lodge at Baptist Shaw or another historically Black college, Saint Augustine's University, also in the state capital of Raleigh. "They wouldn't let Black students in North Carolina go to any of the White hotels," says Sampson, who was taken aback by the double standard confronting the students: come and help us write bills, but don't think of crossing the color line in hotels right next to the statehouse. "When I look at Jesse, it started right there," Sampson says of his fellow activist.

Jackson and Sampson cemented a friendship that week that would last a lifetime, so much so that Sampson became godfather to Jesse Jackson Jr. Both would go on to preach from Chicago. Jackson describes Sampson as a "dynamo," a persuasive orator who reminded him of the charismatic longtime California politician Willie Brown. "Al Sampson is a force to be reckoned with," Jackson says.

Their social consciousnesses stirred, the North Carolina college students pressed a bill that session opening public accommodations to all customers, regardless of race.

"We watched the bubble burst. We won the state legislature's debate," Jesse Jackson recalls. "The White students couldn't justify not letting us in the hotel. Al was so verbal and so prepared, and Al argued our case, brilliantly, really."

Sampson learned about Robert's Rules of Order while studying as a student legislator and saw that the law meant something. As a college student, he supported a voter registration drive to help elect the first Black councilman in Raleigh, a construction contractor named John Winters, in 1961.

After graduating from Shaw, he decided to enroll in the seminary to become an ordained minister. But activism and duty called, and he left the Interdenominational Theological Center and became executive secretary of the local National Association for the Advancement of Colored People. In that role, Sampson was once jailed overnight after protesting Atlanta's segregated marriage license bureau, and he also wrote columns as a staff member of the *Atlanta Inquirer* newspaper. Yet Sampson encountered friction with the local board overseeing the NAACP, which viewed him as being too aggressive in pushing a school desegregation matter, he said. The NAACP forced him and some other leaders out.

When that door closed, another opened. C. T. Vivian, a civil rights groundbreaker, lured Sampson to join the staff of Martin Luther King's Southern Christian Leadership Conference. "When they fired me," Sampson says, "C.T. hired me." There, as assistant director of chapters and affiliates, Sampson worked so closely with Vivian he would grow to view him as a father figure. They teamed up in Birmingham, Alabama, to help children who had missed graduating because of Bull Connor's mass jailing resume their schooling and earn their degrees. That effort, called Project Vision, would serve as a precursor to the Upward Bound program aiding poverty-stricken youth. As the SCLC's director of affiliates, Vivian stared down another infamous sheriff, James Clark of Dallas County, Alabama, drawing the local lawman's ire as he led an effort to register voters in Selma. When Clark turned away from him, Vivian uttered a legendary retort. "You can turn your back on me, but you cannot turn your back upon the idea of justice," he said. Clark later socked him in the mouth.

In Eutaw, Alabama, Sampson challenged squalid conditions at a school for Black students, which he said offered a chemistry lab without equipment and a library without books. One day he led a pack of students in a march toward the school for White students, which featured those and other amenities. A sheriff pulled out a long revolver and put it to his face. "If you make another move, Martin Coon, I am going to kill you," the lawman said, using the derogatory variation on the civil rights leader's name. Sampson glimpsed two FBI agents sitting in a blue Chevrolet watching the scene unfold, and he was chilled to see they were laughing. "I said to them, 'I don't understand what you're laughing about. He's got a gun to my head.' They said, 'Well, reverend, the reason we are laughing is it's kind of funny that we can't do nothing until he blows your head off.'"

"That gun had a long, long, long barrel," Sampson said. He turned to see the children watching the episode unfold, and with the gun still pointed at him, began to sing. *Ain't gonna let nobody turn me 'round, Turn me 'round, turn me 'round. Ain't gonna let nobody, turn me 'round. I'm gonna keep on a-walkin', keep on a-talkin', Marchin' on to freedom land.* He later helped desegregate the school.

At the SCLC, Sampson one day asked Martin Luther King to personally ordain him as a minister. Though Sampson had long felt a religious calling, he was not officially ordained after having left his studies at the ITC, meaning he could not baptize children or officiate at marriages. When he turned to King, he feared rejection. King set him at ease and conducted the ceremony. Being ordained by King, Sampson said, carries with it a "burden and a blessing."

The burden, he says, is that every time he faces a difficult life choice, he asks himself, "*What would Martin do?* The blessing is to have the legacy."

Since his youth, Sampson says, he felt a pull toward what he calls "social gospel responsibility." So, the Atlanta protests after the civil rights act's passage felt like a calling. "It was part of my movement history," he said. "Sit-in demonstrations in North Carolina. Coming to Atlanta, I had to speak out about all these issues."

That the civil rights law was ever passed, and that the young ministers stood poised to insist upon its application in the city of Atlanta, was a testament to shrewd politicking in the nation's capital. The pastors watched as southern Democrats, echoing the sentiments of Lester Maddox, Moreton Rolleston, and other segregationists, tried mightily to snuff out the bill, striving to suffocate it on the Senate floor with the oldest political trick in Congress.

5

FILIBUSTER, POLITICKING, AND THE VOTE THAT SAVED JFK'S PLAN

WHEN PRESIDENT JOHN FITZGERALD KENNEDY urged a national audience to embrace his package of civil rights reforms in June 1963, he pressed the Congress to act with urgency and harmony in helping heal a nation divided.

Five days after President Kennedy's assassination, a somber Lyndon Johnson stood before Congress to address a shocked nation. Johnson appeared in shock, as well, betraying a rare vulnerability as he delivered the first major speech of his presidency.

"My fellow Americans," he opened. "All I have, I would have given gladly not to be standing here today. The greatest leader of our time has been struck down by the foulest deed of our time." His voice choking, Johnson slowed his cadence, collecting his thoughts and his composure. "An assassin's bullet has thrust upon me the awesome burden of the presidency," Johnson admitted.

As president, Johnson said, Kennedy had dreamed of moving the nation forward domestically, had dreamed of tackling poverty, misery, mental illness, education, jobs, care for the elderly. "And above all a dream of equal rights for all Americans, whatever their race or color," Johnson said. From the memory of Kennedy, the nation must derive strength to act, "and act now." Johnson was pivoting from collective despair into a national call to action, astutely tapping into the well of support for Kennedy to urge the Congress to adopt his agenda.

"Our most immediate tasks are here on this Hill," Johnson said, his voice now gaining strength, and the applause now rolling forth. "First, no memorial oration or eulogy could more eloquently honor President Kennedy's memory than the earliest possible passage of the civil rights bill for which he fought so long. We have talked for a hundred years or more. It is time now to write the next chapter, and to write it in the books of law."

Johnson's address aimed to move the country forward amid its shared grief. Behind the scenes, away from the cameras, Johnson would tell anyone who would listen, and even those who hadn't asked, that he would use his ample political muscle and persuading savvy to put his predecessor's words into law and politick right through a congressional logjam that promised to stifle Kennedy's civil rights vision from being realized.

Lyndon Johnson's support was crucial to see the bill through. After Kennedy's death, the legislation could have withered amid the turnover in the White House. Without the new president's aggressive backing, the voices of dissent and delay would win out, and the old ways hold firm. In the evening before his speech honoring Kennedy, advisers had urged Johnson not to burn his political capital on a bill with an undecided fate, a bill whose passage could, in turn, prompt his adversaries to set out to block other administration platforms. "Well, what the hell's the presidency for?" Johnson shot back as the discussion spilled into the early morning hours, according to *The Passage of Power*, author Robert A. Caro's revealing chronicle of Johnson's ascent to the presidency after Kennedy's death.

By early 1964 Johnson was huddling with the chief lobbyist for the NAACP, assessing the political pulse for passage, and expressing optimism the bill would move quickly through the US House of Representatives.

"He thought the bill could and would be brought to the floor some time next week and enacted prior to the Lincoln Day recess," said a summary of a January 21 strategy session between Johnson and NAACP Washington lobbyist Clarence Mitchell. "The President said he wanted the bill passed by the House without a word or comma changed."

The NAACP lobbyist was equally optimistic. "Clarence assured the President that we would have our troops in Washington the week before the Lincoln Day recess helping get the bill passed," the memo said.

Another NAACP strategy memo, crafted March 5, 1964, described how supporters would marshal support in the US Senate. Democrats and Republicans alike were assigned as "floor managers" to gather backing in the Senate, with each politician focused on a specific element of the larger civil rights law. On the Democratic side, for instance, Washington senator Warren Magnuson would handle public accommodations and Michigan senator Philip Hart judicial matters. On the GOP side, New York senator Kenneth Keating would focus on voting rights, Nebraska senator Roman Hruska on public accommodations, Kentucky senator John Cooper on school desegregation, and New Hampshire senator Norris Cotton on nondiscrimination in federally assisted programs.

Yet in the halls of Washington, DC, bill supporters would find neither urgency nor harmony, and backers' optimism that the measure would move ahead unchanged proved out of touch with the political pulse of southern Democrats. Opponents tried, literally, to talk the Civil Rights Act of 1964 to death.

In the House of Representatives, the civil rights bill was choked off by sixty-four hours of debate and underwent 155 proposed amendments. Thirty-four amendments were approved, nearly all involving small technical details. Finally, on February 10, 1964, the bill passed by a 290–130 vote.

The path to passage was far more turbulent in the Senate, where southern opponents recoiled at the notion of the federal government telling local business owners how to run their affairs, mirroring the arguments of Lester Maddox, Moreton Rolleston, and other proprietors who said the US Congress had no right to dictate laws to private businesses. Opponents filibustered the bill on the Senate floor for sixty working days, beginning in late March.

Architects of the strategy of delay included Richard Russell Jr., a Georgia Democrat with powerful influence on the Senate's affairs, who had once compared the FBI investigation of civil rights cases to Adolf Hitler's use of the Gestapo; Strom Thurmond, a Dixiecrat segregationist from South Carolina who had stormed out of the Democratic convention sixteen years earlier to protest its platform on civil rights; J. William Fulbright, an Arkansas Democrat who would gain fame for his foreign policy acumen and his impassioned pleas to end the Vietnam War and who had founded the Fulbright Scholar Program, but who nonetheless stood against the Civil Rights Act of 1964; and Senator Sam Ervin, the self-anointed "country lawyer" from North Carolina who would gain renown a decade later for presiding over the televised Watergate hearings that helped usher Richard M. Nixon out of the White House.

Lyndon Johnson pressed to break through this blockade, targeting politicians from both parties he saw as slowing the bill's momentum. "Say to the Republicans, 'You're either for civil rights or you're not, you're either the party of Lincoln or you ain't,'" he charged. He got in the face of his former Senate mentor, Georgia's Russell, telling him, "If you get in my way, I'm going to run you down."

Bill opponents opened their congressional committees to take testimony from arch segregationist southern governors Ross Barnett of Mississippi and George Wallace of Alabama. Wallace insisted the bill would do nothing less than "destroy free enterprise." He spoke for swaths of supporters across the Deep South.

"That great American, Strom Thurmond, calls the bill 'the biggest grab for power in the history of Congress,'" the *Alabama Farmer* magazine publisher wrote in a column, "Straight Talk": "I intend to hire or fire anybody *because* of race, color, creed, sex or the way they part their hair. If I want to pursue my happiness by hiring only baldheaded, aboriginal idiots, that is my natural right, and I will be uncivil to all who try to deny it."

On March 18, 1964, with the national debate reaching peak intensity, Strom Thurmond took to CBS News to debate a bill advocate, Majority Whip Hubert Humphrey, a Democrat from Minnesota. Thurmond that year would flip parties, taking off his Democratic hat and becoming a Republican to support Barry Goldwater's disastrous bid for the presidency.

Humphrey was a persuasive orator, and he put his public speaking skills to work for the television camera and national audience. The bill's fate had become "one of the great moral challenges of our time," he said. "We know that fellow Americans who happen to be Negro have been denied equal access to places of public accommodation, denied in their travels the chance for a place to rest and to eat and to relax," Humphrey said. The bill "will make sure that no American will have to suffer the indignity of being refused service at a public place."

Thurmond acknowledged the debate moderator, CBS newsman Eric Sevareid, and his fellow senator. Then he disputed every one of Humphrey's points. "This bill makes a shambles of constitutional guarantees and the Bill of Rights," the South Carolina senator said. "It empowers the national government to tell each citizen who must be allowed to enter upon and use his property, without any compensation or due process of law."

The administration, he said, was trying to "railroad" the bill through Congress. "It was only after lawless riots and demonstrations sprang up all over the country that the administration, after two years in office, sent this bill to Congress, where it has been made even worse," Thurmond charged. "The choice is between law and anarchy," he closed. "What shall rule these United States? The Constitution or the mob?"

On one side of the stage, then, stood a bill proponent urging dignity for the oppressed and civil rights protections long past due. On the other side stood a bill opponent, who viewed many of those same people as being nothing more than part of a destructive mob. If the national division over civil rights could present its two faces, they stood there for all to see this night on the CBS stage: a progressive-minded push for change careening into an Old South brick wall.

Another filibusterer was Robert Byrd, a segregationist Democratic senator from West Virginia who had once led a local chapter of the Ku Klux Klan. Decades later, Byrd would apologize for striving to block the civil rights law and admit shame for his earlier ties to the KKK. But in 1964, on the Senate floor, he employed pure political gamesmanship to try to kill the bill. On the evening of June 9, 1964, Byrd took to the Senate floor to begin his talk. He didn't stop speaking until 9:51 AM the next morning, holding the bill hostage for fourteen hours and thirteen minutes.

Finally, bill advocates had had enough and conceived of a way to bust through the filibuster. Behind the scenes, Majority Whip Humphrey and Senate Minority Leader Everett Dirksen, a Republican from Illinois, had been plotting a careful strategy to break through.

President Johnson knew Dirksen's support was crucial to help convince other Republicans to step across party lines, help kill the filibuster, and send the package of civil rights reforms, finally, to the US Senate for a full vote. But Dirksen himself had reservations. While supporting the bill in broad strokes, he was particularly concerned about Title II targeting public accommodations, fearing the measure would go too far in invading private business rights.

"Now you know that this bill can't pass unless you get Ev Dirksen," Johnson told Humphrey. "You get in there to see Dirksen! You drink with Dirksen! You talk to Dirksen! You listen to Dirksen!"

To silence the filibustering politicians, Humphrey and Dirksen would need a two-thirds vote of the Senate, or sixty-seven votes from among one hundred senators. To reach that total, they'd have to draw support from dozens of members of the GOP. Dirksen rose as a defender of the bill, and, counting the votes, ticked off each member he needed to convince to come to their side.

Dirksen sought ways to make the bill more palatable to midwestern Republicans who were generally agreeable to civil rights legislation but opposed heavy-handed government intervention—and to make all of its measures more acceptable to himself. So, among other steps, Dirksen adjusted the bill in the Senate so that primary enforcement of its provisions, such as those related to public accommodations and employment matters, would lie with local and state governments. The big machine of federal government would become involved only if necessary.

Not long after Byrd finally caught his breath, up stood Illinois's Dirksen, rising as an unforgettable presence, as author Todd Purdum described in *An Idea Whose Time Has Come*. "Everett McKinley Dirksen was the single most flamboyant senator of his day, with a rumbling baritone foghorn of a voice," he wrote. "He kept his vocal cords lubricated with a daily gargle of Pond's cold cream and water (which he swallowed) and subsisted on a diet of Sanka, cigarettes, Maalox, and bourbon whiskey. He let his graying, curly hair arrange itself in a deliberate tousle—the better to stand out from the crowd, he once confessed."

The bill had exposed deep divisions not only in the Senate but also across the country, Dirksen said, as a transcript of his speech would attest. "Sharp opinions have developed. Incredible allegations have been made. Extreme views have been asserted." Invoking the names of Lincoln and Jefferson, Dirksen implored his colleagues to end their delay tactic and send the law forward. "I appeal to all senators," he commanded. "We are confronted with a moral issue."

The vote to end the filibuster promised to be so close that, when the tallies were ready to be cast, a terminally ill senator from California, Clair Engle, arrived on the Senate floor in a wheelchair. Engle, once considered a possible running mate for JFK in the 1960 presidential ballot, had battled cancer. Brain surgeries in 1963 and 1964 left him paralyzed on one side of his body and with only a limited ability to speak.

Wheeled into the Senate floor now, Engle slowly lifted his crippled arm and pointed to his eye, signaling his Aye vote to end the filibuster. The Democrat would come back a week later to support the bill's final passage, and once more point to his eye. Six weeks later, he was dead.

The 71–29 vote to stifle the filibuster secured four more votes than the two-thirds required, presaging the bill's passage nine days later. It marked the first time the Senate had successfully killed a civil rights filibuster. In ever-resistant Congress, the civil rights tide had finally shifted.

In the end, bill opponents had been outmaneuvered in a political chess match that crossed party lines, with twenty-seven Republicans joining forty-four Democrats in agreeing to end the marathon delay tactic. The drama behind the vote to quash the filibuster proved to be more dramatic than the final vote in the Senate, where the civil rights bill passed by a vote of 73–27. The House, in turn, adopted this Dirksen-tweaked version of the bill.

The measure then moved to the desk of President Lyndon Johnson. On July 2, President Johnson signed into law the US Civil Rights Act of 1964.

"Its purpose is not to punish. Its purpose is not to divide but to end divisions, divisions which have lasted all too long," the president told a live TV audience. "This Civil Rights Act is a challenge to all of us to go to work in our communities and our states, in our homes and in our hearts, to eliminate the last vestiges of injustice in our beloved country."

Using nearly one hundred pens for the ceremony, Johnson handed souvenir pens to Everett Dirksen and Hubert Humphrey, as well as to Martin Luther King Jr. Johnson handed a half dozen of the historic pens to Attorney General Robert F. Kennedy, the fallen president's brother, whose office would be charged with enforcing the nation's new civil rights laws in federal court.

From Atlanta, Albert Sampson and his ministry school brothers watched the ceremony unfold. The rights King and his flock had sought and preached for, through street demonstrations, Freedom Rides, and sit-ins, through beatings, jailing, and killings, had finally arrived. The nation's top political leader had decreed segregation as an illegal scourge. Black citizens had the same right as White ones to sit down for meals and pull into hotels at the establishments of their choice.

"We were in that path of history at that time," Sampson says. "That was a hallelujah moment for us."

Amid the ceremony and celebration in Washington, the nation's racial wounds continued to fester. But now the federal government had new tools to stanch the bleeding.

Nine days after Johnson signed the law, a Black US Army Reserves lieutenant colonel named Lemuel Penn was driving home with two colleagues after two weeks of Reserves training at Fort Benning, Georgia. The trio, steering a Chevrolet sedan in the early hours of July 11, were headed to Washington, DC, where they taught in the local school system. They stopped briefly in Athens, Georgia, with Penn taking the wheel as they headed north on state Highway 72. None of the men noticed a Chevy station wagon surreptitiously trailing them. As Penn turned on Route 172 near Colbert, Georgia, the wagon pulled alongside them. Two shotgun blasts fired out, with one striking Penn in the head and neck, killing him, and the other blast whistling through an open window. One of Penn's passengers, asleep at the time, awoke at the gunfire and reached over to steer the car to safety.

President Johnson ordered an FBI manhunt to find the culprits, and Georgia's governor, Carl Sanders, expressed shame for the killing in his state. FBI agents gathered evidence showing that the KKK had committed the killing, and state prosecutors brought murder charges against the two White men. A third man in the car with them had signed a confession quoting one of the shooters as their car trailed Penn. "That must be some of President Johnson's boys," he had said. "I'm going to kill me a nigger." An all-White jury promptly acquitted the men, Cecil Myers and Joseph Howard Sims.

Armed with the new civil rights law, federal agents kept pressing their probe and painstakingly built a case they could bring in federal court under a different set of charges involving the abuse of an individual's civil rights. Ultimately, the government charged Myers, Sims, and four other Klansmen with violating the federal civil rights laws in the killing of educator Lemuel Penn. Though the other four men were acquitted, Sims and Myers were convicted in 1966 and sent away to prison for ten years, a tangible victory for the civil rights law passed two years earlier.

With the bill's passage in 1964, racial discord continued to reveal itself in Southern businesses and public gatherings. Several cities paid witness as many hotels and restaurants embraced the new day while others angrily opposed the law.

Northern cities encountered their own racial unrest. Later that month in Rochester, New York, nearly two thousand National Guardsmen and state troopers were called out to quell rioting fueled by a Black population that had grown in size but suffered a staggering unemployment rate compared to White city dwellers. The city's Black residents, a state commission concluded, were "sitting on a pressure cooker whose relief valve has long been choked." The same month in Harlem, New York, six days of rioting broke out after a White off-duty officer shot and killed a Black teenager.

In Atlanta, Texas, a tiny town not far from the Texas-Arkansas line, ninety Black people decided to test the new law by invading a formerly Whites-only public beach. A brawl ensued, with three Black protesters suffering shotgun pellet wounds and one White person shot in the foot by a Black demonstrator. Twenty-two Black would-be integrators were jailed after the mass swim-in.

In Jackson, Mississippi, several hotels and motels swung open their doors to Black customers, heeding the advice of the city Chamber of Commerce that they comply with the congressional mandate. Eleven Black protesters broke the color barrier at the Jackson Municipal Golf Course and public parks without incident. Black patrons ordered meals in previously all-White restaurants, and diners and sat down for the evening without incident.

In the same city, the Robert E. Lee Hotel shut its doors rather than allow Black travelers to cross its threshold. Owners undraped the Confederate flag and closed the hotel restaurant, nightclub, and barbershop. A guest clerk turned away potential patrons, White or Black, from a twelve-story building that had long served as a hub for local pols holding firm to the ways of the Old South. The Jackson Citizens Council urged other businesses to follow the Robert E. Lee's example, pressing White city dwellers to boycott those businesses now integrating their commerce. "Business cannot play both sides of the street," the council said. "They must ultimately choose whether to serve white or Negro customers."

Lester Maddox stood among the southern segregationists expressing deep disappointment with President Johnson, a Texan who for decades in Congress had been a reliable part of the bloc of southern politicians resisting civil rights legislation. For years, Johnson had freely used the word *boy* when talking privately with Black men, according to his biographer, Robert A. Caro, in *Master of the Senate: The Years of Lyndon Johnson.*

On Saturday July 4, 1964, two days after Johnson signed the law, Maddox's "Pickrick Says" advertisement reminded his customers the restaurant would be closed for the Fourth of July holiday, but would reopen the next day, Sunday, in direct defiance of the law the president had just signed. "And remember this, we are segregated," Maddox wrote, "and according to the U.S. Constitution we will always be that way."

This edition of "Pickrick Says" railed against the "race mixing" taking place at city parks and swimming pools. "And if you want to see some rotten things that have taken place in your capital city, visit our swimming pools, that our city officials should not even let operate. They are almost segregated, again, as all of the sensible whites have long ago quit going to the pools, and the property owners left in the communities are now victims of the renegade whites and race mixers."

"AND DON'T FORGET," the ad noted, "that if it is wonderful food at reasonable prices that you are looking for, then come to THE PICKRICK." Sunday's specials included barbecued pork for fifty cents, fried fillet of haddock for fifty-five cents, and the priciest special, roast round of beef, for seventy cents.

Maddox's newest ad also took aim at the White House, Congress, the Justice Department, and anyone else he contended was "not concerned" with the violence arising in cities amid the racial protests.

Maddox had come to view his president as a traitor. "I oppose that legislation and can only hope sincerely that nothing like this again will ever come before the United States Senate," Maddox testified in his own case involving his rejection of Black customers to his restaurant. "And I'm taking the fight that President Lyndon Johnson was taking before he deserted it. And I'm taking the fight that others have taken to preserve my private property rights, the American free enterprise system."

Johnson had not only used his political power to usher in the new law but also was pressing the FBI to snuff out the KKK and unveiling a national platform aimed at reviving poverty-stricken regions. "When Lyndon Johnson came to believe in something, moreover, he came to believe in it totally, with absolute conviction, regardless of previous beliefs," Caro wrote.

Nowhere was Johnson's turnaround more evident than in his support for the sweeping new civil rights legislation constructed to temper the nation's racial ills. In 1956, while holding power as the Senate's wheeling-and-dealing majority leader, Johnson had played a crucial role in shooting down a civil rights bill, a measure that was defeated by the largest margin in Senate history. That opposition fit into a two-decade pattern in which Johnson voted against every civil rights bill presented to Congress. He rejected voting rights bills, measures targeting discrimination on the jobsite, even bills that would protect Black people from being lynched. For years, Johnson was among the Senate "sentries" Georgia's powerful senator Richard Russell "deployed on the floor to make sure that liberals could not sneak a bill through," Caro wrote.

But in 1957, as the nation nursed the still-fresh wounds of the lynching of fourteen-year-old Emmett Till in Mississippi and the arrest of forty-two-year-old Rosa Parks for refusing to give up her bus seat in Montgomery, Alabama, Johnson turned his formidable frame and political prowess to the passage of a civil rights bill focused on voting rights.

Caro described this political about-face in *Master of the Senate*:

> Lyndon Johnson, in an abrupt and total reversal of his twenty-year record on civil rights, would push a civil rights bill, primarily a voting rights bill, through the Senate—would create the bill, really, so completely did he transform a confused and contradictory Administration measure that had no realistic chance of passage; would create it and then, in one of the most notable legislative feats in American history, would cajole and plead and threaten and lie, would use all his power and all his guile, all the awe in which his colleagues held him, and all the fear, to ram the bill through the Senate.

Though Johnson had held fast against civil rights bills for decades, he carried a personal connection with the nation's impoverished, laboring masses, having been raised in Deep South poverty himself and having worked on a road gang building a highway in his Texas youth. At age twenty, he had taught in a Mexican school in the tiny town of Cotulla in south Texas, where he personally tutored the school's janitor before and after classes.

So, in the late 1950s, as Johnson set his sights on national office, and the presidency itself, he hit upon a harsh reality. His steadfast opposition to civil rights would gain him little favor in the northern and liberal states and scant chance of rising to the presidency. Johnson's power in the South would be a crucial reason Kennedy tapped him as his running mate in 1960. But then, three years before he joined the ticket as vice president, Johnson dipped into his oft-hidden well of compassion for minorities, mixed that with a heavy dose of political realism, and rolled up his politicking sleeves, personally pushing through the first civil rights bill passed in more than eight decades.

The Civil Rights Act of 1957 wasn't notable for its substance. It was a limited bill that focused just on voting rights, with the final "watered-down version" removing the most stringent voting protection clauses and failing to address segregation and discrimination in housing, schools, or public accommodations such as restaurants. Far more notable was the fact the bill had passed at all. Since passage of the Civil Rights Act of 1875, literally hundreds of bills had been introduced in Congress to defend the voting rights of Black citizens. All of them had failed, until Lyndon Johnson personally took up the mantle.

Now in 1964, the bill he was signing as president was significantly more consequential than the measure he had backed as a Texas senator. Your restaurant or motel may be privately run, the bill said, but the issue of whom you let in is very much a matter of public concern.

As Lester Maddox joined the chorus of segregationist business owners saying Congress and Johnson were trampling on their God-given rights to free trade, Moreton Rolleston was quietly preparing to take his fight directly to the US government and its president. While Lyndon Johnson addressed a national audience that Thursday evening, Rolleston was putting the finishing touches to the first legal challenge to the law.

6

HEART OF ATLANTA V. USA: THE FIRST LEGAL CHALLENGE ARRIVES

MORETON ROLLESTON JR. was at the end of his studies at the Emory University School of Law in 1941 when the US Navy visited the Atlanta campus offering commissions to serve in World War II. Rolleston seized the chance, signing up to serve the country and its allies battling forces led by Hitler's Nazi Germany.

Rolleston's commission wouldn't begin until 1942, so 1941 became a blur of milestone events spinning one after the other. Graduating law school, passing the Georgia Bar exam, getting married, running off to a honeymoon. Antsy while awaiting his formal orders to serve, Rolleston took a post in the legal department of the Coca-Cola Company, until finally he went to England in 1942 to serve as a lieutenant commander in the Office of Naval Intelligence.

He was forever shaken by the Japanese attack on the US naval base at Pearl Harbor, a cataclysmic event coming one month before his duty formally called. After receiving intelligence training in Washington and New York, he deployed to England, where he drew maps helping the US fight fire with fire. Decades after leaving the service, he choked up recalling the American graves at Normandy, France.

Discharged in 1946, Rolleston came home to Atlanta to raise two children, find pleasure on the water boating and fishing, and launch a legal career. Yet he had trouble putting his law degree to use, hitting dead end upon dead end trying to join a law firm. Rolleston encountered so many *Thanks, but no thanks* he decided to venture into the field as a solo practitioner.

"So, I just hung a shingle out," he later explained. His maiden office was so small he could barely squeeze in a desk for himself and chair for a client. He'd accept any customers willing to pay but soon found himself handling real estate matters, and he quickly developed an interest in making his own investments.

"One of the real estate ventures you may know about is the Heart of Atlanta motel," he told an interviewer decades later.

That structure, at 255 Courtland Street Northeast, just blocks from Peachtree Street, opened on September 5, 1956, as Atlanta's first downtown motel. Occupying an entire city block and rising in the heart of the city core near two major interstates, the resort motel boasted of its amenities. "Each room equipped with telephone, television, radio, Muzak, and individual thermostat for heat and air conditioning," not to mention a swimming pool with underwater lights, restaurant, "ladies lounge," and golf putting green adjacent to the pool.

"$1,500,000 Motel Now Open in City," the Atlanta media announced that day. "Locally Owned 'Heart of Atlanta' Most Luxurious from New York to Miami."

Rolleston, part of the ownership group buying the property, was president and general counsel for the motel corporation, along with its public face and prime operator. Unveiled with 120 rooms and one swimming pool, the Heart of Atlanta did robust business even as other hotels sprouted nearby, with an occupancy rate hovering at 97 percent. With business booming, Rolleston laid plans to expand the motel to 216 rooms and add another pool.

Dapper in his suit and tie, he proudly stood for promotional photographs with his back against a railing overlooking one of its gleaming pools. As he did, a young woman hung in frame midair behind him, her arms reaching high as she jumped off the diving board for a splashdown.

Moreton Rolleston refused to allow Black customers at his Heart of Atlanta motel and took his fight against the government to the US Supreme Court. *Bettmann Archive/Getty Images*

Like everyone else swimming in the pool, she was White. Rolleston shared the deep-seated views of his fellow Atlanta business owner Lester Maddox. Rolleston's segregationist stance would sometimes land him in the local newspaper or before the television cameras, but he'd never gain the same level of attention as Maddox, whose ferocious reply to integrators attracted TV cameras, devoted supporters, and disapproving critics in bunches. Yet like Maddox, Moreton Rolleston refused to allow Black patrons at his establishment. Like Maddox, he was aghast at the idea of Washington politicians telling him how to manage his own affairs. Like Maddox, he never drank alcohol. "I've been in all kinds of scraps and fights," Rolleston once said. "And some folks like me and some folks don't."

In 1959, acting as an attorney, Rolleston helped charter a new organization in Atlanta advocating to keep the races separate in schools, with publicly financed but privately controlled segregated education. Three years later, as NAACP delegates began booking rooms for a convention in Atlanta, Rolleston sent letters assuring his patrons none would be staying at the Heart of Atlanta. "We want to advise you that we have never accepted a Negro guest at this Motel, that we have not agreed with anyone to accept Negro guests now or in the future, and that it is our considered and firm policy that we will not accept Negro guests at this Motel at this time," he wrote. "We believe that a high percentage of our guests will welcome this policy."

Rolleston's son noted that his father opened his motel at a time of deep segregation in the Deep South, when schools, businesses, and communities many times operated with clear lines of racial demarcation.

"This area of the world had a lot of segregation issues, a lot of fear-mongering, and a lot of people saying ugly things," Moreton Rolleston III told me as we spoke in his driveway one day in the summer of 2020. His father's motel, he said, operated in an era in which the races often did not mix. "A sign of the times," he remarked.

Rolleston says his father treated his Black employees with decency. One time, he recalled, a Black cook was booked in jail on some minor charge. "Dad goes down and bails him out," says the son, who worked part time as a front desk clerk at the motel in the mid-1960s before later launching a career as a pilot for Eastern Airlines.

"I never heard him say anything disparaging about Black politicians and activists," Moreton Rolleston III says. "He's been lumped together with all the creepy segregationists out to hurt people." He adds, "He ain't no Lester Maddox, that's for sure."

Moreton Rolleston did share Maddox's view about heavy-handed government interference with his business. When I asked the son why his father operated a segregationist motel, his answer was nearly identical to that given by Maddox's son when I posed the same question to him. "He just didn't want the government telling him how to run his business," said Rolleston III. The son bears a striking resemblance to his late father, the more so, he says, as the years pass by.

When Moreton Rolleston came to a decision, he, like Maddox, stood firm. He presented his views in a legal context, citing the law and the Constitution and addressing reporters or the public as if he were standing in a courtroom. "He was a lawyer, and he had strong views about the law," his son says. "He had a vision of what he wanted the motel to be like."

So even as neighboring hotels began to drop their color barriers and welcome Black patrons inside, Moreton Rolleston refused to budge.

In January 1964, more than a dozen demonstrators, Black and White, had been arrested at the Heart of Atlanta when they tried to integrate the dining room and bar on a Saturday night. Rolleston opposed their entry, even arming himself with a tear gas pistol. "I intend to use it for protection if I have to," he told a policeman called to quell the disturbance. His son says he knew nothing of the pistol episode.

Later that month, a Fulton County grand jury indicted twenty-nine activists for violating Georgia's anti-trespassing laws by trying to integrate the Heart of Atlanta that Saturday and another establishment, the Krystal Restaurant, two days later. Among the indicted was John Lewis, then chairman of the Student Nonviolent Coordinating Committee and later a Georgia congressman. Others indicted on the misdemeanor charges included representatives from the NAACP and Martin Luther King's Southern Christian Leadership Conference. Moreton Rolleston personally brought the charges on behalf of the Heart of Atlanta motel.

A veteran now in the civil rights tensions rocking Atlanta, Rolleston girded himself for the laws descending from Congress to local businessmen like himself. That effort, he believed, "opens a frightful door to the unlimited power of a centralized government in Washington in which the individual citizen and his personal liberty are of no importance. It makes possible a socialistic state and the eventual dictatorship."

So when Lyndon Johnson signed the civil rights act in a nationally televised ceremony on July 2, 1964, Moreton Rolleston Jr. pounced.

Two hours and ten minutes later, at 8:55 PM, he filed suit in federal court in Georgia, *Heart of Atlanta Motel Inc. v. The United States of America and Robert F. Kennedy*, attorney general of the United States. Though the courthouse was closed at that hour, Rolleston, benefiting from a rule requiring clerks to be on duty at all hours, drove to the clerk's home and formally filed the litigation, officially docketing it the same evening the bill was signed into law. Acting as his own attorney, he waged the first legal challenge to the nation's expansive slate of civil rights laws.

"Heart of Atlanta Motel has never rented sleeping accommodations to members of the Negro race, is not now renting sleeping accommodations to members of the Negro race and does not intend to do so unless ordered by this Court to comply with the provisions of the Civil Rights Act of 1964," Rolleston proffered in the seven-page complaint.

He called the new law unconstitutional and, using the legalese of court briefs, said he deserved to operate as he always had. "Before the adoption of said Act, plaintiff corporation operated its motel in any way it deemed fit, provided it complied with local ordinances and statutes of the State of Georgia pertaining to the protection of the health of the guests of said motel," he wrote.

"Before the adoption of said Act," he continued, "plaintiff corporation picked and chose its guests from those people it considered to be compatible with the other guests of said motel and excluded Negro guests because plaintiff corporation determined that such exclusion was in the best interest of plaintiff's business and was necessary to protect plaintiff's property, trade, profits and reputation."

Said another way, Rolleston was urging the government to mind its own business. The city of Atlanta and the state of Georgia hadn't told him how to run his motel, so why did the federal government think it could do so now? Local business owners can manage their own interests, he was saying, a position in lockstep with fellow Atlantan Maddox and with a core of members of Congress who had become wary of liberal-minded Supreme Court rulings and agitated over government laws decreeing how locals should proceed.

The new law, Rolleston said, prohibited him from "exercising and enjoying the full rights inherent in the private ownership of private property." The motel owner said his loss of liberty was "priceless," but he nonetheless affixed a price tag to his potential suffering: $11 million. Of that, Rolleston said $10 million was for being deprived of his right of liberty to refuse service and $1 million for deprivation of his property rights.

His customers, he said, wanted to keep business as usual and had no interest in mixing the races. More than 95 percent of his past guests "prefer not to rent sleeping accommodations at said motel if members of the Negro race also rent sleeping accommodations," his court case maintained. If the law was not overturned, the Heart of Atlanta "will lose a large percentage of its customers, income and good will and will suffer irreparable damages."

Rolleston's pleadings drew a prompt rebuke from the federal lawyers assigned to defend the government's stance. One week later, Justice Department attorneys, including Kennedy and his assistant attorney general, Burke Marshall, fired back with a brisk rebuttal to every one of Rolleston's claims.

His words and actions "constitute a pattern and practice of resistance to the full enjoyment by Negroes of the right, secured by Title II of the Civil Rights Act of 1964, to the full and equal enjoyment of the goods, services, facilities, privileges, advantages, and accommodations of the Heart of Atlanta, without discrimination or segregation on the ground of race or color."

Kennedy's team sought a court order barring Rolleston from refusing to accept Black guests or failing to serve them in the restaurant and barring his operation from "making any distinction whatever upon the basis of race or color in the availability of the goods, services, facilities, privileges, advantages, or accommodations offered" at the Heart of Atlanta.

In short, they wanted an order requiring that the Heart of Atlanta treat its guests equally, regardless of their race, and that the motel adhere to the new law of the land. Attorney General Robert F. Kennedy personally signed the government's answer to Rolleston's lawsuit. The case, he said, is one of "public importance."

Within days, a trio of Atlanta ministers would try to force Rolleston's hand, presenting themselves at the Heart of Atlanta's reception desk and testing the law's application in face-to-face meetings with the owner. Others, including John Lewis, had tried to integrate the Heart of Atlanta before. But those efforts had come before the adoption of the Civil Rights Act of 1964. The difference now was that the ministers set out with a federal rule on the books, one that said Rolleston or any other hotel or restaurant proprietor would be breaking the law if they excluded customers based on race.

One of the visitors was Albert Sampson, who had enrolled in the ITC in the early 1960s but then stopped his studies to become executive secretary of the Atlanta branch of the NAACP. Sampson also wrote a column for the *Atlanta Inquirer* newspaper, where he served as an associate editor.

"It is my contention that this bill presents the white man the opportunity to stand and look at the Negro instead of historically looking down on him," Sampson wrote in one *Inquirer* column days after the civil rights act was passed, under the headline NAACP BATTLEFRONT. "Men like Lester Maddox will be eaten up by the buzzards of equality and his carcass will be like the ostrich, buried in the sands of time."

Though he had left the seminary and had initially studied as a Baptist, his Methodist classmates urged Sampson to join their protests. "They still saw me as a preacher," he said. "They were challenging me to come on and be a part of it. When brothers be talking smack, you got to go."

On Tuesday, July 7, 1964, Sampson called the Heart of Atlanta to make a reservation for the following morning. Out of town at the time, he wired $12.36 to the motel via Western Union, keeping a receipt of his transaction. Sampson's motivations were simple. "Under the new law, they had a responsibility to let me in," he recalled decades later.

He walked into the motel that Wednesday, telling the front desk he was there for his room and that he had wired his money ahead. "I'm very sorry," a dark-haired receptionist replied. "But I don't have your wire." As another receptionist helped a customer, Sampson scanned a list of names on the reservation sheet. There it was. Albert Sampson.

"There's my name!" he told the desk clerk. The second receptionist snatched the guest list. The first worker, seeing the Western Union telegram receipt, told Sampson the motel could not accommodate him.

"You don't have an argument with me," Sampson replied. "You have an argument with the federal government." He demanded his money back and said he'd call the police if the motel didn't oblige. Just then owner Rolleston came out to meet Sampson, leading the NAACP leader away from the front desk so they could speak privately, and looking over the guest list and telegram receipt.

"If the courts decide for me to open up, I'll open up. But until then, I can't accommodate any Negroes," Rolleston told him, returning the $12.36. His access denied and his money in hand, Sampson left the Heart of Atlanta.

The other minister seeking lodging was Charles Wells, a student in the African Methodist Episcopal wing of the Atlanta seminary and among those long advocating for racial equality in local businesses.

The Atlanta protests would become part of a lifelong quest for racial justice for Wells, a tall, commanding figure even in his early twenties. As a child he heard racial slurs and fought back with his fists but always took a seat in the front of the class and scored high grades in his elementary school in Washington, Pennsylvania, a small town a half hour southwest of Pittsburgh.

By adulthood the Reverend Wells would espouse Martin Luther King's vision of peaceful protest, once drawing ten rounds of applause while giving an extemporaneous forty-five-minute speech on the anniversary of the icon's death. His wife Barbara would dub him "The Minister Who Wore Many Hats": musician, orator, civil rights activist, administrator, visionary.

He would protest a Macon, Georgia, laundromat that accepted only White customers, and get arrested in Waycross, Georgia, after leading a march of 130 protesters to demand more job opportunities and better schools for Black students. On Palm Sunday he led a March for Justice in town, with a parishioner walking beside him wearing a WE SHALL OVERCOME sign around his neck. In Waycross, where Wells led services at the Greater Mount Zion AME Church, he chaired a protest committee that orchestrated a six-day boycott of schools by Black students. When he engineered a boycott of downtown businesses, he vowed to march at all hours. "We can walk at night if necessary," he said, "stopping trains, busses, and autos."

Charles Wells was both a minister and a military man, formerly commissioned in the US Army and stationed at posts including Fort Benning, Georgia. "Wells was a military guy, so he moved kind of like with that level of confidence," Sampson recalls. "Wells was stately. He moved like a colonel. He moved like a soldier with bars."

Two days after Sampson was rebuffed, Wells visited the 216-room Heart of Atlanta motel with a friend, the Reverend John Gillison. The athletic Wells stepped to the front desk and asked if the motel had any vacancies, speaking directly to Moreton Rolleston.

"He told me he would not be able to rent me a room. And I asked him why," Wells later recounted. "He told me that it was the policy of the motel not to rent rooms to Negroes until such time as a decision was made on the suit which was pending in the federal courts."

Wells pressed the motel owner. Are you defying the civil rights act signed into law a week earlier? Rolleston repeated his refrain. The motel wasn't renting rooms to Black customers "until such time as a decision had been made on the suit," he told Wells.

Though Sampson and Wells were rejected in their bids to spend the night, their visits would later pay legal dividends and be cited as the litigation reached all the way to the US Supreme Court, helping the US government build a case that Moreton Rolleston Jr. and his Heart of Atlanta motel were violating the new federal law by deciding clientele based on race. The ministers had showed up to a motel with vacancies, with one even wiring his payment ahead, but were turned away because of their skin color. The evidence was clear. Rolleston was skirting the law. During a pivotal court hearing on the Heart of Atlanta case later that month, the government's sole two witnesses were the ITC's Wells and NAACP's Sampson.

Their interactions with the motel owner were cordial, the outcome notwithstanding. The same could not be said for three other seminary students, who would, one day after the Heart of Atlanta lawsuit was filed in court, drive to the Pickrick restaurant seeking a table of their own and a plate of Lester Maddox's hearty fare. Maddox and his brood would repel them with anger, weapons, and vitriol. Soon enough, the Atlanta seminary students would become plaintiffs in a lawsuit against Maddox and his restaurant. As in the Heart of Atlanta case, their attempts to integrate the Pickrick would serve as the legal ballast for the United States government's argument that the two Atlanta segregationists were blatantly violating the law.

In court filings, Burke Marshall and colleague Charles L. Goodson cited the hardships for Black people refused entry at hotels and eateries.

"There can be no doubt that the widespread practice of hotel and motel proprietors to refuse to provide lodging to Negro interstate travelers imposes on such travelers a serious practical burden and inconvenience, and effectively prevents many such persons from traveling interstate," they wrote in their fifty-page memorandum of law challenging the actions of both the Heart of Atlanta and the Pickrick.

"The effect of segregation and discrimination in restaurants—which has notoriously been the major cause of social unrest in large areas of the South—. . . is alone a sufficient basis for Congress to prohibit such practices in restaurants," they added in a supplemental court filing five days later.

Soon, the nation's first two legal tests of John F. Kennedy's civil rights platform would play out, side by side, in an Atlanta federal courtroom. Across the country, cities and towns would pay close attention to how the legal rulings would shake out in Atlanta, Georgia, with staunch segregationists pitted against congressional power and a handful of unrelenting ministry students.

7

PICKRICK SHOWDOWN: AXE HANDLES, GUNS, AND FISTS

THIRTY MINUTES BEFORE 6:00 PM ON JULY 3, 1964, one day after Lyndon Johnson's signature inscribed a new era in American civil rights, three ministry students from the Interdenominational Theological Center drove from their campus three miles north toward the parking lot of the Pickrick restaurant. The men had gone to the restaurant earlier that day, but it was closed when they first arrived, and they told a manager they would be back.

George Willis was driving, Albert Dunn in the passenger seat, and Woodrow T. Lewis in back. Dunn and Willis had been ringleaders of the integration plan, hungry to test the new law at a restaurant that had served its popular diner fare only to White customers, and Lewis felt equally emboldened to demand a seat at the table. As the trio pulled toward the Hemphill Avenue establishment, they witnessed a mass of bodies standing out front, up to one hundred people, anxiously awaiting their arrival. Many held axe handles, the largest of them thirty-six inches long.

"There was a mob of Whites standing there when we drove up to the Pickrick restaurant yard," Lewis says. "Willis was very, very angry and Dunn too. They were saying, 'Look at them, look at them, look at them.' Willis said, 'I should take this car and drive it right through the crowd.'"

Lewis, the quietest of the three, urged restraint from the back seat. "I said, No, brother, let's cool it. Go to the side," he recalls.

Lester Maddox came prepared for combat. He had never fired a pistol in his life but, for the first time earlier that year amid citywide protests over discriminatory businesses like his, had bought a revolver. Maddox kept the weapon handy at all times—in his office, car, home, "or wherever I felt I might need it to protect my constitutional rights."

"If the police would not do their duty and protect my property and my business from these revolutionaries and bums, then they left me no choice but to protect it myself, and this I fully intended doing with every bit of strength at my disposal," Maddox later wrote in his autobiography. "The men who framed our Constitution had to fight for their freedom, and I was ready to fight for mine."

Maddox had been enraged by the downtown demonstrations targeting another Atlanta restaurant, Leb's. For years, integrators both Black and White had picketed the working-class restaurant, demanding that it open its doors to all comers, only to have the restaurant's immigrant owner sometimes evict Black patrons by force. The protests had reached a violent crescendo earlier that year, on a long weekend from Saturday, January 25 through Monday, January 27, months before the Civil Rights Act of 1964 was approved. The discord began when protesters with the Student Nonviolent Coordinating Committee took seats at Leb's that Saturday, only to have the owner refuse to sell them food and lock the bathroom doors, triggering a stalemate. After the reporters left, the owner complained that some of the protesters had busted his furniture and, with the bathroom locked, urinated on the floor.

As Black activists had sought to integrate Atlanta eateries and hotels, the Ku Klux Klan would simultaneously march in protest against the establishments that desegregated. DON'T TRADE HERE. OWNERS OF THIS BUSINESS SURRENDERED TO THE RACE MIXERS, one KKK member's sign said, challenging a hotel near Leb's. And on this Saturday in January 1964, KKK members were picketing a nearby hotel when they got word of what was happening at Leb's. Soon Black and White protesters were encircling each other outside the restaurant in a tense racial standoff that sometimes turned bloody.

Trouble brewed again the next morning, when demonstrators returned to Leb's and another restaurant run by the same owner, sitting on the floor, singing freedom songs, and refusing to leave. Police swooped in and began making arrests. The disturbance continued the next day, with even more arrests of the picketers.

In all, some one thousand White spectators turned out to witness the protesters demanding equal access. The weekend clashes led to multiple injuries to the dueling groups and to a few police officers, plus deep property damage to the restaurant and a black eye for the city of Atlanta.

The weekend fracas was so disruptive, both to the physical operations of Leb's and the psyche of a city that proclaimed it was "too busy to hate," that the Atlanta Restaurant Association soon placed full-page ads in the newspaper. City leaders, the ads said, had placed too much pressure on dining owners to desegregate, and police had not provided enough protection to those operations when agitating picketers had wrought damage.

Two days after the Leb's storm, Mayor Ivan Allen, a staunch supporter of integration in public-use facilities, sought a thirty-day moratorium on demonstrations to allow the city's temperature to cool. Police, he said, would arrest trespassers at sit-ins, though lawful picketing could continue.

Allen pleaded for an end to the discord as he addressed a packed and racially mixed assembly at City Hall. Lester Maddox listened from the front row. "This irresponsible element that chooses to assume a threatening posture and attack our city destructively will find that they cannot undermine Atlanta's solid foundation of fairness and freedom built so patiently over many years by men and women of good sense and good will of both races," the mayor said. "I have asked you to meet here this afternoon to help evaluate and work out a solution to a situation which threatens not only the good name, but beyond that, even the public safety of this city. Atlanta's tolerance has been almost unlimited. Atlanta's desire for every citizen to have liberty, freedom, and equal rights is unabated. Atlanta will not slow down or stop in its efforts to work out solutions to all problems of racial relations."

The rancor continued. The Atlanta Chamber of Commerce and the Atlanta Restaurant Association said they favored voluntary desegregation, not a new federal law that would force the hand of local establishments. Activists from the Southern Christian Leadership Conference and the Student Nonviolent Coordinating Committee, pressing for full integration of all city businesses, refused to adhere to Allen's cooling-off period. The demonstrations continued. Days later, more than a dozen White students from Georgia Tech and Emory University, a mix of men and women, picketed outside the restaurant, hoisting placards saying GEORGIA STUDENTS PROTEST SEGREGATION and ATLANTA MUST BE DESEGREGATED.

Lester Maddox had witnessed the earlier scene at Leb's and put the destructive blame squarely on the shoulders of the picketers. "Leb's," he wrote, "was literally taken over by gangs of civil rights militants, both black and white."

"I could not believe the sight that met my eyes as I stood on the sidewalk across the street from the restaurant," he wrote. "Apparently some of the demonstrators had recognized me when I entered Leb's, for they began to chant: *Maddox is next! Maddox is next! Maddox is next!*"

Maddox had repelled potential integrators before. A year earlier, on May 18, 1963, four Black and three White demonstrators, representing a group called the Committee on Appeal for Human Rights, attempted to take seats at the Pickrick. The owner and his Black employees ushered them out, informing the protesters that the restaurant's minority laborers would lose their jobs if the Pickrick ever integrated. Maddox would close it down before that happened. The same scene had played out in April 1964. More Black and White integrators arriving, but Maddox blocked the doorway and his employees led the visitors away. They never would order a meal.

And now, one day after Lyndon Johnson signed the nation's most far-reaching civil rights law, Maddox braced for more visitors. Black voters had sent him to two losses at the polls. He'd summon all of his inner fire to ensure they didn't conquer him now.

As Willis pulled close, Dunn stepped from the car, eager, as always, to confront his adversaries. Yet as Willis began to park, a crowd led by Lester Maddox rushed to the car, and Maddox himself tried to slam the driver-side door shut so Willis couldn't exit. Willis tried again and again to open the door, but Maddox pushed back each time he did. Then he pulled a pistol and aimed it toward Willis's face, holding it there and ordering the young activist to leave.

"He pointed it toward my face and told me to get off his property or he'd kill me," Willis wrote in his senior ITC essay the following spring. "Mr. Maddox yelled for others to grab axe handles that were on hand and help."

All the while Lewis remained in the back seat, encircled by the mass surrounding the car. "The mob came up and hit the car with axe handles. The mob was not only hitting the car with the axe handles, they said, 'Get the hell away,'" Lewis recalled more than five decades later.

As he witnessed Maddox stick a gun to Willis's face, Lewis was so shaken he was left speechless. In the back seat alone, he said a silent prayer for his colleagues and himself. "I was so shocked and stunned," Lewis says. "No words could come out."

By this time, Dunn was walking back to the car to leave with his brethren. Maddox hurried to escort him off the Pickrick premises, with his pistol in hand as his son stood armed with one of the axe handles Maddox had been selling for two dollars. By gunpoint, Maddox forced Dunn back into the car.

A news photographer captured the surreal moment. Maddox holds what looks to be a satchel or handbag in his left hand and the pistol in his right, walking a few steps behind Dunn. The ministry student looks as if he's trying to remain composed amid the madness, preparing to button his sports jacket as he walks away, with his eyes shaded by sunglasses. Between the two walks a thin White man, Maddox's son Lester Jr., with a pick handle clutched in both hands. The photograph, published and broadcast in news outlets across the country, brought Lester Maddox fully into the national consciousness, as his biographer Short remarked in *Everything Is Pickrick*. "He was hailed by segregationists as a man who would stand up against forced integration," Short wrote.

As Dunn finally reached the car, he couldn't fully bite his tongue. "You're crazy!" he told Maddox.

"Come on," Lewis implored him, "get in the car."

Finally, Willis closed the door to drive off. Before he could, Maddox slammed one of the axe handles on the car, severely damaging it, the men would say in court papers. Lewis confirms that moment. "My impression was this man was out of his mind. He was a real racist. He would have taken the bat and hit Dunn if he could."

Maddox, successfully rejecting the latest attempt to integrate his business, spewed his segregationist beliefs, with the audio captured by Philip C. Flynn of radio station WGST of Atlanta. "I'll use axe handles, I'll use guns, I'll use paint, I'll use my fists, I'll use my customers, I'll use my employees, I'll use anything at my disposal. This property belongs to me, my wife, and my children," Maddox screamed. "The white people

Lester Maddox, armed with a pistol, forces ministry student Albert Dunn off the Pickrick grounds in July 1964. Between the men, holding an axe handle, is Lester Maddox Jr. *AP*

have got enough of this and it's not because of the Negroes. It's because of renegades like Lyndon Johnson and Ivan Allen."

Departing the restaurant, the ministry students were numb by what they had just experienced. "We weren't expecting that. We were shocked to see the mob, because the law had been signed by the president of the United States," says Lewis.

He says it took all of Willis's inner strength to hold back against the crowd and remain faithful to the nonviolent protests they had agreed to practice: "It was hard for Willis to do that. We had nothing to fight back, and it was a mob of Whites. We would have gotten slaughtered."

When the students returned to their dormitory that evening, they were met by Atlanta police and FBI agents, who questioned them about Maddox's gun-toting response. The questioning marked the first step in a legal process that would quickly lead the ministers to file a lawsuit challenging the segregationist's actions.

Before his death in 2012, Willis told his wife of thirty-two years, Kay, about the evening confrontation with the Pickrick owner that Atlanta summer of 1964. "I said, 'You mean to tell me Lester Maddox put a gun to your face?' And he said, 'Yes. The Lord taught me to never be afraid for standing up for what I know is right,'" Kay Willis recounts from her home state of Texas. "They could have easily killed somebody. I thought that took a lot of integrity and stamina."

Her husband's preaching and life credo, she says, was clear-eyed. He believed that "you can go and be civil. You don't have to act like the other person," Kay Willis explains. "You don't want your manhood challenged. But it was challenged. They were ministers, and they had a different calling."

The next day, Maddox organized a Fourth of July rally at a city park that drew more than eleven thousand like-minded White people. He welcomed to the stage segregationist governors Ross Barnett of Mississippi and George Wallace of Alabama, as well as the grand dragon of the local KKK. After the other speakers sat down, Maddox took to the stage, grabbed the microphone, and declared, "Never! Never! Never!" in a steadfast opposition to integration. His words drew the day's most robust applause. When a group of Black protesters turned out to the rally, scores of White participants, gathered in overflowing bleachers to hear the segregationists speak, stood up and began heaving their chairs at the visitors.

As Maddox was rallying his followers, the ministers were retreating to the office of a local lawyer, William Alexander, a veteran practitioner of civil rights cases who would later become a Georgia legislator and sitting judge. Working to bring a lawsuit against the Pickrick, Alexander soon joined forces with the NAACP Legal Defense and Educational Fund, which had been closely monitoring how local businesses were responding to the new federal edict across the country.

On July 9, 1964, six days after the ministry students were forced off the Pickrick property, the lawyers brought the second legal challenge involving the nation's new law in federal court in Atlanta. Plaintiffs Willis, Lewis, and Dunn filed a lawsuit against the Pickrick and Lester Maddox, recounting the events of July 3 and demanding a court order barring the business from continuing to expel customers based on race.

"Plaintiffs were denied and deprived of service at The Pickrick restaurant because of defendants' well established and maintained policy, practice, custom and usage of refusing to serve, and discriminating against, Negroes," said the six-page lawsuit, filed by Alexander along with Jack Greenberg, Constance Baker Motley, and Michael Meltsner of the NAACP Legal Defense Fund in New York.

The state of Georgia and city of Atlanta had no law prohibiting business owners like Maddox from operating a Whites-only restaurant. But the new federal law did employ that power, using the Commerce Clause as ammunition against discrimination in public accommodations. The ministry students' legal team used the Civil Rights Act of 1964 as the basis from which they made their case against Maddox's armed resistance.

"During the time that plaintiffs attempted to enter the said restaurant they continuously received threats from the defendant Maddox and many of the bystanders who were waving axe handles at the said plaintiffs," the lawsuit said. "As a result of the actions of the said defendant Maddox, the plaintiffs were denied service at the defendant Pickrick restaurant solely because of their color."

The complaint stressed that the Pickrick served interstate travelers, bringing it under the Commerce Clause and the new federal law.

So, the lawsuit was saying, Lester Maddox's segregationist policies were not only immoral, but they also fell squarely under the focus of the nation's seminal new civil rights law. And notably, the lawsuit argued, "a substantial portion of the food which it serves moves in commerce."

The Associated Press wire photo of Maddox leading Dunn off by gunpoint was entered as Exhibit A in the students' lawsuit. Exhibit B was one of Maddox's "Pickrick Says" ads. Those two exhibits, the young ministers believed, said all the courts needed to know about Lester Maddox and his Pickrick faithful.

Maddox's forcible ejection of the Atlanta ministers caught the immediate attention of the top attorney in the Justice Department's Civil Rights Division, Burke Marshall, and the Federal Bureau of Investigation.

Within days, Marshall crafted the first in a series of memos to the FBI director's office pressing for a full-scale inquiry into Maddox's actions. At Marshall's request, the FBI interviewed the ministry students and the news media who witnessed their expulsion, and it obtained copies of photographs of the pistol-wielding Maddox and his axe-wielding customers.

Marshall wrote that Maddox again rejected Black customers at his restaurant three days after the ministers' visit. "On this as well as the prior occasion Mr. Maddox was armed with a pistol and pickaxe handles were made available on the premises of the restaurant for white persons to use in intimidating Negroes," he wrote in a three-page memo on July 8, 1964.

The civil rights litigator requested a "full investigation" to determine if Maddox was flouting the new civil rights law. He asked the FBI to research the Pickrick's ownership and management structure, interview its employees about the restaurant's segregationist policies, trace Maddox's permit to carry a gun, study the damage to the ministry students' car, and follow the trail of where the diner got its food supplies from outside Georgia.

The DOJ and FBI were asking the very questions explored by lawyers for the seminary students.

Helping craft the ministers' legal strategy was attorney Constance Baker Motley, the daughter of West Indies Caribbean parents and who knew at age fifteen she wanted to become a lawyer. Her mother said she should be a hairdresser, and her father offered no encouragement. Everywhere she turned, people said a Black woman had no place in the law. The push-back prompted Motley to prove everyone wrong, but she wasn't some agitating hothead. Raised in a working-class household of twelve children where education and religion were most valued, Motley was the child of parents who believed rudeness was a sin. As a girl, she knew better than to call any adult by his or her first name, and adult relatives were to be addressed as Uncle, Aunt, or Cousin So-and-so.

While a student at Fisk University in Tennessee, Motley experienced discrimination firsthand one day in the 1940s as she traveled by train from her hometown of New Haven, Connecticut, through New York and then to the next stop in Cincinnati, Ohio, which stood at the border of the Old South state Kentucky. Motley had to disembark as train workers put another passenger car behind the engine, this one older and rustier than others. When she stepped back to reboard, a Black porter told her she had to now sit in the newly added car. A sign inside the door made clear why. COLORED, it said.

"I was both frightened and humiliated," Motley said years later. It was a glimpse into the Jim Crow South. "Segregation was legal in Kentucky and all other Southern states. Most blacks accepted it as inevitable," she explained.

Motley transferred from Fisk to New York University (NYU), graduating in 1943 with her sights set on Columbia University Law School. But first she took work at a wartime agency in Newark, New Jersey, that aided servicemen's dependents. She did so well on a placement exam she earned a promotion. But she couldn't accept it, she told her boss. She'd be going to Columbia University Law School soon. "That's crazy," the supervisor, a White woman, replied. "Why do you want to waste your time doing that? Women don't get anywhere in the law." It was more fuel for Motley.

Before she finished her studies at Columbia, she landed a job with the NAACP Legal Defense and Educational Fund in 1945. There, the boss was a little-known civil rights lawyer named Thurgood Marshall, who would step into the national limelight as lead NAACP attorney in the *Brown v. Board of Education* case. Later, Lyndon Johnson would appoint Marshall as the nation's first Black US Supreme Court justice. (When Kamala Harris was sworn in as the nation's first Black and female vice president in 2021, she placed her hand upon Thurgood Marshall's Bible.)

In 1961 Constance Motley helped integrate the University of Georgia. A year later she helped James Meredith break the color barrier at Ole Miss, and in 1963 she and colleague Jack Greenberg represented Vivian Malone and James Hood as they entered the University of Alabama.

"Thurgood Marshall threw my letter on her desk and said, 'That's your case,'" Meredith recalled recently. "As far as that organization was concerned, she was the most knowledgeable, the most used lawyer dealing with Mississippi."

Meredith, a famously unpredictable civil rights icon, witnessed Motley bring savvy and self-awareness that made her stand out in the largely all White male legal community.

"She knew how to handle me, and there weren't very many people in the world who could do that," Meredith told me. "Primarily, she knew who she was, and she knew a whole lot about reality."

When she first met Meredith, Motley took stock of her newest client, a US Air Force veteran. "He was dressed in fatigues," she later wrote. "He was slight, no more than 140 pounds and no more than five feet seven inches tall. He was carrying a cane, although he did not have a limp. The thing that did shock me about his appearance was that he was growing a beard, which had come into vogue and which many people of my generation rejected."

She found him reserved, with a "no-nonsense demeanor." Before their first court appearance, "I persuaded Meredith to wear his blue suit, not the fatigues he wore every day, shave off his beard, which gave him a hippie appearance, and leave his cane at home."

Motley soon learned why Meredith carried a cane. "He told me he carried the cane for protection," she said.

His path to admission to Ole Miss was tortuous. Southern judges repeatedly rejected Meredith's bid, and Mississippi once vowed to arrest him. When one of Motley's appeals finally went in Meredith's favor, a segregationist judge made clear he would use all his powers to reverse it. Meredith, "after long study and careful analysis," wrote Motley that he would withdraw his application to Ole Miss and finish his undergraduate studies at Jackson State University, where he was already enrolled. Later, he would pursue a law degree at Ole Miss.

Stunned, Motley asked Meredith to come to New York. We've come too far, she said, to stop now. Had Meredith dropped his appeals and subsequently tried to enter law school at the university, they'd likely have to start the legal battle from scratch. After long discussions with his lawyer, Meredith agreed to continue his pursuit to become the first Black undergraduate student at the Oxford, Mississippi, campus.

He ultimately gained admission, escorted by US Marshals amid bloody protests. On his first day in class, he sat alone when the other students walked out. In August 1963 James Meredith earned his bachelor of arts degree.

Motley won that case and many more. She successfully argued nine of ten cases before the US Supreme Court, visited Martin Luther King Jr. in jail, and sang freedom songs inside churches bombed by supremacists.

News photographers often captured Motley after one big case or another. In nearly every photograph, she is the only woman in the picture, a tall, graceful figure surrounded by men. Five months before the Pickrick lawsuit filing, she had become the first Black woman elected to the New York State Senate, agreeing to take the post so long as it didn't interfere with the NAACP Legal Defense Fund cases on her docket. Two years later, Lyndon Johnson would appoint her as the first Black woman to be a federal judge. (When Harris accepted the Democratic Party's vice presidential nomination in August 2020, she gave a shout out to Motley among the female pioneers who paved the way for future generations.)

"She was before segregationist judges in many cases. She was before cops in Mississippi. And she never lost her cool," says Michael Meltsner, her colleague at the NAACP Legal Defense Fund. "She was a powerful woman physically and mentally. She was tough-minded but courteous and friendly. She would remain balanced regardless of the situation."

Constance Baker Motley broke legal ground, working alongside figures such as Martin Luther King Jr. and lawyer William Kunstler. *Library of Congress, Prints and Photographs Division*

Over the years, Meltsner worked side by side with Motley, battling segregationists from South Carolina to Georgia and beyond. In the Atlanta case, Meltsner had taken the lead in crafting the ministers' complaint against Maddox, and then Motley traveled to Georgia to work alongside local lawyer William Alexander in huddling with the ministry students, filing court briefs, and arguing the case in court.

"She was a great lawyer," Meltsner says of his friend "Connie" Motley. Her legal work was infused with "equanimity, firmness, and intellectual toughness."

He recalls one case, two years before the Pickrick litigation, in which Motley cross-examined a segregationist school superintendent in Charleston, South Carolina. On the stand facing Motley's intense questioning, the superintendent defended his position keeping Black and White students separate. As he stepped down from the witness box and passed her, Motley issued a sharp admonition Meltsner remembered fifty-eight years later. "You should be ashamed of yourself," she said. The superintendent scurried from the courtroom.

In Atlanta, Motley struck an immediate bond not only with her fellow counsel but also with the ministry students who couldn't get past the front door of the Pickrick or the Heart of Atlanta. Her formal role was tied to the Pickrick case, but Motley kept close tabs on the parallel matter involving the motel, as each case was heard by the same judges and litigated on the same issues.

Motley's success came through the quiet, careful preparation she brought to whatever case was on her legal calendar. Never a grandstander, she used the law as the foundation for her arguments. "Her genius on my part is she appreciated our strategies," says Albert Sampson, who shared a connection with Motley through their work with NAACP organizations. "When we talked, it was a great dialogue where, as a student, I am talking to a powerful woman that was a lawyer." Motley exuded an authoritative presence, but "she also had a wit about her," says Woodrow Lewis.

With the Pickrick lawsuit filed in federal court, the lawyer sat before reporters to describe the case's significance, with local attorney Alexander seated beside her. Motley confidently addressed the assembled press, wearing a business dress with white pearls around her neck.

"That's why we're in court, don't you see. He has refused service to Negroes as a matter of fact, he has not just stated it," Motley said to one reporter's question. "By this action we hope to secure a court injunction enjoining Mr. Maddox from continuing his policy of discrimination against Negroes."

A day after the lawsuit filing, Maddox called his own press conference at the Henry Grady Hotel, where he told reporters he'd rather be locked up than integrate his restaurant. "If the president of the United States and the Congress requires that I go to jail, then I will do so gladly," Maddox declared. His family, surrounding him on the platform, choked back tears.

Called to a court hearing over a misdemeanor charge that he put a gun to Willis's face and at Dunn's back, Maddox turned out to the courtroom backed by a wall of supporters. They listened as he told the judge he never pointed a gun in anyone's face, contradicting the testimony Willis had given earlier that he had indeed threatened him with a pistol. "I'm not saying I wouldn't do so to protect my life, my liberty, and my property," Maddox testified. "I was doing what I had to do to protect my God-given property and my life."

Maddox's attorney told the judge his client was not subject to the laws at hand. "Let's get this straight," replied the judge, Osgood Williams. "This court is controlled by the law and the law alone." The judge set a $1,000 bond and directed Maddox to face the gun charge, which stood as a separate legal proceeding from the lawsuit.

The ministers had scored their first courtroom victory over Maddox. "Though this should not have to be true, it does in fact take courage for a judge in Atlanta to have ruled as Judge Williams did under the circumstances present," said an *Atlanta Inquirer* editorial on July 11.

Up next was a crucial hearing on both civil rights lawsuits moving in the Atlanta courts. On July 17, a Friday, a three-panel team of federal judges would hear the Heart of Atlanta and the Pickrick matters on the same day, one case after the other in a hearing that would overflow with spectators. Attorney General Robert Kennedy's office had moved to intervene in both cases, putting the full force of the government against Maddox, Rolleston, and any other proprietors flouting the new act, and behind the activists who could not get past the front door. As he had in the Heart of Atlanta legal matter, Attorney General Kennedy personally signed papers regarding his office's involvement in the lawsuit against Lester Maddox and his Pickrick restaurant.

As they prepared for the hearing, the federal judges directed Maddox and his company to turn over all receipts, bills, and orders involving its purchase of food and equipment. The judges wanted to follow a paper trail to see if the Pickrick was getting food and supplies from across state lines, a practice that would formally bring it under the federal Commerce Clause and the new civil rights law. The judges likewise ordered Moreton Rolleston to turn over his motel's papers, including a guest register for the last six months, the mailing list for his advertising, and all correspondence involving motel conventions for the last year. The paper trail would show that Rolleston advertised out of state and that his customers crossed state lines to spend a night at his resort motel.

When July 17 arrived, the three-judge panel would hear from a score of witnesses, including some surprise visitors to the Pickrick's dining hall. The ministry students, it turned out, hadn't been the only ones to find themselves facing Lester Maddox's pistol.

8

THE COURTROOM
SHOWDOWNS

Fifteen days after President Johnson signed the Civil Rights Act of 1964, both Atlanta lawsuits were heard on the same day by a panel of federal judges, the cases moving with urgency through a court system not known for its rapid resolution of litigation. As the nation had finally moved to pass its most sweeping slate of civil rights laws, the federal courts were giving the measures a place of prominence on the legal docket.

In Atlanta the three-judge panel included US district judge Frank Arthur Hooper Jr., a native Georgian, ardent Southern Baptist, and jurist who was already a veteran of civil rights litigation. Appointed to the federal bench in Georgia's northern district in 1949 by President Harry S. Truman, Hooper became its senior judge two years later. In 1961, Atlanta schools had desegregated upon Judge Hooper's order of two years earlier. He had also been part of a three-judge panel that directed the University of Georgia to admit two Black students.

"It is now well established," Hooper wrote in one of the desegregation cases, "that authorities in control or any state supported school may not refuse admittance to any person solely on account of race or color."

In the Atlanta courtroom in 1964, Hooper was joined by colleagues Elbert P. Tuttle and Lewis R. Morgan, and they presided over a hearing overflowing with spectators, the seats filled with onlookers both

Black and White. The crowd outside the courthouse was so jam-packed officials erected a blockade to try to move participants and spectators into court with some semblance of order. Some of the lawyers involved in the case ran a few minutes late getting into the courtroom, and the hearing room was so crammed that reporters had to sit on the floor. As Maddox walked in, he sent up waves and smiles to his supporters. He drove to court with an American flag fluttering from the antenna of a black Pontiac Grand Prix.

Up first came the Heart of Atlanta case. The government called just two witnesses to the stand: Albert Sampson and Charles Wells, the social justice preachers who had tried to book rooms at Moreton Rolleston's motel days earlier.

From the witness box, Sampson and Wells recounted their experiences. "When I got to the desk, I said, 'I'm here for the express purpose of getting my room reservation. I wired the money ahead of time,'" Sampson told the federal judges. As part of its case evidence, the government lawyers promptly filed Sampson's Western Union telegram receipt with the court.

Wells then matter-of-factly described his encounter with Rolleston two days later. "I then asked him if he was telling me that he was failing to comply with the civil rights law that had been passed, and he told me that he wasn't. He told me that the only thing that he was saying is what he had said before, and he repeated that he wasn't renting guests—renting rooms to Negro guests," Wells testified.

Rolleston personally cross-examined both men, making the point that he had been courteous in his dealings with the activist ministers.

The lawyer-businessman called no witnesses to make his case, instead presenting his legal argument detailing why Congress was wrong to tell him how to run his business.

In arguing that the congressional act was unwise, Rolleston cited an 1883 US Supreme Court ruling decreeing that Congress lacked the power to use the Thirteenth or Fourteenth Amendments to outlaw discrimination by private parties. That high court ruling had dismantled the heart of the Civil Rights Act of 1875, which had, on paper at least, guaranteed Black citizens equal rights in public transportation, public accommodations, and courtroom juries. The court's decision, consolidating five legal matters into one ruling under the heading "Civil Rights Cases," was so lengthy it took more than an hour to be read aloud. By the time Justice Joseph Bradley finished reading the decision, the civil rights act issued eight years earlier, "barely breathing in some places, was now 'void' everywhere," author Steve Luxenberg noted in *Separate: The Story of Plessy v. Ferguson, and America's Journey from Slavery to Segregation*, his book exploring US segregation struggles of the nineteenth century. The court's opinion, one newspaper correspondent concluded, "has affirmed the doctrine that Congress has no right to regulate the social habits and the social customs of the people of the States."

In court, Rolleston cited that Supreme Court case as he invoked the Thirteenth Amendment as one prong of his argument. Only the Supreme Court, not a federal court in Georgia, could rule upon his argument about the 1883 decision, he contended. Though Rolleston had not cited the Thirteenth Amendment when he filed suit against the United States on the evening Lyndon Johnson signed the new law, he quickly amended his lawsuit to include the antislavery provision.

"The Thirteenth Amendment provided there be no slavery and no involuntary servitude," Rolleston told the judges. "In our case, how can we say that we are subject to involuntary servitude? We say that we had the right to run the motel like we wanted to before the act was passed. We now have the right to run the motel like the government says. Sure, we have the alternative of quitting and giving up a four million dollar business; but can that be required of a business by law?"

In a further attempt to persuade the judges to accept his argument, the Emory-trained lawyer cited the writings of the late President Kennedy and his brother, Attorney General Robert F. Kennedy, whose office sat before him in court.

"Well, sometimes in the affairs of man it takes more than one individual to express a thing, and I want to quote a man," he said. "Mr. Robert Kennedy, the defendant in this case, wrote in the prefaced word to the memorial edition of the *Profiles in Courage* that the one thing that President Kennedy admired was courage. It took courage to pass this law. It took a little courage maybe to file a suit against the federal government. And I know this court will follow the motto over the Supreme Court of Georgia's bench which says in Latin, when translated, 'Let justice be done though the heavens may fall.' And I know this court, if it agrees with our legal interpretation, will do that in spite of the consequences which could arise out of such a decision."

With each new law it passed, Rolleston said, Congress was trampling on the "private rights" of individuals and businesses. "This is really the gravamen of the case. This is the guts of it. This is really the reason we brought the lawsuit," Rolleston told the three judges. "We could get along with Negro guests. They would hurt our business as we've alleged, and it's true. We could get along with them. But the next step after this act, there may just be one more step, that's taking over all legislation by Congress, so setting up the stage for a dictatorship in this country."

Rolleston attacked the legal standing of the new law, saying the Commerce Clause had been stretched beyond the use envisioned by the Constitution.

"I'm telling you, this extension of the commerce act to every man, woman, and child in this room and in the United States, business and personal affairs, is not authorized by the Constitution," he argued. "We don't have that liberty under the prohibitions of this act if the act is good. We say that the taking of our liberty has been done by an act of Congress." Rolleston told the judges he would obey a final court order, even if it decided against him, should it come to that. But he would continue to serve only White customers until that order arrived.

Burke Marshall, the assistant attorney general in charge of the Department of Justice's Civil Rights Division, argued the government's case alongside DOJ lawyer Charles L. Goodson.

Marshall had already earned renown as a savvy civil rights litigator. His victories included the government's 1961 ban on segregation in interstate travel. A year later, he helped push the desegregation of the University of Mississippi. He was the government's lead strategist in the season of church bombings, the March on Washington, and Freedom Rides, a skilled and quietly persistent negotiator who strove to bridge divides between figures as diametrically opposed as George Wallace and Martin Luther King Jr.

Whenever some southern city or another was engulfed in a civil rights crisis, "when young people were being beaten by angry mobs in Montgomery and when fire hoses and dogs were being turned on people in Birmingham, people always said, 'Call Burke,'" the late Georgia congressman John Lewis once said.

Marshall had been one of the Justice Department attorneys arguing most persuasively to use the Commerce Clause as a weapon against discrimination in public accommodations. After President Kennedy proposed his civil rights agenda in 1963, he dispatched Marshall across the country to meet with reluctant members of Congress and press them to join the fight. And after the Atlanta ministers were repelled from their first visit to the Pickrick, he urged the FBI to aggressively investigate Maddox's conduct that evening.

So now, in the Atlanta federal courtroom, Burke Marshall stood up for the ministers and any other patrons who could not spend an evening at Moreton Rolleston's Heart of Atlanta motel or any other establishment across the United States still holding to a Whites-only policy.

The law was squarely with the government, Marshall told the three judges, citing a series of legal precedents that showed Congress was fully within its rights to use the Commerce Clause to regulate public accommodations. "These cases hold that Congress has the power to regulate commerce not only in the sense that they can regulate things that move in interstate commerce generally, but that they can pass legislation that deals with problems that affect interstate commerce," he said.

The ultimate question, Marshall said, was not whether Congress was wise in its decision to pass the act and use the Commerce Clause to bar discrimination in local private businesses. The more pointed question, he said, was whether it had the power to make that decision.

"The matter was under consideration by Congress for over a year. It was debated at great length. It is an issue and a problem that involves great emotions. There are great political problems with it. And all of that went into the determination by the Congress to deal with it, Judge Hooper," Marshall told the federal judge. "The decision of Congress on that was made by men that included very conservative men as well as very liberal men. And I think that that kind of a decision is entitled to great weight and has been given great weight by the Supreme Court."

Finally, the lawyers were done making their arguments, and the Heart of Atlanta session adjourned. After a lunch break, the justices would turn to the case generating the most buzz in the city and drawing the most attention inside the courtroom, the ministry students' lawsuit against Lester Maddox's Pickrick restaurant.

After the court docket turned to the Pickrick case, lawyer Constance Baker Motley called to the stand a Black New Jersey high school student named Sheila Agnes Hatcher, who had been in the city that summer as a volunteer for the Atlanta Council on Human Relations.

Eleven days earlier, on July 6, Hatcher and a male friend had tried to eat at the Pickrick about twenty minutes before 6:00 PM, three nights after Willis, Lewis, and Dunn could barely get out of their car, much less enter the restaurant. As Hatcher and her friend walked closer to the door, they saw a large crowd. As they got closer still, Lester Maddox confronted them.

"Mr. Maddox came through the front door and told us to get off his property, get off his property. And he went on to name restaurants that were integrated and told us that we weren't going to—that we niggers weren't going to eat there tonight, and we weren't going to eat there any other time," Hatcher testified.

"And then I offered him my brotherhood button, and he told me to stick it," she told Motley. "There was no place for brotherhood buttons around his restaurant. And then he pulled back his coat and there was a pistol in a holster."

A plainclothes policeman saw the gun too and stepped up to tell the pair to leave. As she began to depart, Hatcher turned back once more to tell Maddox "I still considered him my brother," she testified. The officer escorted Hatcher and her friend, Gary Robinson, back up the hill but did not punish Maddox, even as the proprietor once more brandished his weapon at people who arrived seeking a seat at his restaurant.

Motley's colleague, Atlanta civil rights lawyer William Alexander, called other witnesses to the stand, including several White college students who worked for the Student Nonviolent Coordinating Committee. They had dined at the Pickrick days before the court hearing at the suggestion of the ministers' legal team.

One, George Mark Berkman, a mathematics graduate student at Harvard University working on the research staff of the SNCC, went twice in the days before the hearing, scanning a menu with roast beef, red snapper, fried perch, carrot and raisin salad, and coconut pie.

Berkman reported that the parking lot included cars with license plates from Tennessee and New Jersey, and the ketchup on the table was bottled in California. The relevance? Those cars, and the foodstuffs on the table, moved through interstate travel, bringing the Maddox restaurant under the umbrella of the new congressional act and the Commerce Clause.

Another Student Nonviolent Coordinating Committee witness, Barbara Brandt, dined at the Pickrick six times, also on the suggestion of the ministers' legal team. She spotted cars with Tennessee, Florida, and South Carolina license plates. No one bothered the White woman as she browsed the food offerings of string beans, watermelon, cantaloupe, cherry pie, pork chops, and mackerel. The Tabasco sauce on the table was from Louisiana, and the Worcestershire sauce from New Jersey.

The plaintiff lawyers also called FBI agents, who had scanned the Pickrick parking lot in the preceding days and jotted down the out-of-state plates from Alabama, North Carolina, New York, Illinois, and elsewhere. And they called grocers, who provided food and ingredients for the Pickrick from Oregon, New York, California, and other states.

With this straightforward testimony, the lawyers were proving that Lester Maddox benefited from interstate commerce.

A government lawyer named St. John Barrett called to the stand Philip Flynn, the WGST Radio news reporter whose audio captured Maddox screaming at the ministry students who first tried to integrate his restaurant fourteen days earlier. Now the entire courtroom, along with the three federal judges, heard those words: "I'll use axe handles, I'll use guns, I'll use paint, I'll use my fists, I'll use my customers, I'll use my employees, I'll use anything at my disposal."

Attorneys for Maddox paid the recording little heed. He had always run a segregated restaurant and believed he had the moral right and legal standing to continue doing so. The lawyers pressed the judges to rule the radio tape inadmissible and renewed earlier requests for the court to toss the ministers' case.

When the last witness stepped down, Motley rose to make the plaintiffs' argument. The evidence clearly demonstrated the Pickrick benefits from interstate commerce, she said, with a substantial portion of its food and some of its customers arriving from across state lines.

Motley said the city itself was supporting Maddox's segregationist policies through the actions of the plainclothes policeman who escorted Sheila Hatcher and Gary Robinson off the premises. "The officer enforced Mr. Maddox's admitted custom of refusing to serve Negroes by himself ordering the Negroes to leave," Motley told the judges and packed courtroom, concluding the ministers' case by calling out the city's inaction.

Constance Motley's arguments exposed a rift still dogging a city that had drawn acclaim for its racial togetherness. Lester Maddox felt comfortable enough in his hometown to flash his pistol at any visitor of color, sure that he wouldn't pay a legal price for his actions. Even in a city that promoted harmony instead of hatred, he'd always find himself surrounded by dozens, or hundreds, of like-minded White allies ready to back him up and drive off the integrators. And here, Motley was telling the courtroom, the city police officer provided him cover. Violence against integrators was OK in Atlanta.

The testimony and legal arguments continued until Monday. After the session concluded, the Maddox legal team, Atlanta lawyers William G. McRae and Sidney T. Schell, filed legal papers contending that the Civil Rights Act of 1964 was unconstitutional. Their legal filings attempted to draw a clear line separating the law from the operations of the Pickrick restaurant. The two, the pair argued, were not connected.

The congressional act stretched the Commerce Clause so far "as to effectually obliterate the distinction between what is national and what is local, and to create a completely centralized government, and to place the private activities of every restaurant owner engaged in business under the coercive powers of the federal government," they proffered, echoing the arguments made by Heart of Atlanta proprietor Rolleston.

The Pickrick, they maintained, was a local restaurant and was not subject to the federal Commerce Clause. "Every transaction which the defendants have in the business of operating The Pickrick restaurant is commerce which is completely internal to the state of Georgia," they wrote, even as Constance Motley and her colleagues had just demonstrated the opposite to be true.

As had Moreton Rolleston, the Pickrick lawyers cited the Thirteenth Amendment as part of their defense, saying the century-old amendment offered the restaurant protections against the new civil rights legislation. "There is no room for argument with regard to the rights guaranteed to the individual person, of whatever color or race, under the subsequently adopted Thirteenth Amendment," they wrote. "If this Court should grant the relief prayed for by the plaintiffs and intervenor in this case, the rights of the defendants under the Thirteenth Amendment to the Constitution of the United States would be destroyed by coercing them to render involuntary servitude to members of the Negro race."

As the legal arguments rolled forth, a stark disparity was emerging in the strength of the respective cases. The ministers' legal team had demonstrated in court that it was mounting its case on hard evidence and eyewitness testimony. The restaurant accepted customers and food from out of state, clearly bringing it under the Commerce Clause, and Maddox flouted the act by refusing customers based upon their race. Constance Baker Motley and her colleagues had erected a convincing case against Maddox.

Likewise, the Justice Department lawyers had based their arguments in the twin cases on long-held US law and the focused provisions of Title II of the new civil rights act, which used the Commerce Clause to fight racial discrimination. They bolstered their bedrock arguments with testimony from the ministers who could not book rooms at the Heart of Atlanta motel and with evidence that Rolleston sought out-of-state guests.

The lawyers for Maddox, by contrast, argued that the restaurateur could refuse the law because he did not agree with it and it didn't apply to his operations. Likewise, Moreton Rolleston's case was built upon the tenuous legal premise that he and his clientele had long prospered under the old ways and that Congress lacked the authority to tell him to operate any differently.

As the Pickrick lawyers scrambled to poke holes in the ministers' lawsuit, Maddox again weighed in through his "Pickrick Says" ads. His newest ad, appearing in the wake of the court hearing, hit upon familiar themes of anti-Communism, pro-Constitution, and a government peering into his affairs.

His newest ad derided the "agitators who have attempted to force me into 'involuntary servitude,' in violation of my 'rights under the Constitution,' plus the invasion of my private property by the FBI, the imported lawless and Communist-inspired white renegades who worked with them, and others who would destroy my 'Civil Rights.'"

Maddox was casting himself as the victim and his opponents—the ministers, the government, the law, the "race mixers"—as the oppressors. Their effort, Maddox told his faithful readers in Atlanta, "is intimidation of the first order."

9

TWO MAJOR RULINGS, AND A BACKLASH AGAINST THE SUPREME COURT

Five days after the court hearing began, word had spread through Atlanta's legal community. The federal judges were about to issue rulings on the Heart of Atlanta and Pickrick integration battles. The pending decrees would be historic, issued simultaneously as the first two judicial decisions nationwide assessing the legality of the Civil Rights Act of 1964's section on public accommodations. The Atlanta federal courts would be formally adjudging a core component of the late president's civil rights legislation.

Reporters raced to the courthouse to get their copies. There, they saw that Lester Maddox had turned out as well. He was as eager as anyone to see how the judges would rule. But regardless of what the federal judges would say, "I'm not going to integrate," Maddox told the journalists. "I've made a pledge."

He and the media horde unfurled the rulings to see that Judge Hooper and his colleagues had issued a definitive rebuttal to the restaurateur's latest advertisement and his defense team's arguments and to the legal strategy conveyed by Moreton Rolleston.

Brisk and conclusive in their opinions, the justices directed Rolleston and Maddox to open their doors to all races. Their rulings, issued July 22, 1964, under the auspices of the US District Court in the Northern District of Georgia, said Congress had the legal right to apply the Commerce Clause to bar racial discrimination.

"Congress had the power to go this far," the judges wrote in their four-page order in the Pickrick case. "It follows, therefore, that the defendants' attack on the constitutionality of the Act as applied to their operation must fail."

The judges echoed those sentiments in their six-page order in the Heart of Atlanta matter. "It is clear that the attack by the complainant on the constitutionality of these sections of the Civil Rights Act must fail," they wrote. "It is equally clear that the United States is entitled to the injunction prayed for it by its counterclaim."

A day later came a pair of brief two-page orders making clear what was expected. The Heart of Atlanta was enjoined from "refusing to accept Negroes as guests in the motel by reason of their race or color." Maddox likewise was barred from "refusing to admit Negroes to the premises of The Pickrick Restaurant upon the same basis and under the same conditions that non-Negro members of the general public are admitted."

The Atlanta rulings suddenly became required reading across the country. The county attorney's office in metropolitan Dade County in Miami sought a copy—as did the attorney general's office in Baton Rouge, Louisiana, and a First Amendment lawyer in Hollywood, California. A Vanderbilt University office on race relations in Nashville, Tennessee, and the city of New Orleans, were among others seeking copies.

"My constituents in New Orleans have been asking me for a copy of the decision in the case involving the Pickrick and the Heart of Atlanta Motel," New Orleans city attorney Alvin J. Liska wrote to the court clerk in Atlanta. "I would appreciate it very much if you would send me a copy of this decision."

To each request, the clerk's office collected a modest copying fee, and then shipped out the rulings, from coast to coast.

The judges gave Maddox and Rolleston twenty days to appeal, closing that window on August 11. Moving with haste, the men filed petitions to the US Supreme Court to stay the three-judge panel's ruling. The federal court decision, they said, would bring their businesses great harm while trampling upon their rights to act free of government intrusion.

In their appeal to the high court, Maddox's lawyers raised fundamental questions about the Georgia panel's decree. "Is Title II of the 'Civil Rights Act of 1964' a valid exercise of the power of Congress to regulate commerce?" the attorneys asked. "Will such compulsion by the court subject the defendants to involuntary servitude, in violation of their right to be free from involuntary servitude under the provisions of Article XIII of the Constitution of the United States?"

––––––––––––

The stay requests landed before US Supreme Court justice Hugo Black, the high court jurist assigned to oversee federal appeals from the Eleventh Circuit covering Georgia, Florida, and Alabama.

Black's ruling was eagerly awaited across the country, most notably in southern cities still waged in a race war over public accommodations. His opinion would mark the high court's first foray into the legality of the new civil rights act. Though the law was on the books, segregationists were praying for a reprieve and looking for Black to provide it. He would deeply disappoint them.

Black considered the evidence in both cases and then drafted a single ruling in longhand, using pencil on lined notebook paper, scratching through some passages as he crafted a decision. The high court staff typed up his prose and issued his analysis in a four-page ruling under the heading of the Supreme Court of the United States.

On August 10, Justice Black rejected Rolleston's and Maddox's requests, deeming the lower court's ruling legally sound. "The court's findings adequately supported by facts show that the motel and restaurant have refused and unless enjoined intend to continue to refuse to serve Negroes with food or lodging because of their color," Black wrote. "This refusal plainly violates Title II of the Civil Rights Act of

1964 unless Congress in passing that Act went beyond its powers under the Constitution."

In passing the civil rights act, Black concluded, Congress properly turned to the Commerce Clause, "which grants Congress power to regulate all commerce among the states—a very broad power to regulate commerce itself as well as what affects or conduct might affect that commerce." And Congress justifiably turned to the Fourteenth Amendment, which forbids any state to "deny any person, within its jurisdiction the equal protection of the laws," Justice Black wrote.

The burden to overturn a congressional act was exceedingly high, Black said. "Thus, judicial power to stay an act of Congress, like judicial power to hold that act unconstitutional, is an awesome responsibility calling for the utmost circumspection in its exercise," the jurist reasoned. "This factor is all the more important where, as here, a single member of the Court is asked to delay the will of Congress to put its policies into effect at the time it desires."

Rolleston and Maddox had not come close to reaching that bar, he ruled, particularly on an issue of such public importance. "Moreover, the constitutionally chosen policies of this Act are not the result of sudden, impulsive legislative action but represents the culmination of one of the most thoroughly debated subjects concerning which Congress has ever passed a law," Black added. He closed simply, "Stays are denied."

Even as he rejected the appeals, Black made clear he was eager for the full court to consider the core questions posed by the legal challenges, and to do so quickly. His ruling denying the stay requests was limited to whether the high court should, in effect, block the execution of the lower court's ruling. Yet Black and his colleagues stood ready to fully explore the legality of the civil rights act's section on public accommodations.

"Under these circumstances, a judicial restraint of the enforcement of one of the most important sections of the Civil Rights Act would, in my judgment, be unjustifiable," Black wrote. "I agree with appellants, however, and with the Solicitor General as to the wisdom of having the specific constitutional issues here involved decided at as early a date as orderly procedure will permit."

Black's opinion, heartening to the government and ministers, rattled constituents across the country who made their views clear in a stack of letters that began arriving in his mailbox.

"That bill is a disgrace to the human race," an elderly woman wrote Black one day after his ruling. "I would like for you to tell me if you feel deep down in your heart that you really think that the negras are your equals. I want to say here and now they are not my equals & never will be and we don't want them going to school with our children."

She continued, "They are entitled to go to school—but not with our children and we don't want them eating in our restaurants & going to our churches & theaters. They rape white women & young girls & what does the law do about them. They should be put behind bars to stay. This country is in the worst mess then I can remember it being in, in my 79 yrs."

A self-described "An American Mother" corresponded three days later. "You persecute someone like Lester Maddox to do the will of Communist trained Martin Luther King, Jr.," she wrote. "If Goldwater loses in Nov. I think I will just move out of America. . . . As I view the riots by the Negroes in the North I feel that anarchy has come to America and unless a Conservative government wins out we will have rule by mobs just as do Latin America countries."

A seventy-seven-year-old Saint Louis, Missouri, property owner told Black he was "ashamed" by the ruling and shared his own personal bill of rights, including his right to choose his own clientele and vote against any public official who supported civil rights and its public accommodations section. Another writer made his point in a pungent few words. "You are not [going] to force niggers on us," he wrote the justice.

Also landing on the justice's desk was literature from the Pennsylvania-based National Association for the Advancement of White People, which shared its platform of "White Equal Rights" as it launched a petition drive to put the civil rights bill up to a public referendum. "We are not as much ANTI-NEGRO as the NAACP is ANTI-WHITE—we are PRO-WHITE," the group said. It had cast a wide net seeking "any suggestions to offer as to how we can best keep the U.S. WHITE."

Lester Maddox was every bit as entrenched as the letter writers. After Black's ruling, Maddox appeared before reporters to deride the

Civil Rights Act of 1964 as "unconstitutional" and President Johnson as a traitor to the cause of free enterprise.

"I am shocked, and I am hurt," Maddox said. Attired in a dark suit and tie, he stood before a giant billboard decrying the death of liberty. "And if we close, it won't be Lester Maddox closing. It won't be the Pickrick closing. It will be the president of the United States and my government turning the key in my lock," he later added.

Some Pickrick patrons had turned away as the nation's new civil rights law officially took hold. But Maddox said many regulars continued frequenting a restaurant that refused to change even as almost every other hotel and eatery in Atlanta accepted or embraced desegregation. Even after the federal court's ruling, Maddox boasted, "Well wishers came by the hundreds."

With the courts now against him, too, joining Congress and the president, Maddox placed a manikin on a bench in front of his restaurant. Then he thrust a knife in its back. "This manikin represents what has happened to the American private enterprise system," he wrote.

10

THE MINISTERS AND PICKRICK: BACK FOR SECONDS, THIRDS

WITH THEIR QUEST TO BLOCK THE FEDERAL court's order summarily denied and with August 11 formally upon them, the two Atlanta businessmen responded in markedly different ways.

Moreton Rolleston Jr. reluctantly opened his Heart of Atlanta to all comers, just as he had told the judges he would, upon a formal court order. Yet even as Rolleston prepared to provide a night's lodging to the occasional Black patron or family who would arrive to register at the front desk, he kept working his legal appeals in a case he would take all the way to the US Supreme Court. Lester Maddox, on the other hand, kept operating as if there were no court order at all.

With the August 11 deadline having arrived, three seminary brothers set out to see if Maddox would finally comply with the law and accept their patronage. Albert Dunn, Albert Sampson, and Charles Wells, all dressed in suits and ties this Tuesday afternoon, didn't want to allow Maddox a single day to flout its provisions. They headed out about 1:30 PM that day with a fellow activist named Barbara Pace Suarez.

"We knew that we had to implement the law five minutes after the ink dried," Sampson recently recalled. The ministers shared their plan with their lawyers, including Constance Baker Motley and William Alexander, and briefed government lawyer Burke Marshall. All were in agreement: the activists must test the ruling right away and send Maddox the clear signal he was not above the law.

"That first day, I was scared," admits Sampson, who was fully cognizant that he and his colleagues would likely be encountering "deepseated Klanspeople." A second woman who was to join the group decided against confronting Maddox and his backers, saying she was frightened by what may occur and would stay back. Sampson ultimately put the fears aside. "We had to do it," he knew.

Sampson was already "seasoned" in the landscape of civil rights sitins and demonstrations and found a peaceful calm as he readied to confront Maddox. He had been the NAACP's North Carolina college leader at the time of the Greensboro Four sit-in movement and, with a friend named James Fox, had been arrested when they tried to patronize a Whites-only lunch counter in Raleigh in March 1960. "I had already come out of the heat or been a part of the sit-in demonstrations in North Carolina from 1957 to 1961," he said. "And then as executive secretary of the Atlanta branch of the NAACP, I was fighting for school desegregation."

As he ventured out to challenge the Pickrick restaurant, Sampson felt emboldened by his experience as a college student in North Carolina, when he saw laws being passed in the capital and then put into action in the community. He felt the Civil Rights Act of 1964 was at his back. "My background of the law gave me the responsibility to challenge the law," Sampson says. "Once we understand we had the law, Lester Maddox is no different than me. We both had to function because of the law."

Maddox would promptly and forcefully reveal that he didn't share the young activist's view. Earlier that day, Maddox and his staff had repelled three Black seventeen-year-olds who tried to enter. He'd block the next visitors, too.

As Sampson's group pulled into the familiar low-slung diner, Maddox stood ready for them, armed with a pistol at his side and a mob of some two hundred supporters. Nearby, a barrel held axe handles available for sale.

Maddox rallied his supporters for another stand against his would-be invaders. "We are never going to integrate!" he yelled. "The Pickrick belongs to Lester Maddox, not to Lyndon Johnson or the news media or the agitators or Nikita Khrushchev!"

Then he turned his attention toward the ministers at his door. "You're dirty Communists and you'll never get a piece of fried chicken here," Maddox shouted, keeping his firearm in its holster as he thrust his fingers at the men. Maddox still had to resolve his earlier gun charge so, while he was sure to let the ministers know he had the weapon on hand, he didn't point it at anyone's face this time.

As he witnessed Maddox packing a pistol, Sampson braced for an attack, knowing that he or one of his friends could suffer serious injury or worse. The most haunting image, he said, was the barrel filled with pickaxe handles nearby and the specter of Maddox supporters grabbing them as weapons.

"We were really under the impression we were really going to die there. It was not only his gun," Sampson said recently. "I can never forget the barrel."

Wells likewise saw that the crowd was "very hostile," but the visitors held their ground as they stood surrounded by a swarm of Maddox faithful. While most of the faces were White, some were Black. Maddox had one of his Black laborers, a sturdily built cook named Ozell Rogers, tell the ministers their efforts would force his boss to close the restaurant and put him and other Black employees out of work. Rogers later told the press he enjoyed his job and had no hesitation blocking the integrators. "I feel like a person should not go where he is not wanted," he said. Maddox had other Black employees stand out front as well—Black people blocking Black people, a turn that astounded Sampson.

One of Maddox's White supporters tried to punch one of the preachers, but missed, and local police stepped in to separate the factions. But they took no action to punish the segregationists flailing fists at their nonviolent visitors. Another White patron hollered, "Push that black boy out of the front of that door," reported the news media paying witness to this newest confrontation.

Ministers Charles Wells and Albert Dunn are swarmed by Maddox patrons and supporters, who block them from entering the Pickrick restaurant in August 1964. *AP*

"You're not here to eat," Maddox shouted. "You're here to run us out of business."

"The government has told you to integrate," Sampson replied. "We would like to enter."

"If you live to be one hundred years old, you'll not get a piece of my fried chicken," Maddox said.

Undeterred, Sampson asked, "Are you calling President Johnson a Communist?"

"No," Maddox replied. "But you're a Communist and you're not coming in."

Maddox dashed into the restaurant at one point, speaking to his supporters through a loudspeaker. Wells, Sampson, and company tried again to inch forward but could not move past the mob. "Shut your big boy mouth!" Maddox bellowed at Sampson, a United Press International journalist reported.

As Sampson and his brethren stood their ground against Maddox's attack, the NAACP leader said he relied upon his faith for protection.

"As a minister I am deeply rooted in the idea of death," he told me. "When you work out the question of death, it's kind of comfortable to go on to live. Because it's all in His hands."

By now the regular lunch contingent would normally peter out, so Maddox moved to close the restaurant for a few hours before the supper crowd arrived. When he did, the ministry activists and their friend Suarez agreed to depart, knowing they could not break through the throng of resistance but aware that this newest confrontation further enhanced their case that Maddox was blatantly violating the most significant component of the new civil rights law.

As they left, Maddox blockaded the streets around his restaurant and let local police have it for having rerouted traffic earlier, saying their efforts had made it harder for some of his regulars to come in that day.

Why did the ministers keep turning out when they knew the odds of crossing past the restaurant's front door were slim to nonexistent? Dunn said they kept returning not to put the spotlight on themselves—he said he never watched the television reports on the confrontations—but for a simpler reason. "I could never as a human being accept the fact that anyone could deny me entrance in public places," he later said. Their visit, unsuccessful on its face, became fuel for government lawyers arguing that Maddox was a habitual scofflaw to the Civil Rights Act of 1964.

The next day, August 12, Robert F. Kennedy's office filed a motion seeking a court order holding Maddox in contempt of court for continuing to disobey the law. Each time Maddox refused the pastors' entry, the government and the ministers' lawyers replied with new legal filings citing his blockade as additional proof he was in contempt of court. The battle had emerged as a legal game of chicken. Which side would blink first? The ministers and the government, every bit as dug in as Maddox and his followers, showed no sign of retreat.

Attached to this newest motion, the government lawyers included an affidavit from Charles Wells, filed with the court to document Maddox's latest resistance to the new law.

"When we reached the door, the people who had been standing around on the sidewalk gathered around us, and we were completely encircled," Wells said. "Mr. Maddox called us Communists and agitators. He was applauded and cheered by the other people while he made a speech."

Wells recounted how, when he asked Maddox if he were open for business, "he said we would be putting seventy-five people out of jobs. Mr. Maddox brought several of his Negro employees to the door where we were standing. One of the Negro employees was a big man about fifty years old. He told me that I was supposed to be a man of the gospel and I was doing something which could cost him his job. I told him I could get him another job."

Sampson also filed an affidavit, attached to a similar court filing made by the attorneys for the pastors, that provided more documentation to hold Maddox to account. "It was not possible for us to enter the restaurant as the door was physically blocked by Mr. Maddox, some of his employees and by other unknown persons," he wrote. "The crowd was very hostile and many persons in the crowd were carrying ax-handles."

A federal judge immediately acted on the motions, the next day setting a hearing for one week later to adjudge whether Maddox was in contempt of court for refusing to serve Dunn, Sampson, Wells, and Suarez. The court served the papers on Maddox on August 13, saying he would have to show cause why he shouldn't be held in contempt. That same day, FBI agents and even more "agitators" tried to enter his restaurant.

Maddox blocked their entry, but he had had enough. He was about to blink first.

———

That Thursday, August 13, Lester Maddox closed the Pickrick. He'd rather shut down his business than cave to pressure from the president, Congress, and local integrators. "The Pickrick is closed!" he declared. "Now get out of here!"

Maddox later wiped tears as he closed his restaurant while he grieved for the loss of the "southern way of life." Behind him, a Black worker, with a white Pickrick cap atop his head, bit his own lip at the reality of his job loss.

Two weeks later, Maddox traveled to the Democratic National Convention in Atlantic City to protest the new civil rights law. Joined by relatives and coworkers, he and the group paraded on the boardwalk with signs saying the new law was "ungodly." Maddox told reporters he would refuse to dine at integrated restaurants in the city. Soon enough, the segregationist faced heckling himself. "Take down those lousy signs!" a young man shouted at him. "You're standing out here making an idiot of yourself."

"You're a liar!" Maddox shot back.

He returned home to more legal challenges. On September 4, with his restaurant still not serving diners, the federal court once again issued an order barring Maddox from refusing to serve Black patrons. Though he wasn't serving food, Maddox was open for other business, selling even more axe handles, segregationist pamphlets, and a fizzy drink called "Gold Water," a play on words for his support for Barry Goldwater's 1964 presidential campaign against Lyndon Johnson. Two months later, Johnson would destroy Goldwater at the polls with the largest share of the national vote in 144 years.

The restaurant closing was short-lived. Maddox, bleeding money with his dining room's closure, decided he needed to reopen for food service to maintain his income. He did so with a Lester Maddox twist, showing that his temporary shutdown was ultimately a short-term diversion as he plotted his next chess move to beat the government and the ministers.

Later in September, on the same Hemphill Avenue site, the doors of the Lester Maddox Cafeteria swung open. The proprietor promptly affixed signs on the front door making clear the new rules of the establishment. One said, NOTICE: I DO NOT OFFER TO SERVE EITHER: 1.) INTEGRATIONISTS, OR, 2.) INTERSTATE TRAVELERS, REGARDLESS OF RACE, COLOR, CREED OR NATIONAL ORIGIN. Maddox vowed to serve only "acceptable" Georgians.

He added, "A person entering this Restaurant for service will be considered as representing to me that such person is neither an Integrationist nor an Interstate Traveler. If such representation is believed to be false, service will be refused." He signed the note, "Lester Maddox, Owner, Lester Maddox Cafeteria."

After the courts ruled he had to serve Black patrons, Maddox opened a new restaurant with new rules for admission on the same site as the Pickrick. *Kenan Research Center at the Atlanta History Center*

Maddox was trying to outsmart Congress and its civil rights act by saying he served only in-state customers. For years Maddox had rigidly refused to serve Black people, a position well known to anyone who knew him or had frequented his restaurant. "We perfectly knew and everybody knows that we did not serve Negroes, under the Pickrick Corporation," Maddox testified under oath in the court case.

But now, with the Civil Rights Act of 1964 telling him and all other dining hall owners they couldn't discriminate based on race, Maddox was adjusting his posture. The sign on his door was saying he barred integrationists and interstate travelers. Thus, he was not subject to the interstate Commerce Clause and could continue operating exactly as he had since the day he opened his restaurant seventeen years earlier, free from government interference.

His lawyers cited this shifting position in one of their legal filings after he changed the name of his restaurant. "The policy of The Pickrick corporation in the operation of the Pickrick Restaurant in refusing service to members of the Negro race on the ground of race alone has not been continued by Lester Maddox Cafeteria," they noted.

As he opened his new restaurant that Saturday September 26, Maddox changed the title of his weekly "Pickrick Says" ads to "Lester Maddox Says." His message did not change with the new name. "The soul of America is being destroyed," he told his followers.

The ministers and their legal team saw through the smoke screen shrouding the Lester Maddox Cafeteria's new rules of entry. Once more, they plotted a visit to the Hemphill Avenue edifice.

Two days after the Lester Maddox Cafeteria began serving practically the same menu the Pickrick restaurant had offered, the civil rights leaders were back at his doors at noon that Monday.

This time, it was Dunn, Lewis, Wells, and Willis, all wearing dark business suits and journeying over from the offices of Martin Luther King's Southern Christian Leadership Conference.

"We were a little bit more bold and radical in those days, but reasonable," Woodrow Lewis later recalled. "He would not serve us no matter what, so we said we were going to test the water. We're going to go in and get some chicken in the restaurant. The law was on our side."

Lewis says one attribute drove the men as they tried, once more, to enter through Maddox's front door: determination. They were angry they couldn't get in, and their patience was wearing thin over the blockades that had greeted them each time they tried. But Albert Dunn, Lewis says, led the charge. We need to keep going back until we finally get a seat.

"We were determined to fight this battle, and we were determined to persevere," Lewis recounts. "There was a sense of frustration, anger, and I guess a bit of impatience too, and I would give Albert Dunn the credit of leadership in pursuing the effort not to be patient but to move forward.

"We're not going to give up. We're not going to let this go," he continues. "They thought we would give up. That's where they read us wrong."

As the pastors set out for their third attempt to eat at Maddox's restaurant, the Atlanta proprietor would have none of their business. "Get off my property! I'll run my place the way I want to," yelled Maddox, wearing a GOLDWATER FOR PRESIDENT button and surrounded by hordes of allied White faces.

Maddox pushed and shoved the men to the sidewalk, some twenty feet from his front door. One of the men told Maddox he was crazy, and he retorted, "Yeah, I'm crazy—crazy enough to want my business." The ministers didn't strike back. "I've never laid my hands on Mr. Maddox other than to extend my hand for him to shake it," Wells later said.

"I don't make threats to anyone," Dunn echoed.

With the hostility hovering around them this Monday afternoon and no chance to step through the restaurant's doors, they departed. "You are a disgrace," Dunn told Maddox as the activists headed back to their dorms. He wouldn't use his fists, but Dunn always had to speak his mind.

After he again forced the ministry students off his property, Maddox disparaged the men in a chat with local reporters. "We're not ever going to integrate," he said. "They ought to know that by now. If the sorry rascals would get jobs, we wouldn't have any of this trouble."

To the press and the Atlanta reading public, the ministry students were largely invisible, often unnamed and not quoted. An *Atlanta Journal* account of this latest confrontation, headlined MADDOX BARS FOUR NEGROES, includes a photograph of Maddox pushing back against one of his visitors. "Owner Lester Maddox Shoves Negro Attempting to Integrate Cafeteria," says the cutline under the picture. The photo does not identify the man, sharply dressed in a dark suit and tie, who is the focus of Maddox's fury. It is George Willis. The news account describes the men simply as "all reportedly ministers or ministerial students."

Invisible or not, Lewis could see that their nonviolent protests had gotten under the skin of Maddox and his supporters. Had the ministers fought back, the Lester Maddox faithful would have surely pounced upon them and said they had ample cause to do so, with hordes of witnesses to back up their story. Instead, the ministers pressed forth with words, exuding a calm that contrasted with the barbs and screams of the Pickrick mob.

Lester Maddox pushes back upon a sharply dressed visitor in September 1964 after opening his restaurant under a new name, the Lester Maddox Cafeteria. In the photo published at the time, the target of Maddox's fury was not identified. It is George Willis III, one of the Atlanta ministry students who kept knocking at Maddox's door. *UPI/Bettmann Archive/Getty Images*

"They couldn't stand it. I think we got to them," Lewis says. "It wasn't easy for us from a human standpoint to be nonviolent, but the teachings of Martin stuck with us. We stayed on the battlefield of the Lord."

Another blockade meant more evidence documenting the restaurateur's violation of the civil rights law, and additional momentum for the ministers' legal quest to hold Maddox accountable. Once again, their lawyers were back in court, seeking another contempt of court hearing for Maddox.

"On September 28, 1964, four members of the Negro race, George Willis Jr., Woodrow T. Lewis, Albert Dunn, and Charles E. Wells Sr. were denied admission to and service at The Pickrick and Lester Maddox Cafeteria by Mr. Maddox solely because they are members of the Negro race," wrote Atlanta attorney William Alexander, Constance Motley, and her colleagues with the NAACP Legal Defense Fund in New York.

The attorney general's office filed a similar motion, including an affidavit from Willis. "He ordered us off the property and pushed me backwards toward the sidewalk. I saw him push Charles E. Wells, Sr. backwards toward the sidewalk, also," Willis reported.

Once more, a federal judge ordered Maddox to stand before him to say why he shouldn't be held in contempt of court.

Not long after, Lewis says, Lester Maddox reached out to the men and invited them to come sit across from him in the restaurant during off hours. For a moment, their hopes rose that their adversary had finally agreed to relent. When they sat across from Maddox, it was clear he had not changed.

"If you tell me you believe in segregation, I'll buy you dinner and I'll have dinner with you," Maddox told them, Lewis recalls. They said no and left, chagrined by the owner's words. "We thought maybe he was going to give in and accept us for who we are," Lewis says.

The Maddox defense team continued to insist their client had broken no laws. To them, the ministers were the scofflaws, not Maddox. Charles Wells "used offensive and insulting language," they said, "calling him a crazy man, and otherwise insulting him in an attempt to provoke him to do and say things he would not have said but for such provocation and harassment."

His lawyers crafted a legal strategy they hoped could finally block the law from applying to his place of business. Title II of the Civil Rights Act of 1964 "is not applicable to him, or to his said business, because such discrimination and segregation as is practiced by him in the conduct of said business against prospective customers is not upon the ground of race, color, religion or national origin, but upon the ground of the political beliefs and ideas espoused and promoted by integrationists which are exceedingly obnoxious to him, and with whom he does not desire to associate," wrote the lawyers, William G. McRae and Sidney T. Schell. Forcing Maddox to serve the ministers "would constitute depriving him of his personal dignity and subject him to humiliation before his family, his friends, and his community," they continued.

It was, once more, a legal filing relying upon the argument Maddox was above the Civil Rights Act of 1964. Forcing Maddox to follow the law, the lawyers argued, would bring him humiliation.

The lawyers ticked off a string of constitutional amendments they say empowered Maddox to operate his private business as he saw fit. One, once more, was the Thirteenth. "It would subject said respondent to involuntary servitude in violation of the Thirteenth Amendment to the Constitution of the United States," the Maddox lawyers argued.

Maddox was more succinct than his team's legal filings. After the ministers' newest failed attempt to enter through his doors, he confided to reporters. "They'll kill me before they force me to integrate my place," he vowed.

11

"THE PEOPLE'S COURT" AND THE HEART OF ATLANTA MOTEL

As the integration chess game played out in Atlanta, the nation's highest court wheeled forth with one ruling after another cementing its image as a proponent for equality and social change.

For sixteen years, from 1953 until 1969, the US Supreme Court was chaired by jurist Earl Warren, a judicial activist who believed the Constitution should be interpreted with the times. Under Warren's watch, the high court would issue some of its most earth-moving, lasting, and occasionally contentious rulings. Warren himself penned the court's unanimous *Brown v. Board of Education* decision in 1954, ordering public schools be desegregated "with all deliberate speed," a decree bitterly fought for years in communities resistant to racially mixed schools.

After serving as a local district attorney in California, Warren would go on to become the state's attorney general in 1938. Then, beginning in 1942, he won three successive elections as California governor, leading one of the country's most influential states. Warren was a moderate Republican and populist figure who curried support with voters from both parties. His political outlook had been cast at an early age, when, while working on the Southern Pacific railroads as a youth, he witnessed the industry's abusive treatment of workers. "I was dealing with people as they worked for a gigantic corporation that dominated the economic and political life of the community," Warren later said. "I saw that power exercised and the hardship that followed in its wake."

The Supreme Court under his stewardship issued a series of rulings permanently altering the nation's laws involving racial equality and the rights of the accused in criminal justice proceedings. Such cases served as an affirmation of Earl Warren's view of the legal body as "the people's court." Scholars say Warren's liberal views became more pronounced as he led the nation's highest court.

In *Mapp v. Ohio* in 1961, the court held 6–3 that evidence collected in violation of a suspect's Fourth Amendment right against unlawful searches would be inadmissible in court. That ruling centered on a case in Ohio where Cleveland police, without a legal warrant in hand, invaded the duplex of a woman they believed was harboring a suspected bomber. When the woman pressed to see the warrant, police kept searching. They didn't find the bomber but arrested her for possessing pornographic material. The Supreme Court reversed her conviction. "The ignoble shortcut to conviction left open to the State tends to destroy the entire system of constitutional restraints on which the liberties of the people rest," said the opinion authored by Justice Tom Clark.

A year later, the court weighed in on the issue of school prayer, taking up a New York case in which several families filed suit after the school district in New Hyde Park adopted a daily prayer. In the 6–1 *Engel v. Vitale* ruling authored by Justice Hugo Black, the court held that the state could not hold prayers in public schools, even if participation was not a requirement and the prayer was not linked to any specific religion.

In *Gideon v. Wainwright* in 1963, the court, in a unanimous vote once more authored by Justice Black, said impoverished criminal defendants had an absolute right to a lawyer even if they could not afford one. The case involved Clarence Earl Gideon, who stood accused of breaking into a Florida pool hall but wasn't given legal counsel even though he asked for one in open court. "Mr. Gideon, I am sorry, but I cannot appoint Counsel to represent you in this case. Under the laws of the State of Florida, the only time the Court can appoint Counsel to represent a Defendant is when that person is charged with a capital offense," the judge replied.

Gideon represented himself at trial, and he "conducted his defense about as well as could be expected from a layman," the Supreme Court noted. Convicted at trial and sentenced to five years in prison, Gideon kept pressing his case, filing an appeal saying he was entitled to counsel. The Supreme Court agreed, reversing his conviction in a ruling affirming the rights of all defendants with no money to be represented by counsel in a felony proceeding.

In the latter years of the Warren court came two more landscape-changing rulings: *Miranda v. Arizona* in 1966 and *Loving v. Virginia* in 1967.

The *Miranda* case, passed by a razor-thin 5–4 vote, held that police had a lawful obligation to advise suspects of their right to counsel and to remain silent. No statements could be taken from suspects without the Miranda warning first being issued and understood, a protection well known by any viewer of modern-day law-and-order crime sagas.

The ruling initially drew deep rebukes from police, who feared they were losing vital weapons to protect citizens from criminals. "We might as well close up shop," a Texas police chief griped. Others said the ruling essentially granted criminals a shield of protection. Chief Justice Warren, preparing to craft the final opinion, believed the fundamental legal protections at stake were most paramount. "This will be one of the most important opinions of our time," he correctly assessed.

The Miranda ruling involved four cases in which defendants were "cut off from the outside world" and questioned without being given any sense of their legal rights. The primary case centered on an indigent twenty-three-year-old suspect with a ninth-grade reading level who had been convicted of kidnapping and raping an eighteen-year-old young woman after confessing to Phoenix, Arizona, police he was guilty of the crimes. His confession came although he had not been advised of his legal right to remain silent or to have a lawyer present.

Warren said the rights of criminal suspects could not be trampled simply to secure convictions, even in crimes of such a serious nature. "The cases before us raise questions which go to the roots of our concepts of American criminal jurisprudence: the restraints society must observe consistent with the Federal Constitution in prosecuting individuals for crime," he wrote. The high court tossed Miranda's conviction. The state of Arizona retried him, this time without introducing his confession, and again won a conviction. Like *Gideon*, the Miranda ruling remains among the bedrock rights of criminal justice suspects to this day.

In the *Loving* case, a grand jury in Caroline County, Virginia, had indicted a couple, Richard and Mildred Loving, for violating the state's ban on interracial marriage. "Almighty God created the races white, black, yellow, malay [*sic*], and red, and he placed them on separate continents," said the trial judge hearing their case in Virginia. "The fact that he separated the races shows that he did not intend for the races to mix."

In a unanimous decision once more authored by Warren, the Supreme Court adjudged the Virginia law unconstitutional under the Fourteenth Amendment, which held that no state shall "deprive any person of life, liberty, or property, without due process of law; nor deny to any person within its jurisdiction the equal protection of the laws." The couple's quest to overturn the Virginia county ruling was years later featured in Arkansas-born director Jeff Nichols's Academy Award–nominated feature film, *Loving*.

Writing in the *Loving* case, Justice Warren encapsulated another watershed moment for civil rights under the court's watch. "Under our Constitution the freedom to marry, or not marry, a person of another race resides with the individual, and cannot be infringed by the state," he wrote. "There can be no doubt that restricting the freedom to marry solely because of racial classifications violates the central meaning of the Equal Protection Clause."

Now, in the fall of 1964, the Warren court prepared to hear evidence and pass judgment on the case of *Heart of Atlanta v. USA*.

Motel proprietor Moreton Rolleston had earlier appealed the Georgia federal court's July 22 ruling barring him from refusing Black patrons, arguing that the Civil Rights Act of 1964 was unconstitutional and an infringement upon his rights as a private businessman. And then when

Hugo Black denied his request for a stay of that order, Rolleston pressed his case to the full Supreme Court.

One of his appeal prongs turned to the Fifth Amendment. Rolleston contended the act took his liberty and property without due process or compensation. It was the same argument South Carolina's Strom Thurmond had made in his CBS debate against Hubert Humphrey over the bill in Congress. And once more the motel operator founded his argument on the Thirteenth Amendment. The civil rights law, "by requiring plaintiff to serve Negroes at plaintiff's motel against plaintiff's will, subjects plaintiff to involuntary servitude," he wrote.

The Supreme Court moved with dispatch to schedule the *Heart of Atlanta* case, setting it for hearing three months after Rolleston had brought his case against the government. The justices wanted to apply the weight of their court to adjudge a core component of the civil rights law, scheduling oral arguments during a week normally set aside for administrative matters.

So, the Supreme Court readied to take up the *Heart of Atlanta* case and a companion matter involving a barbecue eatery in Alabama, which had filed suit on July 31, 1964, alleging the Civil Rights Act of 1964 was invalid. Both cases landed on the docket for oral arguments that first week of October. Rolleston and the government had filed a joint motion to accelerate the oral arguments, the rare occasion in which the parties had come to a consensus.

Justice Black had made clear his eagerness to hear the *Atlanta* case in August, even as he denied Rolleston and Lester Maddox's request to stay the federal court ruling, and now he stood ready to weigh both the Georgia and Alabama arguments. "I would welcome motions to the Court to expedite both cases in the hope that they could be made ready for final argument the first week we meet in October," he wrote.

As they prepared to hear the cases, Supreme Court justices described the Civil Rights Act of 1964 as "most comprehensive," noting that it set out to bar discrimination "in voting, as well as in places of accommodation and public facilities, federally secured programs and in employment."

But their focus now would be squarely on the act's Title II, which said: "All persons shall be entitled to the full and equal enjoyment of the goods, services, facilities, privileges, advantages, and accommodations of any place of public accommodation, as defined in this section, without discrimination or segregation on the ground of race, color, religion, or national origin."

That section targeted hotels and motels, cafeterias and restaurants, and movie houses across the country, providing for civil sanctions and permanent injunctions against scofflaws. The issue before the court justices was whether Congress had the authority to regulate such local businesses using the Commerce Clause. "The sole question posed is, therefore, the constitutionality of the Civil Rights Act of 1964 as applied to these facts," the justices wrote.

What happened in Atlanta would now play out in the august chambers of the US Supreme Court as the first and most significant legal test of the new civil rights act. Standing before the jurists would be an Emory-trained lawyer who contended the law was not only unjust but also discriminatory, barring him and any other business from running their operations as they saw fit. The case, then, zeroed in on a battle between private rights and the public good, between Moreton Rolleston's quest to manage his own affairs free from government dictate and the wishes of Black customers looking for a night's lodging at his big city motel.

12

ARGUMENTS BEFORE
THE HIGH COURT

CHIEF JUSTICE EARL WARREN OPENED the two-hour-and-twenty-two-minute Supreme Court hearing for *Heart of Atlanta v. USA* by noting that jurisdiction was proper and that the court had granted the joint motion for an expedited hearing.

"We will proceed," Warren said. "Mr. Rolleston."

Rolleston dressed conservatively, like the lawyer and businessman he was, and he spoke with crisp blasts of dialogue. On October 5, 1964, he put his voice, and his training, to use before the nine justices.

"Mr. Chief justice, may it please the court," he began, taking a few moments to gather his thoughts and legal papers.

"Now the facts in this case are very simple," he told the nine jurists. "As a matter of fact, the parties tried to make it simple." Rolleston quickly summarized the facts of the case, and then turned to his fundamental opposition to the new law, spelling out five areas in which he believed the Civil Rights Act of 1964, and specifically Title II, were unconstitutional. One argument was that the act was "an unlawful extension of the power of commerce, out of the Commerce Clause."

He ticked off the other areas he believed were problematic, including its violation of his Fifth Amendment rights, and then concluded, "And lastly, it violates the Thirteenth Amendment to the Constitution." If he could sway them on any of his five theories, Rolleston told the jurists, "then this act has got to fail."

"The fundamental question I submit is whether or not Congress has the power to take away the liberty of an individual to run his business as he sees fit in the selection and choice of his customers," the lawyer continued. "And the fact of alleged civil rights of the Negroes involved is purely incidental, because if Congress can exercise these [powers] . . . it is possible that there's no limits to Congress' power to appropriate private property and liberty."

As Rolleston argued why he had the legal right to keep Black patrons from entering his motel, he fielded queries from Justices Warren, Black, Potter Stewart, Byron White, William Douglas, and Arthur Goldberg.

"The real question in this case: How far can Congress go?" Rolleston asked.

With Rolleston nearing the end of his time limit, Justice Hugo Black asked questions revealing a skepticism of the motel owner's argument.

Justice Black had joined the high court twenty-seven years earlier, arriving through a circuitous and controversial path and beginning his first day by entering through the building's basement door to avoid the protesters decrying his membership in the nation's most pristine legal body.

Born the youngest of eight children to an Alabama farmer, Black became a lawyer who stood up in the Birmingham courts for Black people and the poor facing unfair treatment, and he gained renown for representing striking miners and laborers. In 1923 he joined the Ku Klux Klan, a decision that would haunt his path to the Supreme Court in 1937. Black left the White supremacist group two years later and soon won election to the US Senate. During his confirmation hearings for the high court, details of his KKK membership spilled out, and Black went on the radio to acknowledge his earlier membership, all the while saying he never took part in Klan activities. Before his death, Black told the *New York Times* why he joined the KKK. As a lawyer, he said, he saw that many of his adversaries were members. Many jurors were too. "People think it was politics, but it wasn't politics," he said. "I wanted that even chance with the juries."

Black would go on to become a prominent voice on the high court, voting to strike down school prayer and guaranteeing legal counsel to poor defendants. Two months earlier, he had denied the stay orders sought by Rolleston and Lester Maddox. With each social justice ruling, his earlier Klan membership receded a little more deeply to the background, though it would never permanently erase from his personal backstory. Courtly in his judicial robes, Black was fiercely competitive outside the court, whether swatting tennis balls or during judicial deliberations. In his pocket he carried a worn copy of the Constitution.

Now, as Rolleston's oral argument reached its final minutes, Justice Black, speaking in his customary soft and cordial tones, told the lawyer he hadn't really touched upon "the most important" issue for both parties, spelled out in prior legal rulings: the right of Congress under law to regulate interstate commerce, even for businesses that are local.

"Congress has not only the right to regulate interstate commerce itself, it has the right to regulate local activities," Black told Rolleston. "It seems to me that you have not touched on that yet. That to me is a very important part of this case." The rule of the land, Black said, demonstrated that "Congress has the right to take care of interstate commerce, to foster it, to care for it, and to see that it is not adversely affected in any way, even going so far as to regulate the purely Intrastate Railroad rates in every state in the union."

Rolleston promised to respond to Justice Black's concerns in rebuttal, but for now his allotted time was up, and Justice Warren called the government to make its presentation. "Mr. Solicitor General," the chief justice said.

As Rolleston sat down, up rose US solicitor general Archibald Cox Jr., who had been picked for the post in 1960 by John F. Kennedy. A decade later, Cox would gain renown as the bow tie–wearing Watergate prosecutor fired in President Richard Nixon's infamous "Saturday Night Massacre." Cox would forge a career as a Harvard Law School professor and expert in constitutional law.

In court now, Cox promptly put the *Heart of Atlanta* case into its historical context. "The fact that the court is sitting to hear argument on the day that usually marked only an opening ceremonial occasion testifies more forcibly than any words of mine can do to the importance of the issues being presented today," Cox told the justices.

"The Civil Rights Act of 1964 is surely the most important legislation enacted in recent decades. It's one of the most important laws, I think, enacted in the last century," the solicitor general continued. "No legislation within my memory has been debated as widely as long or as thorough. Certainly, none has been considered more conscientious." Above all, he said, the law enforces the standard that "all men are created equal."

"Now the failure to keep that promise lay heavy on the conscience of the entire nation. North as well as South; East as well as West," he went on. "We should solve the problems as one people and thus escape the consequences of the sins of the past, only if we act in the spirit of Lincoln's second inaugural, without malice, with charity and perhaps above all without that spirit of false self-righteousness that enables men who are not themselves without fault, to point the finger at their fellows."

"Happily," he added, the legal question before the justices was not nearly as complex as the political path required to achieve the new civil rights law. The US Constitution clearly empowered Congress to regulate commerce among states, Cox maintained, and Title II of the Civil Rights Act of 1964 rests upon those clearly defined powers.

"The constitutionality of Title II under those provisions is sustained by principles that are so familiar because they have been enacted over and over again, applied indeed throughout our entire history," Cox continued, speaking in a relaxed tone with the jurists.

The Heart of Atlanta motel, the solicitor said, clearly fell under the umbrella of interstate commerce. Seventy-five percent of its guests visited from out of state, and the motel had long run an advertising campaign targeting visitors outside Georgia.

Segregation like that enforced at the Heart of Atlanta created a "grave national problem," mounting unrest, and practical barriers for Black Americans, Cox added, citing specific examples to support his argument.

Black travelers driving from Washington, DC, to Miami would have to traverse 141 miles on average before finding decent places to stay, he noted. "And when we think of the frequency by which we go by other hotels and motels open to everyone, the significance of a three or four-hour drive between the hope of accommodation is very significant indeed," he said.

Racial unrest over such barriers triggered economic problems nationwide, Cox maintained. In just two months in the summer of 1963, he told the jurists, 174 cities, 32 states, and the District of Columbia had been targeted with more than 630 protests over civil rights. Fully one-third involved discrimination in public accommodations. This racism was morally unacceptable, Cox said, but it also affected interstate commerce, driving away tourists and scaring businesses with no interest in becoming entangled in protests in the streets. Some hotels lost business once it was known they were not open to all guests.

"The effect of those demonstrations, picketing, boycotts, other forms of protests, upon business conditions and therefore upon the interstate commerce was dramatic," Cox said.

Cox cited the experience of Little Rock, Arkansas. In the two years before an ugly school integration crisis there, when protesters spat upon Black teenagers trying to enter an all-White school and the National Guard and US Army troops had to be sent to Arkansas to personally escort the students to ensure their safety, Little Rock had gained ten new plants worth almost $3.5 million and thousands of new jobs. In the next two years following the racial strife, the city saw no new industry involving businesses of more than fifteen employees, Cox told the justices. Another example surfaced in Louisiana. When the city of New Orleans could not guarantee equal public accommodations, he said, an American Legion convention expecting fifty thousand visitors transferred to another city.

When businesses opened their doors to all comers, patrons responded. One day after fourteen Atlanta hotels announced they had desegregated, the solicitor said, the Atlanta Convention Bureau received lodging commitments from four organizations expecting more than three thousand delegates. Those patrons "would not have gone to Atlanta if segregation were continued to be practiced," the solicitor general argued.

Finally, Cox took up Rolleston's use of the antislavery amendment as a defense of his actions, quickly dismissing it. "But surely it would turn the world quite upside down for anyone to seriously suggest that the Thirteenth Amendment was intended to prohibit either Congress or the state governments from guaranteeing Negroes equality of treatment in places of public accommodation," he offered.

Cox's arguments were persuasive, and when Rolleston stood again to rebut the US solicitor general, his tone sharpened noticeably. "In my opinion, the argument of counsel and of the government that this is done to relieve a burden on interstate commerce is so much hogwash," he charged. "This is a court of law to decide whether Congress had the right on the Constitution, the legal right, not whether it was a good thing to do, or whether it's a human thing to do, or the kind thing or the moral thing."

During Rolleston's rebuttal, Justice Hugo Black asked the lawyer about the burden on commerce when hotels turn away certain guests. The jurist asked, Isn't it Congress's right to regulate commerce?

Rolleston argued that his decision not to integrate didn't hurt commerce at all, telling the justices he had firsthand knowledge to prove it. "Because I probably know more, personally, about the travel of the Negro race than any white man in this room," he said. Rolleston informed the Supreme Court members that he had operated a twenty-room hotel specifically for Black patrons in Atlanta for a decade. He said he had trouble keeping that small business full.

Since the federal court ruling officially went into effect two months earlier, Rolleston said, the Heart of Atlanta motel had three requests from Black lodgers in that time.

"At one time, we were full and had no rooms. The other two times we took them. We've had three requests and Lord knows this case has been in the papers and every member of the Negro race in the United States knew" about the legal dispute.

So, Rolleston asked, what harm had been caused by his stance not to open his doors to Black customers? He said his longtime customers embraced his policy. His business, he said, had sent out five thousand surveys to customers who had stayed at the motel at least twice, asking the question: "If a member of the Negro race were using our recreation facilities . . . would you use the swimming pool and would you use the recreation area?"

"And 90% of those people said they would not," he told the jurists.

His time winding down, Rolleston challenged Archibald Cox's argument that segregation hurt communities and businesses. "Counsel seems to think that the act was passed for the benefit of the people in Birmingham and Little Rock and other people who had racial disturbances in the South," Moreton Rolleston said. "There are forty-three million white people in the South, and I'll say it for all of them—so loud that Congress can hear: Please don't do us any more favors!" Rolleston charged, drawing some laughter from the assembled spectators.

"I believe that the rights of individuals, the rights of people, the personal liberty of a person to do what he wants to, to run his business, is more important and more paramount than the commerce of the U.S.," he maintained, espousing the core belief that had initially prompted him to file suit and attempt to take on the US government.

Rolleston quoted a verse from Shakespeare's *Julius Caesar*—"There is a tide in the affairs of men"—signaling that when the flood comes, citizens must choose a pathway out. Is the power with the people, or the government? Take the path for the people, the Atlanta motel owner urged. "It's as simple as that."

He closed his argument succinctly. "Under the Constitution," he told the nine men before him, "the decision is yours."

13

JUDGMENT DAY: THE US SUPREME COURT RULES

Two MONTHS AND ONE WEEK LATER, on December 14, 1964, the justices delivered their answer, a resounding, unanimous ruling that affirmed the civil rights law, its section on public accommodations, and the notion that Congress had a legal right to correct the nation's wrongs.

With Justice Tom Clark authoring the twenty-page opinion, the high court held that the Commerce Clause allowed Congress to regulate local businesses and decreed that the Civil Rights Act of 1964 under review passed constitutional muster. Public accommodations, such as hotels and restaurants, had no right to select guests as they saw fit. The ruling further unraveled the Jim Crow system, affirmed the power of Congress to regulate local businesses across the United States, and sent a clear-eyed message to segregationists nationwide: the law was against them.

In its lengthy discussion of the case facts, the court cited the hardships Black Americans had encountered in trying to gain lodging in cities across the country, so much so that special green guidebooks had been published letting minority travelers know where they could safely spend a night. While acute in the South, the discrimination also festered in the North, West, and Midwest, the justices noted, citing congressional testimony submitted as part of the government's briefs.

"In framing Title II of this Act Congress was also dealing with what it considered a moral problem. But that fact does not detract from the overwhelming evidence of the disruptive effect that racial discrimination has had on commercial intercourse," the justices wrote. "The voluminous testimony presents overwhelming evidence that discrimination by hotels and motels impedes interstate travel."

Congress properly applied the Commerce Clause in regulating such abuses, the court ruled, citing case law dating back 140 years. "It may be argued that Congress could have pursued other methods to eliminate the obstructions it found in interstate commerce caused by racial discrimination. But this is a matter of policy that rests entirely with the Congress not with the courts."

Thirty-two states had laws on the books similar to those adopted by Congress, "and no case has been cited to us where the attack on a state statute has been successful, either in Federal or state courts," the judges wrote.

Some opponents to the Civil Rights Act of 1964 had argued that motels were local businesses, but the court did not buy into that reasoning, nor did it agree with the contention that Congress had overstepped its bounds. "One need only examine the evidence which we have discussed above to see that Congress may—as it has—prohibit racial discrimination by motels serving travelers, however 'local' their operations may appear," the opinion said.

The jurists point by point rejected the arguments of Moreton Rolleston and his Heart of Atlanta. Rolleston sought not only to continue his business as usual, but to collect millions of dollars in damages against a government he accused of trampling upon his rights.

The court was easily persuaded by the government's argument that the Civil Rights Act of 1964 applied to his motel. The Heart of Atlanta stood near Interstates 75 and 85 and two well-traversed state highways, attracting most of its customers from out of state. Rolleston plastered fifty billboards throughout the state attempting to lure customers driving through Georgia to pull into his motel along their journey, so long as they were White.

Justices expressed incredulity that Rolleston tried to use the Thirteenth Amendment to support his case. Maddox had also tried, and failed, to use the amendment as a defense in his own civil case in Georgia. "We find no merit in the remainder of appellant's contentions, including that of 'involuntary servitude,'" the justices wrote of the Heart of Atlanta proprietor. "We could not say that the requirements of the Act in this regard are in any way 'akin to slavery.'"

And, the justices dismissed Rolleston's contention that his Fifth Amendment rights were trampled, citing a "long line of cases" affirming the principle that banning discrimination in public accommodations in no way "interferes with personal liberty."

In his oral arguments to them, the justices said, Rolleston offered "no evidence" to support his sweeping claims, instead trying to win the case with his legal rhetoric. The government, by contrast, "proved the refusal of the motel to accept Negro transients after the passage of the Act," they said.

Without naming them, the jurists were referring to the ITC's Charles Wells and the NAACP's Albert Sampson, who had been turned away from the Heart of Atlanta days after Lyndon Johnson signed the Civil Rights Act of 1964 into law. Even as their attempts to book rooms enhanced the federal government's case against Rolleston, and as their courtroom testimony helped Robert Kennedy's lawyers secure victories in the Georgia federal courts and now the US Supreme Court, Wells's and Sampson's role receded to the background. They were unseen foot soldiers, the grunts on the front lines, in this civil rights engagement.

Building from their testimony and other evidence assembled by Kennedy's team, the high court affirmed the lower court's permanent injunction barring Rolleston from excluding Black customers.

In doing so, the Supreme Court also passed judgment on a companion case involving Ollie's Barbecue, a family-owned restaurant in Birmingham, Alabama. Ollie's refused to serve Black patrons inside its dining room since opening in 1927 and continued to refuse service after the Civil Rights Act of 1964 was passed. Black customers could pick up food to take out, but they couldn't sit among the White customers eating barbecued meats and homemade pies. An Alabama court had ruled that

Title II did not apply to Ollie's but the Supreme Court justices, in the *Katzenbach v. McClung* opinion authored by Clark, reversed that ruling.

———————

Constitutional and civil rights law scholars find the *Heart of Atlanta* ruling meaningful. While its ultimate impact is to bar local businesses from discriminating in their clientele, the actual question before the Supreme Court judges was much more specific, says Rachel Moran, a distinguished professor of law at the University of California Irvine.

"It doesn't turn on a claim of equal rights. It doesn't turn on the transgressions against the freedom to travel. It's all about a contestation about who gets to decide about these issues when businesses are effectively public," Moran says. "It becomes a contest over individual liberty to manage your business and the federal government's ability to regulate interstate commerce."

Ultimately, she said, "it becomes more of a contest of the federal government against individual shop owners and shop keepers" rather than a battle pitting civil rights activists against those businesses, even as the ruling itself meant those activists, or anyone else, could frequent the hotels and restaurants that had previously precluded them.

By its unanimous passage, *Heart of Atlanta* became among the panel's least contested landmark social justice decisions. The law, the justices said, was abundantly clear.

Michael Meltsner, the former NAACP legal fund lawyer who helped bring the initial Pickrick lawsuit, said it's not surprising the court's ruling has remained unshakable over the decades. "It was very important at the time, and it has the virtue of having held. Nobody anywhere says, 'That should change,'" says Meltsner, now a distinguished professor of law at Northeastern University in Boston. "It was simple justice."

The justice was so simple and clear-eyed, in fact, that the ruling's legacy has faded over time. Mention the *Heart of Atlanta* decision to most people and you'll likely be met with blank stares. Southerners of a certain age recall Lester Maddox and his pickaxe handles, but few, beyond law scholars and students, can tell you much, if anything, about the Supreme Court's landmark public accommodations ruling involving a Whites-only motel in Atlanta. In recent years, entities ranging from the American Bar Association to *USA Today* to the US Courts to CNN produced listings of the most consequential Supreme Court rulings; *Heart of Atlanta* made none of those lists.

The National Museum of African American History and Culture in Washington, DC, displays one of Maddox's axe handles among its exhibits. "Lester Maddox once brandished an ax handle to keep black patrons from his restaurant," the display tells visitors. "When he ran for governor of Georgia, he used the ax handle to symbolize his opposition to civil rights legislation."

And the highly lauded, deeply popular museum showcases multiple Supreme Court civil rights rulings, from the 1857 Dred Scott decision declaring that African Americans held no rights as citizens to the 1896 *Plessy v. Ferguson* "separate but equal" ruling to the groundbreaking *Brown v. Board of Education* and *Loving v. Virginia* cases in 1954 and 1967, respectively.

Nowhere among the museum's exhibits is *Heart of Atlanta v. USA*.

Brown v. Board of Education was an earth-moving ruling at the time and has remained fresh in the public's consciousness as school integration battles continue to fester. "The high-profile busing cases are also seared into people's memories, and for all that struggle, schools are generally still highly segregated," says Moran. "Yet with this case, I would be very surprised if there were many cases where property owners excluded people on the basis of race and tried to keep segregated restaurants and hotels."

"The success of the ruling," she said of *Heart of Atlanta*, "has also become a source of its invisibility." But some legal scholars believe *Heart of Atlanta* merits greater attention. In 2015, when *Time* magazine canvassed legal experts for what they viewed as the best Supreme Court rulings since 1960, University of Texas law professor Cary Franklin, a Yale University–trained Rhodes scholar, was the rare voice singling out *Heart of Atlanta*. "In this case, the court upheld Title II of the 1964 Civil Rights Act, which granted African Americans full access to public accommodations such as hotels, restaurants, and movie theaters," Franklin wrote. "The court confirmed that Congress has broad powers, under the commerce clause, to address important national problems—many of which are still with us and still need addressing today."

When the decision was issued in December 1964, the ruling's weight was not lost on those who had risked bloodshed for a seat at a restaurant or a bed at a roadside hotel.

Roy Wilkins, the NAACP's executive director at the time, said the high court's decision "should promptly end discrimination in public accommodations everywhere in our country." For years protesters' lunch counter sit-ins had attempted to tear down the color barricades that remained in countless hotels and diners across the country. Now, the Supreme Court was affirming that the protesters were right. The barricades must fall.

John H. Sengstacke, editor and publisher of the *Chicago Defender*, a newspaper closely read by Black American during the civil rights era, called the court's opinion a rejection of the segregationist senators who had so fiercely fought the civil rights bill. "In upholding the public accommodations section of the new civil rights Act, the Supreme Court dealt a fatal blow to the Southern racist's hope of defeating this essential feature of the law," he told his readers. "The defeat is a further repudiation of Sen. Goldwater and Gov. Wallace of Alabama who used their rustic rhetoric in a vain attempt to prove the unconstitutionality of the law."

At the White House, Lyndon Johnson welcomed the court's decision, viewing it as an affirmation of his plea to the nation, thirteen months earlier, that Congress pivot from the killing of John Kennedy to ensure the assassinated president's civil rights vision took root. "There already has been encouraging widespread compliance with the act in the five months it has been law," the president said. "Now that the Supreme Court also has ruled I think we all join in the hope and resolution that this kind of reasonable and responsible acceptance of the law will continue and increase."

With the legal opinion now in the books, his team of Justice Department lawyers stood poised to legally challenge any hotel, restaurant, or movie house that continued to accept patrons based upon skin color. Integrators who had previously been stopped at the door or forcibly removed by police or proprietors now had the nation's highest court saying they had the legal right to frequent any hotel or restaurant of their liking.

When he heard news of the court's *Heart of Atlanta* opinion, Albert Sampson took a moment of quiet contemplation to absorb its meaning. Sampson was heartened by the Supreme Court's decree that all races had a legal right to public accommodations. He was thankful that neither he nor any of his colleagues had lost their lives or suffered serious injury in their fight for equal accommodations. "We understood we lived in a segregated world because of the color of our skin," Sampson says. The nation's highest court had decreed that this segregated world was coming to an end.

Jesse Jackson, Sampson's friend from their North Carolina college days who would go on to seek the presidency two decades later, said the rule of law meant everything for the activists who had so long risked injury and arrest trying to gain a seat at the table. "In 1964 white race supremacy was the law of the land," Jackson says. "White supremacy was law. We couldn't eat at Rich's downtown, the law. We couldn't stay at the Heart of Atlanta, the law."

With the Civil Rights Act of 1964 affirmed by the nation's highest court, everything had changed. "We were free," Jackson told me recently. "It opened up the whole world. Once the freedom flame was lit, it never went out."

Three months later came Bloody Sunday in Selma, in which Dallas County, Alabama, Sheriff Jim Clark's officers and posse joined state troopers in brutalizing protesters marching over the Edmund Pettus Bridge in a peaceful press for voting rights. The police tactics "were similar to those recommended for use by the United States Army to quell armed rioters in occupied countries," Alabama federal judge Frank M. Johnson Jr. wrote in scolding Governor George Wallace and his police forces in a lawsuit brought by civil rights activists Hosea Williams, John Lewis, and Amelia Boynton. Troopers, armed with tear gas, nausea gas, canisters of smoke, and billy clubs, pursued the marchers before sending them scurrying with twenty canisters of tear gas and smoke.

"The Negroes were then prodded, struck, beaten, and knocked down by members of the Alabama State Troopers. The mounted 'possemen,' supposedly acting as an auxiliary law enforcement unit of the Dallas County sheriff's office, then, on their horses, moved in and chased and beat the fleeing Negroes," the judge wrote. Some eighty marchers were beaten, many of them so badly they had to be hospitalized. The vicious attack presaged passage of another seminal civil rights law, the Voting Rights Act of 1965, which outlawed discriminatory literacy tests long employed in Southern bastions to arbitrarily block Black citizens from becoming registered voters.

And then in August 1965 the Watts race riots in Los Angeles revealed how underserved urban hubs, stifled by years of police oppression, economic poverty, and inadequate housing, would explode in a blaze of sometimes violent protest. The Watts rebellion would force President Johnson to press for more federal laws to address unemployment and inadequate housing for long-ignored communities. "A riot," Dr. King said, "is the language of the unheard."

After the *Heart of Atlanta* decision in December 1964, integration's staunchest opponents feared what the ruling meant for the South they knew. Moreton Rolleston expressed surprise at the justices' ruling, saying he believed he would prevail. As the weeks passed after his October legal arguments, he grew more assured he had won the day in his presentation to the nation's most venerated court.

Seeing that he lost by a unanimous vote, the motel owner had trouble coming to grips with the court's reasoning. "I don't think the people of the South will ever like it. They'll have to become accustomed to it," Rolleston told Atlanta TV reporters moments after the ruling was issued, dressed formally in coat and tie, his dark hair combed neatly back. "Congress now has the power to do almost anything it wishes to regulate individual conduct," he added.

Reading from a statement he had written out after the opinion was issued, Rolleston continued. "This decision nullifies the rights and principles which the Constitution was designed to perpetuate," he told reporters. "This is a sad day for the cause of individual freedom."

Almost immediately, his hotel's clientele changed from entirely White to racially mixed, beginning to mirror the city. Once the Supreme Court formally ruled, a wave of Black customers lined up for lodging, eager to officially dismantle the Heart of Atlanta's color divide and make history by being among the first African Americans to experience its amenities.

"I checked in a lot of people and checked out a lot of people," says the proprietor's son, Moreton Rolleston III, who worked at the front desk part-time in 1965, just as the high court's ruling took effect. "We had all kinds of Black church groups. Everybody wanted to come to the Heart of Atlanta motel. It was a big victory for civil rights."

Lester Maddox erected no such welcome signs. The restaurant owner was chagrined but not surprised by the ruling of the court, which had already rejected his stay appeal and had now shot down the Heart of Atlanta's case. "I held out faint hope that the Supreme Court would see that what was happening was clearly against the Constitution, even though the Warren court was the most liberal in the country's history, and Earl Warren had already done more to destroy our system of government than any Chief Justice before him," Maddox wrote in his autobiography.

With the court's newest civil rights ruling made public, Justice Warren sent a final word to his colleague Tom Clark, who authored the body's opinion. "I agree," Warren wrote of the *Heart of Atlanta* decision. "Bueno." He heavily underlined both comments, to be sure their meaning was clear. The ruling was a victory for equal rights and the notion that public accommodations were open to all. The people's court had once more spoken. Three months earlier, the Warren Commission, chaired by the chief justice himself, had issued its Warren Commission Report into the assassination of President John F. Kennedy, whose 1963 nationwide address had laid the groundwork for the law jurists had adjudged.

Segregationists had lost another deeply significant round in their quest to keep the races separate and unequal. In five rapid-fire, momentous months of change, the Congress, the president, the federal courts, and now the US Supreme Court had all adjudged segregation in hotels and restaurants as illegal, demanding a sudden and resounding end to the American private industry's apartheid-era ways.

In Atlanta, Lester Maddox girded for one more defense of his segregationist line in the sand. At his newly renamed Lester Maddox Cafeteria, he readied for his most violent pushback against integration, prepared to use his fists, his axe handles, and his venom to resist from entering this new world of racial equality. Once more, the Atlanta ministry students would show up at his door and seek to be served like any other customer.

14

MORE SHOVES, VENOM, AND AXE HANDLES

AS THE CALENDAR CLOSED UPON THE HISTORIC and conflicting events of 1964, with a multilayered civil rights law passed in Congress as Black and White activists were killed across the country, the *Heart of Atlanta* case was put to bed by the US Supreme Court. Across the land, one business after another opened their doors to integration, many willingly, some begrudgingly.

Lester Maddox would have none of it. When the year turned to 1965, the Lester Maddox Cafeteria continued to serve its diner fare, and Maddox continued to allow White customers only to sit at its tables. No integrators allowed.

The ministry students dug in once more, showing themselves to be every bit as resilient as their adversary. On Friday afternoon, January 29, 1965, emboldened now by the nation's highest court, four Interdenominational Theological Center students turned out to the front door of Maddox's business. Charles Wells, George Willis, Albert Dunn, and Woodrow T. Lewis, donning winter sports coats, ties, and hats on this chilly afternoon, came knocking now for the fourth time in six months.

Maddox rushed to the men, shoving them over and over away from the front steps and toward the sidewalk. It was as if Maddox were sickened by the thought of any of the men actually crossing through the threshold of his restaurant's front door, and he pushed back as if his life depended upon it. Maddox would indeed later say his life, liberty, and freedoms stood at the precipice as the young ministers again pressed for a plate of food.

He reached for their necks and sport coats and top hats. At one point, Maddox wielded axe handles in both hands as he stormed toward his visitors. He pushed and swiped so hard he had to catch his breath a moment. Then, as the ministers held their ground and began walking again toward the front door, he pushed and shoved some more.

The ministry students stood calm amid the Maddox storm, holding their fists and tempers. Some of the proprietor's customers jawed at the men, but Wells and Willis responded calmly, saying they merely sought a seat in the dining room. At one point, Wells extended his hand to shake Maddox's, but the segregationist wouldn't return the gesture. Dunn spoke assertively to one of the restaurant's customers, but, like his classmates, kept his hands to himself. All the while, Atlanta police officers passed by on motorbikes or on foot, never stopping Lester Maddox's newest physical attack on the nation's integration movement.

A soundless four-minute, thirty-seven-second black-and-white video, among the collections of the Walter J. Brown Media Archives of the University of Georgia Special Collections Libraries, captures the stunning scene. The archives, preserved at the Civil Rights Digital Library, identify just one of the four men, the Reverend Charles Wells. The other three are not named.

I sat down with one of them, Woodrow Lewis of South Carolina. Sitting at his dining table one morning in 2019, Lewis viewed the footage for the first time. Until I clicked on the grainy newsreel video, he had no idea it existed.

Lewis glimpsed Maddox holding two axe handles, one in each hand, and pushing, shoving, and haranguing the ministers as a mob of supporters, including his son, shouted at them. Lewis, peering closely at the five-decade-old footage, sees himself and identifies the others, Wells, Dunn, and Willis.

Wells is the tall man with a hat and a leader of the group this afternoon. He puts his hands up several times peacefully, even as Maddox forcefully pushes him away from the restaurant and at one point aggressively put his hands upon Wells's neck.

Albert Dunn, also wearing a hat, speaks assertively to a White man angrily waving his arms at him. Dunn stood his ground, forcefully but peacefully.

Woodrow Lewis is in the middle of the group in several scenes and the only ministry student not wearing a hat this day.

Of the four, Lewis engaged the least with Maddox and the crowd. "I was the coolest among the group. I recall trying to keep my classmates calm and not to get too emotional. Somebody had to keep a level head. Lester was going crazy and acting crazy. The spirit of the Lord told me to keep cool," he says. As for his ministry classmates, "I think they fought more with words than with a physical attack."

In one scene, Maddox swipes at the neck of Willis, trying to knock him down. Kay Willis, the late reverend's widow, had not seen the video either, until I reached her in Texas to ask about her husband's activism in Atlanta five decades earlier.

"It was very emotional," she says after watching the footage. "I was proud of him. But I didn't like the fact that he put his hands on him."

Her husband would never back down, she said, but sought ways to rise above his adversaries. Long before his death in 2012, George Willis had told his wife about the integration battles earlier in his life in Atlanta. "I said, 'Boy, you could have been killed a long time ago.' He said, 'If I'm going to die, I can die for civil rights.'" When I connected with Kay Willis, she was eager to speak of her husband's activism in Atlanta. It was important, she says, "for keeping this history alive."

Woodrow Lewis was part of that history. Watching the footage at home that morning in South Carolina, long-dormant emotions were suddenly rekindled within him. It was as if he were experiencing the fight with Maddox for the first time, and he was surrounded once more by his seminary school brethren.

"I suspect we had some nerve during that day," Lewis says. "I'm amazed. I'm astonished. I don't know whether I'd believe it if I didn't see it." Absorbing this footage, even with the physical force and intensity of hatred spewed upon the four men, is "touching and very much invigorating," he says. "I knew that it happened, but after all of these years to

George Willis III, who pushed for integration of restaurants in Atlanta and later pastored for decades in Texas. *Courtesy of Kay Willis*

see the reality happen, it was almost unbelievable. So real." Sitting for a second viewing, he says, "The reality is right there. You can't escape the reality of what happened."

A brief *Atlanta Journal* account of this latest fracas, "Maddox Bars Negroes with 'Body Force,'" did not name the ministers and quoted only Maddox. He told the newspaper the men tried to "push their way inside and I wedged myself between inner doors to keep them out." Once more, the ministers were faceless and voiceless. Maddox surely would like to forget their names.

15

CLOSING TIME
AT THE PICKRICK
AND LESTER MADDOX
CAFETERIA

LESTER MADDOX SOON WOULD FACE the cold truth that his opposition
to integration came at a considerable cost. His wounds would be self-
inflicted.

On February 1, 1965, federal judge Frank Arthur Hooper presided
over another hearing in the case of *Willis, Lewis, and Dunn v. The
Pickrick and Lester G. Maddox,* called to decide whether Maddox was
once more in contempt of the court's already affirmed order. The legal
dispute, then, continued as if it were a record played on repeat, the same
refrain spinning over and over again.

The cycle played on. Maddox, ordered more than six months earlier
to integrate his restaurant, continued to serve White customers only,
prompting the ministry students to press again for entry, only to have
the restaurateur and his group of supporters shove and scream them
away. The court would issue another order directing Maddox to comply
with the law, and the cycle would start anew: resistance, rebuke, repeat.

Six weeks after the US Supreme Court had affirmed the nation's civil rights law as legally sound, Maddox was still pushing back.

Willis, Wells, and Dunn all took the stand, recounting the group's four overall attempts to integrate Maddox's restaurant since the civil rights law had been passed the previous July, including the most recent attempt days earlier. Their statements, transcribed into the court record, would attest to their repeated efforts to hold Lester Maddox accountable, and provide clear evidence that the Atlanta business owner remained an outlier at a time every other business in the city had adhered to the federal law.

Wells described how he had asked Maddox if he was shutting his doors on the men simply because of their race. Each time he asked, Maddox responded that he wouldn't serve integrationists, Black or White. Yet each time Wells managed to peer into the Pickrick, he saw only White faces seated at its tables. Maddox himself had made clear, in court papers and other forums, that his restaurant had a long-standing policy of not serving Black customers.

"Mr. Maddox pushed me from the premises of the Pickrick several feet," Wells told plaintiffs' attorney William Alexander. "He also choked me. Also struck me in the face, knocked my hat off."

Another time, he said, he was pushed to the sidewalk and choked again.

"Can you state the person who choked you at that time?" asked Alexander.

"Mr. Maddox," replied Wells, who had taken part in three of the four visits to the Pickrick, turning out on every occasion other than the first.

"Did anyone else assault you on that date?"

"Mr. Maddox's son ripped some buttons off my clothing," Wells said. "From the time I left the vestibule of the restaurant, I was repeatedly pushed, shoved, struck, choked till such time as I departed from the premises."

Wells continued. "I was standing there and Mr. Maddox spun me around and pushed me out of his restaurant and repeatedly pushed me afterwards until such time as we left the premises," he said.

"Now," Alexander asked, "when you stated that you were choked by Mr. Maddox, which Mr. Maddox are you referring to?"

"Lester Maddox," Wells replied, pointing to the restaurateur sitting in court. "The one sitting there."

One of the lawyers representing Maddox, Sidney T. Schell, then rose to cross-examine Wells. Did you ever personally threaten Maddox? Schell asked.

"No, I did not," Wells said.

Then Schell veered into broader terrain, touching upon one of Maddox's strident themes, anti-Communism, while harkening back to the infamous McCarthy Senate hearings a decade earlier.

"Are you now or have you ever been a member of the Communist Party?" Schell asked Wells. Beyond serving in the ministry, Wells had enlisted in the military and worked as a distribution clerk at the US Post Office.

"I have not been a member of the Communist Party," he replied. "If I had I would not have been working for the federal government."

After Wells stepped down, Dunn took the stand, recounting the group's most recent visit. "All of a sudden Mr. Maddox came running through the door and twirled Brother Wells around, and at that point he was pinned in the door, and he started pushing and shoving until he pushed the three first out back towards the sidewalk. And of course, someone said, where is the other one? And then they came back and got me and started pushing me."

"Get out of my door," Maddox had yelled at them, "so my customers can enter."

Alexander asked whether Dunn had seen Maddox hit Wells. "Yes. As a matter of fact, I put Brother Wells' hat back on him after he knocked it off."

"After who knocked his hat off?" the lawyer asked.

"Mr. Maddox," Dunn replied.

"Mr. Lester G. Maddox knocked his hat off?"

"That's right."

Did Dunn fear for his safety? "Well, when two of the buttons off my coat were snatched off and we were shoved, I think I had reason to believe that," he testified.

Defense counsel Schell asked Dunn, as he had pressed Wells, whether he had threatened Maddox.

"I don't make threats to anyone," replied the ministry student, who had turned out every time the ministers tried to enter through the Pickrick's doors.

"There was hostility, a hostile crowd here saying, 'Nigger, why don't you go somewhere else,'" Dunn testified. "And 'Why don't you quit disturbing and making trouble?' And we simply said then we had a right to eat there, and we would eat there, and we would eat or he could close his business. As long as he stays open, we have a right to eat. Simple statement."

The defense counsel then homed in on the core question on his client's mind.

"Are you a segregationist?" Schell asked Dunn.

"I'm a human being," Dunn replied. "Person."

Next to the witness stand rose Willis, who had joined three of the integration attempts and who told Judge Hooper the ministry students never could get inside the door of Maddox's restaurant.

Willis recounted how he saw Maddox push and shove Wells until he was on the sidewalk, slapping him and knocking off his hat.

"Then I told him there was no need of all this. I said, 'We have only come to eat,' and then he slapped me. And then his son came over and he collared me and he pushed me up against the car which was parked right there and he bounced me off of it once, and then he bounced me off again, and at this time he backed away. And in the meantime, Mr. Maddox had two, looked like many or two bats in his hand," Willis testified.

Then the Maddox son approached Willis again "and asked me if I wanted the button off my coat and he jerked it and it came off. And he asked me about the other one and he jerked it and it came off."

Alexander asked, "Did you at any time strike Mr. Maddox's son?"

"No sir," the ex-boxer replied. "Not at all. He is just a small fellow. I wouldn't hit him."

I sought Lester Maddox Jr.'s view of those altercations one morning in 2020 when I knocked on his door in Georgia. Maddox said he was watching over an ill family member but agreed to chat in the driveway of his rental home, donning a protective mask during the coronavirus pandemic. Maddox Jr. says his father treated his Black employees with respect, sometimes making them supervisors, but took deep offense that the government told him whom he could serve. Why did his father push back so hard against the ministers at his door? "Because the federal government," the son says. "The government ordered him to."

In the infamous photo of Lester Maddox leading Albert Dunn off the Pickrick premises by pistol, a young Maddox Jr. seems to tower over his father. Decades later in his driveway, Maddox Jr. said he shrunk several inches over the years amid health issues. He invoked religion into the conversation several times and added, "There's too much hate in the world."

When I asked about his own experience with the ministers, Lester Maddox Jr. said he simply did not recall those events through the fog of the decades. "I don't remember," he said.

The courtroom archives of 1965 affirmed how his father remained a scofflaw to the civil rights law. The ministers could never break through the Maddox wall of resistance and grab a seat at one of his tables, never order a grilled steak, slice of coconut pie, or get endless refills on their cups of coffee, as the establishment's White customers had since 1947.

The ministers weren't the only witnesses to take the stand this day. Barbara Brandt, secretary of the Student Nonviolent Coordinating Committee, once again testified about her experiences dining at the restaurant, including the Friday afternoon in which the ministers tried to gain entry.

"Everyone eating there was white," said Brandt.

Brandt paid witness as the ministry students tried to enter the dining hall. "They stood, and when Mr. Maddox pushed them, they would not move back, and they didn't strike him, but they stood. And every once in a while they would attempt to walk back to the restaurant, and Mr. Maddox would push them again," she told the court.

Brandt had eaten at the restaurant before a prior court hearing without incident. On this most recent visit, she said, Maddox approached her as she sat for lunch, striking up a conversation not long after he forced the ministers off his property.

"Do you belong to any civil rights organizations?" he asked her. "And I said, I belong to the American Civil Liberties Union."

"And he said, are you an integrationist? And I said, how do you define that? And he said an integrationist is a person who believes in mixing the races and doesn't mind mingling with a person of another race. And I said, I believe in only one race, the human race."

Maddox instantly grew enraged, she said. "You are an integrationist!" he called to her. "You lied when you came in here. You saw the sign but you came in here and lied. Get off my property. Get out of here!"

Maddox lawyer Schell questioned Brandt about her motivations, three times referring to the witness as "young lady." "Would you answer my question now, young lady?" he asked once.

When it came time for the defense to call witnesses, Schell presented Allan Maddox, the restaurateur's brother. The gas service station owner had been at the restaurant on August 11 when the ministry students were repelled from the Pickrick. The lawyer asked Maddox to identify the men in the courtroom who had been there that day.

"The colored man far back is one and this boy here with the watch on is another one," Allan Maddox said, pointing to one of the plaintiffs in the courtroom and identifying the master's student by the still-ingrained Old South phrase *boy*.

Maddox said no one, his brother included, had assaulted the men that August day. His brother did talk with them, he said, painting a much different scene than that described by the ministers and captured by news reporters. "He told them if they came through the doors that the Pickrick would be out of business," the brother testified. "That he was not refusing them service, refusing them entrance, but if they did go through those doors that they would be responsible for the jobs of some sixty employees."

In the city of Atlanta, Maddox had remained the sole holdout to accepting the law of the land in the wake of the Supreme Court ruling. Every other restaurant, hotel, and movie house in Atlanta had opened their doors to all races, including the Heart of Atlanta resort motel—but not Lester Maddox.

Finally, Maddox took the stand to defend the business practices set forth by his newly named restaurant. Maddox said he wasn't discriminating based on race but, rather, on the larger issue of his deeply held segregationist beliefs. Anyone could dine at the Lester Maddox Cafeteria, so long as they were not integrationists or interstate travelers. The Commerce Clause, he argued, did not apply to him.

It took little time for his flimsy defense to be shredded, and this time by the sitting federal court judge. But first Maddox answered questions from his own lawyer and from counsel for the ministry students he had come to view with a visceral disregard.

Yes, he said, he had told his baker, Ozell Rogers, to talk to the ministers and to explain the consequences if they ever passed through the threshold of his restaurant's front door. "And I told my colored baker, I says, 'Tell them if they insist on eating that we're not going to stop them. But if they do come in, tell them we're going to lose our jobs and our business,'" Maddox testified.

His lawyer asked, Did you strike, slap, or abuse any of the men?

"I hadn't," Lester Maddox said. "I've never struck one or slapped one. I have pushed them when they pushed against me."

The words were untrue, as the grainy archive footage from the January 29, 1965, altercation showed. In every instance, Maddox was the one pushing, shoving, and slapping the men as the ministry students stood their ground, held their fists, and even once reached out for a handshake that wasn't returned.

"Mr. Maddox," Schell wanted to know, "presently in your Maddox Cafeteria, is it your policy to exclude both persons white and colored because of their political beliefs?"

"Mr. Schell," Maddox answered, "the color doesn't have anything to do with the rejection of any customer. Only, I reject customers who I know to be integrationists."

OK, Schell asked next, "If a Negro comes to your place of business and informed you that he was not an integrationist, would you feed him?"

"If he convinced me he was not an integrationist, I would be happy to have him," Maddox testified. But he would not, under any circumstances, serve food to the ministers sitting across from him in the courtroom, Maddox told the judge. "I want everybody to understand the world over that I would never, if my life depended on it, serve any of these four people who have threatened my life, property, and liberty and says they're going to close my business," he said.

Maddox recounted his conversation with Willis, sitting before him at the plaintiff's table. "He says, 'We are going to eat some of your chicken, Lester.' And I said, 'You're still lying too.' He'll never eat any of my chicken unless he gets its secondhand. I might serve a lot of the others but I wouldn't serve him if somebody shot me down in the door," he testified, his fiery resistance on display for the entire courtroom. Several contempt of court hearings in, Lester Maddox would not retreat from his island of segregation.

Maddox said the legal fight had drained his resources and that his business was now losing money compared to prior years. He blamed the new civil rights law as the cause of his financial decline, even as his own accountant took the stand and testified that other Atlanta hotels and restaurants had been prospering.

To help him raise money, Maddox said supporters created the Lester Maddox Defense Fund, opening an account in an Atlanta bank where like-minded residents could help bankroll his defense against the congressional edict. He was a segregationist, but he was not alone in the fight.

The plaintiffs' lawyer Alexander then began his cross-examination, opening with a question exploring Maddox's curious process of shuttering the Pickrick and reopening the restaurant under a new name, the Lester Maddox Cafeteria. Alexander was joined in court by civil rights lawyer Donald L. Hollowell, renowned for freeing Martin Luther King from prison and arguing to admit two Black students to the University of Georgia.

"Mr. Maddox, isn't it true that you changed the name of your restaurant to avoid serving Negroes?" Alexander asked.

"No, it is not," Maddox responded. "I closed down my restaurant. It was forced to close by those agitators and court decisions and things that said I could no longer operate and discriminate in any manner." So, he decided to close the Pickrick and opened a new restaurant "that had no connection whatsoever with the former restaurant that used to operate there."

But you opened the new restaurant on the same spot, right? Yes, Maddox replied. And you employed many of the same workers? Yes, again. And the telephone number was the same? Yes.

"Now the food you are serving at the Lester Maddox Cafeteria is the same food as you served at the Pickrick last year, isn't that correct?" Alexander asked.

"It's the same kind of food," Maddox said, though the menu changed from time to time in both establishments.

No matter what the restaurant's name, Maddox said he would not open his doors to integrationists, Black or White. "I think most people are honest, and I don't think a white integrationist would come into my place unless he had been told to by you or the Justice Department. They don't want to associate with me. They don't like me. They don't like my philosophy. So they stay out," he said. "They're honest."

He recounted how three or four Columbia University students had come to his restaurant in the last month and approached him as he and his wife sat for a meal. "They got after us about our stand, and I gave them two minutes to get out of my place," Maddox said. "And one of them looked at his watch and he said, 'We've got a minute and a half left.' And I said, 'No, you've shortened it down to thirty seconds.'" He had his Black workers escort them out.

Maddox cited Bible verses to disparage the intentions of the seminary students who kept knocking, saying their actions had "forced" him out of business. "The Pickrick had to close because four people who claimed to be reverends, acting in quite an opposite way from Jesus ever acted, came into my place as moneychangers to destroy my business and to violate the Commandment, 'Thou shalt not steal' and again to violate the one, 'Thou shalt not covet that which is thy neighbor's,'" he said. "And I was forced out of that business in an attempt to be free and a part of the American free enterprise system."

Maddox said he had received letters of support backing up his segregationist stance, and not just from southerners but from like-minded people across the country. He painted a bleak picture of other Atlanta restaurants that had integrated, claiming that brawls, stabbings, and shootings had followed their decision to mix races.

"I'm not going to subject my wife and my children and my customers to any such thing to where they think they are going to walk in my place and be stabbed or walk out and be stabbed or be beaten or be shot," he told the courtroom. "I'm not going to turn it into a lawless place where paid agitators at their will can subject my customers and my family to any such circumstances."

It was another falsehood from the witness stand. In every case in which the ministers tried to enter his restaurant, it was Maddox who was the aggressor, brandishing weapons and assaulting the integrators.

With Maddox done talking, presiding judge Hooper had a few questions for the proprietor. "You make the contention and refer to the government ruining your business, Mr. Maddox," the judge said. "Your certified public accountant, Mr. Cheek, testified in your presence and hearing that since July 1964, that your business lost money and all the other restaurants around here have been doing real well. How do you explain that?"

Maddox started to answer, but the judge wasn't done.

"They complied with the law and without orders of the court, and they didn't even have a case against them, but they complied with the Civil Rights Act as to restaurants, and they're making money and you have refused to comply," the federal judge continued, "and yet your revenues went way down."

"Does that bear out your statement that this new act of Congress is ruining your business?" the judge asked.

"Yes sir," Maddox proffered.

"Or is it the way you've met this act that's ruining your business? The civil rights bill was passed and has been upheld by the Supreme Court. All the other restaurants around Atlanta complied with it except you and yet you are the only restaurant whose business has gone down. Can you explain that?"

Maddox held firm. The civil rights act and integration agitators had hurt his business. No matter how compelling the evidence to the contrary, even when stated by the presiding federal judge, Maddox wouldn't budge.

"You can come down," Judge Hooper said. "Court is recessed."

No one but Maddox's most die-hard supporters could agree that what he said on the stand was true. The Civil Rights Act of 1964, Congress, President Johnson, and the ministers hadn't drained his business; he had done the damage himself, as federal judge Hooper quite pointedly demonstrated. Once more the law and societal norms were telling Maddox his ways of operating were a relic of America's dark past.

Four days later, on Friday February 5, 1965, Judge Hooper formally ruled, finding Maddox in civil contempt of court and fining him $200 a day for continuing to violate one of the core tenets of the civil rights law. Maddox had an easy solution to "purge" the contempt order and the daily fine. He could simply serve all customers, Black patrons included.

The next day Maddox, his voice shaking, said he would abide by the court ruling and allow Black customers through his doors. "I have been bound by things I think unjust, but I must obey the law," he told reporters from his cafeteria, reading from a prepared statement. He then cited a verse from the Bible: "No man can enter into a strong man's house and spoil his goods, except he will first bind the strong man; and then he will spoil his house."

A day later, when a Black customer turned out for a piece of Sunday skillet-fried chicken, Maddox locked the restaurant doors. Dressed in a suit and tie, he then posted a sign on the door. CLOSED, it said. OUT OF BUSINESS RESULTING FROM ACT PASSED BY THE US CONGRESS, SIGNED BY PRESIDENT JOHNSON AND INSPIRED AND SUPPORTED BY DEADLY AND BLOODY COMMUNISM.

Finally, Maddox had had enough. The ministers' integration efforts, and the law of the land, told him he could no longer decide who could enter through his doors and who would be forced out by pistol and axe handle. Maddox said he'd rather go to jail than serve integrationists. Now he decided he'd rather shutter his business than comply with the law. He'd never serve a piece of chicken, cherry pie, or fried perch to a Black patron or a known integrator. To Lester Maddox, that was victory in itself.

That Sunday, February 7, 1965, Maddox closed his restaurant for good. He blamed LBJ, Communists, and myriad other forces for running him out of business and soon etched his views again on a giant placard:

PUT TO DEATH BY:

- MY PRESIDENT
- MY GOVERNMENT
- THE COMMUNIST
- THE LEFT WING NEWS MEDIA
- WEAK AND COWARDLY BUSINESS LEADERS
- CHRISTIAN MINISTERS WHO TEACH SOCIAL SALVATION RATHER THAN CHRIST

After he shut his business, Maddox sat for a press conference with local reporters, with his wife Virginia seated beside him. She arrived formally attired in a dress and pearl and occasionally dabbed her eyes as he spoke. In the back of the room, a crowd of supporters sat and stood absorbing every word, and they broke into applause once or twice, as if at a political rally.

Maddox waxed religious and philosophic, saying he had come to terms with his decision to follow Judge Hooper's order. The night before,

The Pickrick was Lester Maddox's home away from home, but he closed the restaurant after the courts told him he could no longer discriminate. *Kenan Research Center at the Atlanta History Center*

he told reporters, he had gotten his first good night's sleep since the civil rights bill had been passed the previous July.

His tone sharpened only when he spoke of the activists who had tried, time and again and again, to join his loyal customers at his personal and professional sanctuary. Those who would do him harm, Maddox said, were not "Negroes" but "niggers," and he used that contemptuous pejorative to describe his adversaries either Black or White.

"Their purpose has never been to integrate. Their purpose has been to destroy," Maddox said. "In that the Civil Rights Act of 1964 demands that I admit these thieves, murderers, liars, and Communists to my business and property, I am forced to close my business to protect my family and customers from these gangsters."

A reporter asked if Maddox planned to open another restaurant, possibly outside Atlanta. "No, sir," he replied. "The Communists put me out of the food business, sir."

Maddox would later recall the thoughts running through his mind as he hung up the permanent CLOSED sign on his door. "It was a sad and tragic moment, not merely for Lester Maddox, but for every American citizen," he wrote in his autobiography. "The sign was symbolic of the door that had been closed to individual opportunity and private property rights all over this land."

Maddox later leased the property to two White employees, who opened the restaurant under a new name and erected no racial blockades. He refused to step through its doors.

The Maddox legal team would appeal his contempt citation all the way to the US Supreme Court. Once more, they would lose the day in court. On October 11, 1965, the high court dismissed his appeal in a brief one-page order.

Woodrow Lewis and his ministry schoolmates took the news of the Pickrick's closing with bittersweet feelings. "My thinking was that we won, but our intention was not so much to close up the restaurant; our intention was to be able to be served in the restaurant," Lewis says. "This man would rather close the restaurant than open it up to serve Black folks."

"In the end, who lost?" Lewis asks. "He lost the income."

Maddox still had to grapple with a misdemeanor charge involving the ministers' first visit to his restaurant on July 3, when he stuck a pistol in George Willis's face and led Albert Dunn off his land by gunpoint. Two months after closing his restaurant, Maddox appeared in the courtroom of criminal court judge Dan Duke, and he listened as Willis and Dunn recounted that first heated encounter.

"He pointed the gun directly in my face," Willis told the all-White jury. "I was looking down the hole in the barrel."

Dunn described his mindset as Maddox forced him off the property with his pistol. "I just politely turned around and headed back to the car," the minister testified. "It was the pistol that determined my moves from there on."

Four Atlanta newsmen, who had been witness to the July 3 altercation, testified that Maddox freely waved his pistol in the direction of the integrators.

Maddox lawyer William McRae alleged the ministers had threatened Maddox, not the other way around, recounting how Willis once told the proprietor they would keep coming back to his restaurant. Maddox, the lawyer said, felt "threatened" by this vow.

"Is that a threat?" asked Judge Duke, who, two decades earlier as a young prosecutor, had aggressively prosecuted several Georgia Klansmen for whipping a Black man later found frozen to death. "That's having to stretch the English language a long way."

Maddox lawyer Sidney Schell put on the stand a string of character witnesses to vouch for his client's integrity, including three judges and Maddox's own pastor at the North Atlanta Baptist Church. Maddox had come into the crosshairs of the local newspaper, the federal government, the new civil rights law, and activists White and Black who could never attain a seat at his restaurant—but he still had plenty of friends in Atlanta.

Maddox also took the witness stand, confidently describing how he was legally and morally within his rights to defend his property against the agitating pastors. "I pulled my gun because I had reason to believe that my life and property were under threat," he said. Speaking directly to the jurors, he added, "The action I have taken is what I would expect you to take."

He spoke to a sympathetic audience. The jurors took little more than a half hour to clear him of the misdemeanor charge. "Thank God we still have juries," Maddox later said. Once more, he would have the last word, and his beating back of the gun charge would not represent his final victory in a public forum.

In closing his restaurant, Lester Maddox had finally blinked. But the story of the Pickrick's violent integration clashes doesn't end so neatly there. In quick fashion, Maddox would surface from this loss, in many ways gain fuel and oxygen from it, and rise all the way to the governor's mansion. For his many opponents, that ascension would serve as a cruel twist to his courtroom losses. Lester Maddox lost the fight over the Civil Rights Act of 1964 and lost money as the last Atlanta holdout refusing to integrate his business, with his restaurant's closing a symbolic image of his failed and dated cause. The shuttering of the Pickrick restaurant didn't shut down Lester Maddox. If anything, he now felt compelled to take his message to a larger arena.

Maddox couldn't win the mayor's seat in Atlanta, where the Black vote went entirely against him in two bids for office in the years before the Pickrick showdowns. Governor of the state of Georgia, though, was another matter. Even as he lost his legal effort to keep integrationists out of the Pickrick, Maddox felt sure of his actions and considered himself blessed as like-minded friends told him he had pursued a righteous path. As he fought every effort to integrate his restaurant, Maddox's picture and words were splashed on the TV news and cited in the local and national newspapers. His name recognition statewide shot up, even as courts ruled against him on every count. Friends stood ready to back him, including Alabama governor George Wallace. Other Georgia cities were not nearly as progressive and integrated as his Atlanta. Maddox would find plenty of pockets of support in his home state.

Friends pressed him. "Lester," an old friend promised, "this thing will make you governor." Maddox chewed on the notion, and then, in September, nearly a year to the day after he unveiled his Lester Maddox Cafeteria, announced he would seek the governor's office in his hometown of Atlanta. Now Maddox would aspire to be the one writing the rules of government, presenting himself as the face of the Old South and seeking to connect with like-minded voters across Georgia. He would ultimately win a razor-close election in a campaign in which neither major candidate secured 50 percent of the vote.

His gubernatorial tenure would surprise many, including the ministers he viewed as archenemies, revealing multiple facets of Lester Maddox's views on poverty, race, and redemption as he pushed to clean up state prisons, hired numerous Black employees, and set free born-again prisoners committed to second chances. But on many matters, Maddox remained an unyielding, unmovable, unapologetic force. He would never forget his enemies, he would never accept integration, and he would bring shame on his administration and his legacy on the day Martin Luther King was laid to rest.

16

A NEW GOVERNOR IN GEORGIA

LESTER MADDOX RAN A CAMPAIGN for governor that was every bit as homespun as the man himself. He tapped his brother Wesley as his campaign manager and his sisters to be campaign aides. He hired no political strategists or media handlers. He didn't even have a secretary. Instead, in an era long before social media and instant news and commentary, Maddox sidled into his Pontiac station wagon and, with a driver, ventured across the Peach State, stepping out to shake hands with voters and ready with a hammer and nail to place MADDOX COUNTRY signs on the lawn of any homeowner who would allow them. He wrote his own speeches and maintained a daily log of campaign events in a green "National Diary 1966" book he kept with him at all times.

"As a campaigner, he was indefatigable," wrote his biographer Short, who had been working on state senator Jimmy Carter's gubernatorial campaign but would shift to join Maddox after his own candidate dropped from contention.

Maddox's campaign platform was built around a "Society of Liberty" that urged voters to think about their future, their liberty, and their security. "Georgians love their liberty and know that with Lester Maddox as governor they will stand guard and defend it," said his campaign brochure.

When he ran for governor, Lester Maddox was a tireless campaigner, traveling the state to seek support. *Kenan Research Center at the Atlanta History Center*

Maddox surprised the political apparatus of both parties by making the 1966 Democratic runoff for the governor's seat, finishing in second place among six candidates to former governor Ellis Arnall, long viewed as the front-runner. Jimmy Carter, who would win the nation's highest office ten years later, finished in third place and couldn't even make it to the runoff in his native state. Then the Maddox shock waves continued, when he easily defeated Arnall in the runoff to set up a statewide election against a Republican, Bo Callaway, whose background could not have been more divergent than his own.

Callaway was a dashing and well-liked sitting congressman, a West Point graduate, and a Korean War veteran whose family had made its riches through the Callaway Textile Mills and operated the Callaway Gardens magnet for well-heeled tourists. Though governors in Georgia had long come from the Democratic Party, the state GOP believed it now had a real chance to seize the state's top elected position in the persuasive persona of Bo Callaway.

When Maddox emerged as the Democratic contender for governor, Atlanta mayor Ivan Allen captured the view of the city's progressive bloc. "The seal of the great state of Georgia lies tarnished," he said. Weeks earlier, on September 6, 1966, Atlanta had confronted its own racial reckoning. Hundreds of Black residents erupted in violent protest near the newly built $18 million Atlanta–Fulton County Stadium after police shot and wounded a Black suspected car thief; Mayor Allen stood atop a police car begging for calm, but his pleas were met with virulent catcalls, and the rioting triggered more than sixty arrests.

Reese Cleghorn, profiling Maddox on the eve of the election for the *New York Times*, synthesized the Atlantan's string of political upsets in a richly reported feature entitled "Meet Lester Maddox of Georgia: 'Mr. White Backlash.'"

"Maddox's victory was an ironic joke on many politicians. During the earlier six-man primary race, Arnall had hoped Maddox would run second because he thought Maddox's racial extremism—his only claim to public attention—would make him the easiest man to beat in the runoff," Cleghorn wrote. "Many Republicans had invaded the Democratic primary to vote for Maddox because they thought he would be the easiest candidate for *their* man to defeat in the general election. But Maddox won so resoundingly (in the runoff), carrying 136 of the 159 counties, that everything suddenly was topsy-turvy."

Topsy-turvy, indeed, and now the Republican contender wondered if more shock would surface on election day. The conservative Democrat Maddox headed into the statewide vote with the hearty support from Alabama governor George Wallace, whose own term was coming to a close that year. "It is apparent from Lester Maddox's victory that the people of Georgia want to return to those bedrock principles of our Constitution which guarantee us individual liberty and freedom, the free enterprise system and private property rights," Wallace said, beaming with the news of his friend's victory in the Democratic runoff. "I think we are reaching the turning point in our struggle against federal tyranny and we are well on our way to destroying it. I hope that the people of Georgia and of this nation will continue to make their feelings known in the November election." The KKK in Georgia also supported Maddox, Cleghorn reported, with one leader dispatching a note to its members to get out and work hard for "Bro. Maddox."

When the ballots rolled in late that November election evening, nothing was settled. Callaway barely edged Maddox in the overall vote, 453,665 to 450,626. But nearly seventy thousand write-in votes had gone to Arnall, the loser of the Democratic primary, meaning neither Callaway—who collected 46.6 percent of votes, nor Maddox, with 46.2 percent—could claim the governor's mansion. Arnall collected just 7 percent of the statewide vote, but it was enough to deprive Callaway or Maddox direct entry to the governor's office. Neither had more than the 50 percent required to take office.

Maddox had won just 4 percent of the Black vote statewide. But in a twist, the Black vote may have impeded Callaway's direct path to the governor's mansion. After the Republican failed to aggressively court Black voters, some local voters' leagues urged communities to cast write-ins for Arnall. In the end, Arnall captured enough votes to ensure Callaway could not claim a majority total and take office.

Under the rules of Georgia, the decision was now in the hands of the Democrat-laden state legislature, operating from a capitol that had long been a one-party power. To no one's surprise, the legislators chose their fellow party nominee. On January 10, 1967, Lester Garfield Maddox was anointed as the seventy-fifth governor of Georgia. He professed that God had been his campaign manager. The high school dropout who later completed his degree through correspondence courses had just given the state's political power base an education in old-school politicking.

During his first press conference, Maddox set the tone for his administration. Visitors to the governor's mansion, he announced, "will get a cool sip of cow's milk or a soft drink, if they're thirsty, but no alcohol." Each day he was in the office, prayer services would be held promptly at 9:30 AM, and Governor Maddox made clear he preferred that women not wear miniskirts in the capitol. Days after he was sworn in, he sent a delegation of state legislators to Montgomery, Alabama, to attend the inauguration of Lurleen Wallace, who was elected state governor as a stand-in for her husband George, who had been term-limited out.

The election results shook that part of the electorate hoping for a new day in Georgia politics, those voters seeking a further expansion of the civil rights legislation that had been set in Washington, DC. Atlanta's most famous son, Martin Luther King Jr., said the vote results had made

After stunning the state's political establishment with his victory, Lester Maddox is sworn in as Georgia governor. *Kenan Research Center at the Atlanta History Center*

him "ashamed to be a Georgian." Three months later, amid a sermon entitled "Three Dimensions of a Complete Life" he delivered at the New Covenant Baptist Church in Chicago, King addressed the political problem in his home state of Georgia and the Deep South.

"We were made for God, and we will be restless until we find rest in him. *Oh yeah.* And I say to you this morning that this is the personal faith that has kept me going. *Yes.* I'm not worried about the future. You know, even on this race question, I'm not worried. I was down in Alabama the other day, and I started thinking about the state of Alabama where we worked so hard and [they] continue to elect the Wallaces. And down in my home state of Georgia, we have another sick governor by the name of Lester Maddox. *Yes.* And all of these things can get you confused, but they don't worry me. *All right.* Because the God that I worship is a God that has a way of saying even to kings and even to governors, 'Be still, and know that I am God.' And God has not yet turned over this universe to Lester Maddox and Lurleen Wallace." Lester Maddox would not forget the minister's words. King, he said, was "an enemy of our country."

With Maddox taking residence at the governor's mansion, the reverend's disciples knew their fight to integrate the Pickrick had fortified and inflamed Maddox's support in pockets of Georgia where voters were most comfortable keeping the races separate, not equal. "We propelled him to the governorship," says Woodrow Lewis, the South Carolina–born preacher who had never been able to dine at the Pickrick.

One of his classmates, Albert Dunn, took a more pointed view. Years later, recalling their repeated attempts to crash through Maddox's segregationist doors, Dunn would think back to the wisdom Martin Luther King's father, himself a celebrated Baptist minister and civil rights activist, had shared. If you confront the Maddox horde, it will only boost his popularity. "Daddy King was right," Dunn said in 1994, eleven years before his passing, in an interview with the Atlanta newspaper. "We helped make Lester governor."

Like the Reverend King, Albert Sampson was "ashamed" by the Georgia election results. "I was embarrassed that it dramatized the depth of the Confederate movement because he became the face of the Confederate movement. He became the chairman of the board of the Confederate movement," Sampson told me. "We were confronted with the Confederate flags. It was like racism was resurrected. . . . For him to end up being the governor was a historical mindblower."

Segregationists had won the governor's seat in Georgia, and, for one election at least, the days of the Old South were restored with Maddox's ascension to the state's highest office.

In his early years as governor, Maddox revealed that he couldn't be typecast as a one-note racial demagogue. In noteworthy ways, his own poverty-stricken background came to the forefront as he assumed his first-ever political office, and he pushed efforts to help the working class. Twice a month he welcomed to his office anyone who wanted to bend his ear, setting aside regular hours for "the little people."

He installed the first Black Georgia state trooper and the first Black member to the state Board of Pardons and Paroles, appointed some forty Black people to county draft boards, and instituted food assistance programs in 158 Georgia counties. His administration boasted that he appointed more Black citizens to state government than any segregation-era governor before him, though Atlanta news accounts noted that most of these were in lower-level government positions. Maddox also devoted considerable time probing the state prison system and instituted reforms to clean up the seventy-three county work camps and sixteen prisons.

And he favored a narrowly focused early release program for inmates, so long as their crimes had not involved serious felonies. "The releases granted these people, none, of course, of whom were incorrigibles or in for heinous crimes, were effective December 1 so that they could find jobs before Christmas and have a little money to brighten up the season with their loved ones," he explained in his autobiography.

"Lester Maddox is an aggressively affable, bald, red-faced man with twinkly old-fashioned steel-rim eyeglasses," author Melissa Fay Greene described him in *Praying for Sheetrock*, her exploration of a civil rights awakening in McIntosh County, Georgia, in the 1970s. "This once venomous and outspoken racist surprised everyone in the late sixties by serving as a decent and honest governor."

Bob Short, the Maddox staff advisor who later wrote a biography of him, says the Democratic Party asked him to help manage Maddox's campaign to ensure the GOP didn't win the governor's mansion. Having the governor's ear, he says, he pushed Maddox to think more broadly about race relations. "We were working on him to try to make him see the right path," Short told me. "I think that he became more mellow, and I think that his experience as governor softened him a great deal, in a lot of ways, not just racially but otherwise."

Short recalls urging Julian Bond, the Morehouse College–educated civil rights activist who had won a House seat in Georgia, to visit Maddox to personally impress upon the governor the importance of appointing Black people to the state draft board. Maddox saw the civil rights leader's point. "As Julian told me later, [Maddox] said if Black people serve in the military, they should have representation on the draft board," Short recounts.

Maddox freely corresponded with constituents who wrote him about state affairs, their own run-ins with the law, Communism, school integration, and myriad other issues. To one letter writer in 1968, Maddox shared his views on segregation. "It is my judgment that a member of any race should be permitted to eat with any other race so long as the rights of the other race are not violated," the governor wrote. "The right to integrate must not be greater than the right to segregate. . . . The choice to disassociate one's self from others must not be subservient to the choice of associating with whom we please."

The official state portrait that would hang in the capitol showcased Maddox, his wife Virginia, two state peaches—and a copy of the *Atlanta Journal-Constitution* wrapped around a fish, revealing Maddox's long memory and sharp-tongued wit.

Enraged by his hometown newspaper's critical coverage of a special session he planned to call in 1970, Governor Maddox called a press conference to announce a ban on the sale of newspapers on state grounds. When a worker refused his order to remove ten newspaper vending machines, Maddox and backers lifted *AJC* boxes themselves and carried them away. Then the governor led a throng of supporters to picket the local newspaper, with a mass of bodies swarming the building's front door that June.

Maddox connected with portions of Georgia voters. When he turned ill in 1970 and had to be hospitalized at Georgia Baptist Hospital, he was deluged with two Bankers Boxes full of get-well letters and cards. On other fronts, Maddox held firm, with the yin and yang Short witnessed up close on display for all of Georgia and the country to see.

Whenever Lester Maddox found himself in a pinch, Short recalls, he would keep turning back to his fight at the Pickrick, seeking a connection to the unyielding stance that drew him just enough support to win the state's highest office. "Any time he was under any sort of stress he would become a homing pigeon and he would go back to the Pickrick and bring that stuff up all over again," Short recalls. "He would go right back to his harangue about how man's property was his private property. For some reason, it appeared to me he always got great pleasure out of saying those things. And I think he thought he was speaking for Joe Six-Pack out there who thought the government was running over them, and that's who elected him."

"Regardless of what history might call him," Short concludes, "he was loyal to his following."

In his State of the Union speech after his first year in office, delivered in January 1968, Governor Maddox announced he wanted to target "the crime of rioting and making it a felony." Sophisticated political analysis wasn't required to see that Maddox was trying to exorcise some of the ghosts of the integration battles at his Pickrick restaurant, when he repelled ministers and activists he would forever view as militants and agitators before finally closing his beloved business. Now he wanted to extract state-sanctioned revenge, pushing a law to punish any like-minded demonstrators, including those who did not engage in violence. The proposed law would make rioting a felony if a demonstrator was present at the scene of a riot but refused to leave when told to do so. It took little stretch of the imagination to see how the nonviolent Atlanta seminary students, had they engaged in their protests with Maddox as governor, would be handcuffed away had his idea been written into the books. The state's Black elected leaders took immediate offense. Atlanta senator Leroy Johnson, the first Black elected to the state senate since Reconstruction, called the Maddox plan "vicious, dangerous, abusive, and unconstitutional."

The governor suggested that the state's White residents "flatten the tires" of school buses rather than allow them to serve integrated schools, and, after the Supreme Court issued a ruling affirming civil rights, had the state capitol flag lowered in a sign of mourning. And Maddox would upset US congressional leaders and Black Georgia legislators when he handed out commemorative axe and pick handles at the House of Representatives restaurant in Washington.

His most divisive and ignominious moment in office arrived on the crisp morning of April 9, 1968, and the occasion was the massive and emotion-filled funeral procession for native son Martin Luther King Jr., who had been assassinated five days earlier in Memphis, Tennessee. Schools, banks, and businesses shuttered in the city as mourners, from King widow Coretta Scott King to presidential widow Jacqueline Kennedy Onassis, and politicians and celebrities, from Hubert Humphrey to Harry Belafonte to Wilt Chamberlain, made their way through some two hundred thousand well-wishers to the services for the fallen civil rights leader.

Atlanta mayor Ivan Allen ordered liquor stores not to sell alcohol on the day, while at City Hall a funereal black bunting was draped on the facade of the building. The funeral procession, in fact, would have to first pass the glittering golden-domed Georgia capitol before reaching City Hall en route to its ultimate destination, the Ebenezer Baptist Church. Along the way, mourners paid witness to Maddox's bitter disregard for the civil rights leader, with the governor taking a stance so rigid the *Atlanta Journal-Constitution* would later headline its account THE GOVERNOR'S FORTRESS.

Maddox—never forgetting how King's followers cost him two bids to become Atlanta's mayor, nor how his preacher disciples pressed so often to integrate his restaurant that he ultimately and angrily shut the place down—refused to give state employees the day off to mourn the civil rights legend in his hometown. It was a Tuesday, Maddox noted. "Why shouldn't they be on the job?" he asked. Though all Atlanta public schools were closed to honor King, Maddox declined to order districts across the state to follow suit. Then he fought fiercely against lowering the state flag at half-staff to honor King, even as President Lyndon Johnson directed that flags at all federal buildings be lowered in a symbol of respect. Finally, the longtime Georgia secretary of state, Ben Fortson Jr., rebuffed Maddox and ordered the state's flag lowered.

Governor Maddox not only refused to attend the funeral for Reverend King but also stayed bunkered at the capitol and, anticipating violence to erupt in the streets, ordered masses of armed guards to stand ready inside and outside the state building. In all, some 160 state troopers, decked out in riot gear, stood guard with orders to act with violence, if necessary. If any mourners tried to break through the capitol front door, the troopers were to "shoot them down and stack them up," Maddox demanded. His prophecy proved to be wildly off base, and his actions embarrassing both in the moment and for his legacy. As mourners passed by this veritable state of Georgia war zone, they sang, "We Shall Overcome."

Maddox ultimately dispatched state workers to leave for the day if they wanted, but he wouldn't apologize for his actions on the day Martin Luther King Jr. was buried. To Maddox, being true to his core beliefs was a higher calling than ensuring that, as the governor of Georgia, he paid any semblance of respect upon the death of the Atlanta-born Nobel Peace Prize winner. "Against the protests of many of Atlanta's liberals, I kept the Capitol open," he wrote in one of his book chapters, entitled "Four Short Years." He continued, "My political and philosophical differences with Martin Luther King were well known, and in view of this my attendance at the funeral would have been the grossest hypocrisy."

During that spring of 1968, Governor Maddox would return to the grounds of his former restaurant, joining a group tour of the Georgia Tech campus. After he shuttered the restaurant in 1965 (and after a stint when ex-employees reopened the restaurant as the integrated Gateway Cafeteria), the august university had bought the property as part of an expansion of its campus and built a job placement center on the former Pickrick grounds.

Maddox was returning to the scene for an official visit, stepping upon the site of the restaurant he had built from the most modest of means, the grounds upon which he had embraced regulars like neighbors but rebuffed Black patrons with pistols and axe handles.

A young woman leading the tour turned to the governor, remarking that he surely recognized the location and suggesting that everyone take a peek inside. As others followed her, Lester Maddox stood still. He refused to step inside the property he would forever believe had been stolen from him by his government and a group of ministry school students, young preachers whose determination had outlasted his own. "No, y'all go ahead," he said. "I'll just wait out here."

He would never again walk through those doors.

Georgia Tech later razed the structure. In 2021 the university erected three pillars on the site, permanent landmarks honoring the three ITC students who brought a federal lawsuit after they were driven off the Pickrick by a gun-toting Maddox and his axe handle–wielding faithful. Now the names of George Willis, Woodrow Lewis, and Albert Dunn are forever etched upon the grounds of a former restaurant that would never welcome them inside.

EPILOGUE

Legacy

IN JUNE 2020, FIFTY-SEVEN YEARS to the month after President John F. Kennedy's speech urging a national shift toward racial decency, President Donald Trump walked a clear path to the Saint John's Episcopal Church after police used tear gas to disperse crowds of peaceful demonstrators in the nation's capital. There, with the TV cameras rolling and the nation's eyes upon him, Trump held a Bible in the air, a blatant political photo opportunity meant to galvanize his hardline supporters as the country once more underwent a wrenching civil rights reckoning. Trump vowed to unleash the full power of the nation's military muscle to silence protesters' quest for justice.

Precisely one week earlier in Minneapolis, on Memorial Day, May 25, an unemployed restaurant bouncer named George Floyd was suffocated to death when a White city police officer, Derek Chauvin, forced his knee upon Floyd's neck and kept it there for nine-and-a-half minutes, kept applying pressure even as the unarmed Black man begged for air. "I can't breathe, man. Please!" cried Floyd, sprawled upon the pavement facedown aside a police car as Chauvin and two other officers pressed their weight upon his powerless frame. "The knee in my neck!" At least sixteen times, Floyd pleaded for relief, at least sixteen times telling Chauvin and his fellow police officers he could not breathe.

Officer Chauvin, unmoved by Floyd's urgent cries for air, kept his knee upon the man's neck even as the forty-six-year-old became unconscious. Chauvin appeared to cavalierly keep his left hand in his pocket as his knee continued applying its force against the unmoving figure below. Another police officer forced his weight upon Floyd's torso and a third upon his legs, as a fourth officer stood sentry. Floyd, a towering former college basketball player, never fought back. As bystanders demanded that Chauvin let Floyd up, the officer pulled out Mace, threatening them away, but never taking his knee off the neck of George Floyd. As Floyd began his descent into unconsciousness and ultimately to his last breath, he twice uttered the word *Mama*, a searching plea for help. The cry of a father now made helpless like a child.

Police had been called out on suspicion that Floyd, who had lost his restaurant job amid the coronavirus pandemic and economic meltdown, had passed a counterfeit twenty-dollar bill at a corner mart to buy cigarettes—a petty offense. And soon the nation was paying witness to the punishment.

Surveillance and cell phone footage of the killing of George Floyd sparked protests across the country and then across the globe, with demonstrators turning out en masse in big cities and small towns to demand an end to police brutality. The protests were often peaceful, but sometimes filled with agitation toward police, vandalism toward businesses, and violence toward demonstrators or law enforcement. I CAN'T BREATHE, the demonstrators' signs said. BLACK LIVES MATTER. A young Black child, wearing gloves and a protective mask amid the coronavirus pandemic, held a sign: AM I A THREAT?

The mass movement was even more stunning as it formed in city streets during the global public health lockdown. That Minneapolis police fired all four officers, and that Chauvin had been arrested on murder and manslaughter charges, had done nothing to quell demands for an end to police-sanctioned abuse of unarmed citizens. On Saturday, June 6, 2020, nearly two weeks after the killing, thousands of protesters filled the nation's capital, and even more would turn out on the fifty-seven-year anniversary of the March on Washington on August 28. Earlier in June, Washington mayor Muriel Bowser had city staff paint the BLACK LIVES MATTER slogan in giant yellow letters on a street leading to the White House, in a direct rebuke to President Trump.

A bigger rebuke arrived on election day, when Trump lost the presidential race by seven million votes to Joe Biden. The state of Georgia turned blue for Biden-Harris, an important piece of their larger national victory, and Fulton County, the racially diverse base of Atlanta, was pivotal to the Democrats' victory in the state. Fulton County went 73 percent for Joe Biden and 26 percent for Donald Trump. Biden won Georgia by some 12,000 votes—but Fulton County by a stout 240,000-plus margin. Six decades after Black Atlanta sent Lester Maddox to two mayoral election defeats, Black Atlanta helped remove Donald Trump from the presidency.

And then Georgia turned blue again in the Senate runoffs of 2021, sending two Democrats to Washington in a historic vote that cemented the party's control of Congress. One was the Reverend Raphael Warnock, the Morehouse College–educated pastor of Martin Luther King's Ebenezer Baptist Church, who had been raised in public housing by a mother who once picked cotton and who now was heading to the halls of Congress. The runoff results were a repudiation of Trump's desperate bid to overturn a just election, in which the outgoing president bullied and badgered election and justice officials in Georgia and elsewhere to award him states he had clearly lost.

"It's vindication for a lot of people who have really suffered," CNN commentator Van Jones said in an emotional response to Trump's loss. "You know, the I can't breathe. You know that wasn't just George Floyd. That was a lot of people who have felt they couldn't breathe." As Congress gathered to certify Biden's victory, Trump inflamed a mob of supporters who invaded the Capitol and did nothing for hours as the extremists terrorized the halls of democracy and sent Vice President Mike Pence and members of Congress scrambling for safety. George Floyd could not breathe, but Trump's Confederate flag–wielding faithful could lead a deadly insurrection on the house of Congress.

Just as Lester Maddox shattered the norms of political decency by refusing to attend Martin Luther King's funeral in 1968, Donald Trump shattered the norms of presidential decorum by refusing to attend Joe Biden's inauguration in 2021. He was the first president in 152 years to rebuff his successor, declining to witness the peaceful transition of power.

Watching that season's racial unrest unfold, from the lethal indifference Chauvin and his colleagues showed to a man pleading for air, to the tear gas and rubber bullets fired at the peaceful BLM demonstrators, to the election revolt played out in Washington, I returned to thoughts of the events I was researching in the 1960s in Atlanta and the Deep South. After Floyd's killing, citizens and even some police officers across the country kneeled upon the ground in a plea for equality, and activists from coast to coast rejoiced in April 2021 when Chauvin was convicted of second- and third-degree murder and manslaughter in Floyd's death. Six decades earlier, student demonstrators staged sit-ins in diners and hotels serving White customers only. As police spewed tear gas and aimed painful rubber bullets at protesters in 2020, echoes of Bull Connor's fire hoses of 1963 raced to mind. The 2020 DC demonstrations recalled the March on Washington for Jobs and Freedom of 1963, twin oceans of races and ages marching, chanting, and praying for a sea change in the government's treatment of minorities.

A more fundamental parallel connected Trump's most strident supporters with the Atlanta segregationists, and it showed itself through the debilitating coronavirus pandemic of 2020. In 1964 Lester Maddox and Moreton Rolleston cited heavy-handed government intrusion as their prime reason to lock the doors on Black customers, adopting a libertarian view that too much government causes grave harm. Fifty-six years later, Trump supporters cited heavy-handed government intrusion into their personal affairs when they refused to wear masks to help stop spread of the disease. Thousands of Trump faithful descended on Washington a month after his defeat to rally behind his fabricated claims of election fraud. As the spread of COVID-19 was at its most lethal in the United States, many of the deposed president's backers proudly wore no masks as they destroyed Black Lives Matter signs and fought with counterprotesters.

I was immersed in the reporting and writing for *Heart of Atlanta* when George Floyd was killed by Minneapolis police and a nation's rage played out nightly. One day that late May, I reached out to one of the key players in the earlier events in Atlanta, Chicago minister Albert Sampson. Reverend Sampson was on the ground pressing for equal rights in the 1960s, first as a seminary student, then as a leader with the Atlanta chapter of the NAACP, and then working at the Southern Christian Leadership Conference. In Atlanta Sampson tried to enter segregating restaurants and hotels but had been repelled from one establishment by a pistol and pickaxe handles.

I was calling Sampson on May 27, 2020, to ask some follow-up questions about those events. Before I could get deep into the interview, the reverend told me he wanted to talk about George Floyd. Sampson had been weeping earlier that day. "Why am I in tears all the way in Chicago?" Sampson asked me. "This one here is making me cry because we're in 2020."

In 2020 the nation was once more engaged in an urgent fight for equality. Sixty years earlier, the mission was for equal rights for all in voting booths and places of commerce, for minorities to have a seat at all-White businesses, and for an end to KKK murders and bombings. Today the struggle is for people of color to be treated lawfully by police, that Black lives matter. Even after Floyd's killing, abuses continued. In August 2020 in Wisconsin, a White police officer fired seven shots in the back of Jacob Blake as the twenty-nine-year-old Black man tried to enter his car, paralyzing him. Prominent athletes responded by refusing to play or postponing games in historic shutdowns for professional sports, with basketball stars, baseball players, and other athletes using the power of their silence to demand an end to police abuses.

"Watching the continued genocide of Black people at the hand of the police is honestly making me sick to my stomach," wrote tennis Grand Slam champion Naomi Osaka, among those to step away. "When will it ever be enough?"

The Civil Rights Act of 1964 created lasting weapons to target the nation's racial ills, setting out ironclad rules barring discrimination in private businesses and public places. The path to that landmark legislation was paved with so much bloodshed, with the toll of KKK killings finally forcing an intransigent Congress to act. But history shows that legislation alone cannot wipe clean racism's legacy. The Library of Congress, in a summary of the Civil Rights Act of 1964 compiled long before Derek Chauvin forced his knee upon George Floyd's neck, presciently forecast that struggles would continue and that they would be waged in city streets.

"As transformative as the Civil Rights Act of 1964 and its successors have been," the summary said, "the exclusion, exploitation, and discrimination that it targeted were deeply entrenched and have proved difficult to end. The act and its subsequent enforcement continue to prompt new debates about what equality means, what government can do to promote it, and how ordinary Americans can continue to achieve it. The future of civil rights, like its past, will be shaped by citizens' participation in lobbying, litigation, politics, and public protests."

Martin Luther King made this point more succinctly, with an eloquence that echoes through the decades.

"The arc of the moral universe is long," King said, "but it bends toward justice."

The central figures in Atlanta's engagement over civil rights and public accommodations took varied paths once the legal books closed on the cases. Here is a look at what the key players did after the courtroom battles.

The Segregationists

Lester Maddox

The Atlantan died in 2003 at age eighty-seven. After his gubernatorial term, he was elected lieutenant governor in 1970, serving under political enemy Jimmy Carter. Maddox would go on to lose a string of future bids for office, including for Georgia governor in 1974 and a run for president in 1976, when he gathered two-tenths of one percent of the vote running on the American Independent Party ticket. He opened a souvenir shop in Underground Atlanta, where he sold axe handles. He then performed stand-up comedy with a Black man released from prison during his term, a duo called "The Governor and the Dishwasher." In 1990 Maddox ran again for Georgia governor and finished last in the Democratic primary. After his death, his family published a lengthy tribute that detailed his growth from poverty to the state's highest office. The four-thousand-word obituary notes that Maddox owned restaurants but does not once mention the Pickrick by name.

Moreton Rolleston Jr.

The losing lawyer in the *Heart of Atlanta v. USA* Supreme Court case died in 2013 at age ninety-five. His motel was demolished in 1973 and replaced by a Hilton. Continuing as a lawyer, Rolleston engaged in long-running litigation against multiple figures, including a failed property dispute against entertainer Tyler Perry. He was repeatedly scolded by Georgia courts for conduct unbecoming his profession and once jailed for contempt of court. In 2007, the Georgia Supreme Court debarred Rolleston. "After repeated disciplinary actions and admonitions from Georgia courts at every level, Rolleston has shown no remorse for his actions," the debarment order says. "To the contrary, he has continued to plague the judicial system with untenable claims for purposes unbefitting any member of this State's Bar."

The Groundbreaker

Constance Baker Motley

The renowned civil rights lawyer who would become a public official and federal judge died in 2005 at age eighty-four. As a judge, Motley in 1978 upheld the right of female sports journalists to enter the locker rooms of professional sports teams. As Manhattan borough president, she secured funding to revitalize communities in Harlem and East Harlem. In 1993 Motley was elected into the National Women's Hall of Fame following a career in which she successfully argued nine of ten cases before the US Supreme Court and was the first Black woman anointed a federal judge.

The Ministers

Albert Dunn

The Reverend Albert Lee Dunn, who graduated from the Interdenominational Theological Center in 1966, died in 2005 at age seventy in Texas. Before his death, he was a minister in Clarkston, Georgia, and for years was the dean of chapel at Paul Quinn College, a private historically Black institution in Dallas affiliated with the African Methodist Episcopal Church.

Woodrow T. Lewis

After graduating from the ITC in 1965, the Reverend W. T. Lewis returned to his native South Carolina as a pastor. He hosted gospel music radio shows; raised eight children, one a minister he personally ordained; and helped lead the Congress of Racial Equality. In the 1970s Lewis argued that too many Black children were being bused into schools in White communities. "He was in the eye of the storm with that issue," says the Reverend Waverly V. Yates, a former CORE colleague. Lewis later encountered another storm involving bingo-funded charities he operated to help fund crime prevention and job training. The state, citing inconsistencies in his paperwork, denied renewing his bingo licenses. Lewis admitted making unintentional paperwork errors. After both sides filed suit, Lewis kept the charity efforts going. "We overcame," he says.

Albert Sampson

After leaving Atlanta, the Reverend Albert Sampson became pastor of Fernwood United Methodist Church in Chicago in 1975 and operated the church for several decades until semi-retiring in 2013. In 2003 the Illinois House of Representatives had issued a resolution honoring Sampson's small church for making an outsize difference. "Fernwood United Methodist Church has served as a beacon in the Chicago community with a broad array of services including computer classes, senior programs, energy assistance, and youth enrichment services," said the resolution. Among its initiatives, his Chicago church launched a farmers market intended to help struggling Black farmers survive by encouraging his congregants and neighbors to buy produce shipped from southern farms. Sampson is now leading an effort to reopen the church.

George Willis III

After graduating from the Interdenominational Theological Center in 1965, the Reverend George Sylvester Willis III pastored at Texas churches, including in Waco, Dallas, and Houston, before his death in 2012 at age seventy-seven. The US Army veteran continued his studies after leaving Atlanta, pursuing his passion for justice and equality. Even as he led churches, Willis served as a substitute teacher in Texas.

Charles Wells Sr.

The Reverend Charles Wells, a 1966 ITC graduate, died in 2004 at age sixty-five after pastoring in Georgia for four decades with the African Methodist Episcopal Church. He died on the job in Atlanta as he was renovating his church. Wells's last breath came as he sat in a church library chair, with his arms at his side and "his head looking up to God."

ACKNOWLEDGMENTS

In striving to re-create Atlanta's civil rights epoch of 1964, I was aided by the oral histories of key participants, as well as by archivists who helped me gain access to crucial documents that framed the spine of this story.

I owe a debt of gratitude to the Reverends Albert Sampson and Woodrow T. Lewis. I called each in 2019 and, after explaining my goal to bring this forgotten piece of the nation's civil rights history to the page, each enthusiastically agreed to discuss his role in the battles to integrate the Pickrick restaurant and Heart of Atlanta motel. I sat down with the reverends after those initial calls, and then reached out to both more than a dozen times apiece to gain further details. They answered every call. I thank Kay Willis, widow of the Reverend George Willis III, for meeting me in Texas and fielding all my follow-up calls about her husband's activism. Like the Reverends Sampson and Lewis, Kay Willis was committed to preserving this history.

Several other figures who witnessed, participated in, or studied these events took time to speak with me. I thank civil rights icons the Reverend Jesse Jackson and James Meredith, Lester Maddox biographer Bob Short, legal experts Rachel Moran and Michael Meltsner, Atlanta academics Andra Gillespie and Deirdre Oakley, writer and educator Paula Young Shelton, the Reverend Waverly Yates, and Moreton Rolleston III and Lester Maddox Jr., the sons of the key figures in this story. Thanks also to Angel Parks of the Interdenominational Theological Center in Atlanta.

Public documents provided historical heft to these oral histories and insights, and I am indebted to several researchers who helped me attain vital records. I thank Leah Lefkowitz of the Atlanta History Center, Jeffrey Flannery of the Library of Congress, and Nathan Jordan of the National Archives at Atlanta.

I am indebted to my agent, Esmond Harmsworth, president of the Aevitas literary agency, who helped shape my proposal for *Heart of Atlanta* and provided invaluable guidance from start to finish. Thanks also to Jerome Pohlen, senior editor at Chicago Review Press, who saw promise in this story and worked to bring these words to the page; to his colleague Frances Giguette; and to copyeditor Rebekah Slonim and proofreader Joseph Webb.

My wife and fellow journalist, Beth Reinhard, remains my staunchest supporter and toughest critic. As in my first two books, Beth read every word of my draft and sent back detailed notes. Thank you, Beffy, for helping me see the story with clarity and purpose. And a heartfelt thanks to our daughters, Abby and Emma, both now college age, who have grown into creative and impassioned advocates for justice and equality. You both inspire me each day.

I am deeply grateful for the feedback from my friend and colleague Chris Hamby, who took the time to read my working manuscript and offer tangible suggestions to enhance the storytelling. Chris's insightful comments reminded me to keep the characters on each page.

Finally, an indirect, but meaningful, thanks to two other sources of inspiration. First, to the writer Roya Hakakian, who led a nonfiction workshop I participated in, THREAD at Yale, in 2019. Roya pushed me to find my next book, and I left the conference for the three-hundred-plus mile journey home committed to doing so. The next morning, I thumbed through my book ideas and saw *Heart of Atlanta* in a new light. I reimmersed myself in the story the following day. And, thanks to writer-director Jeff Nichols, whom I have never met but whose 2016 movie *Loving* inspired me nonetheless. After leaving the theater, I told myself I wish *I* had written that story, describing a seminal US Supreme

Court civil rights ruling while peeling back the personal story of the oft-forgotten figures behind the saga. That led me on a quest to find a Supreme Court civil rights ruling that had, perhaps, been lost to history. I found *Heart of Atlanta*.

ABOUT THE RESEARCH

HEART OF ATLANTA IS A NONFICTION NARRATIVE account of events in the city of Atlanta and across the country during the sea-changing civil rights movement of the 1960s. The book is built from thousands of pages of historical public documents obtained from archives in Atlanta and Washington, hundreds of other records and video footage, and interviews with key participants. The documents include the federal court archive for the two 1964 lawsuits that serve as the spine of this book—*Heart of Atlanta Motel Inc. v. USA and Robert F. Kennedy* and *Willis, Lewis, and Dunn v. The Pickrick and Lester G. Maddox*. The lawsuits were filed within days of each other in Atlanta, serving as the first two legal challenges over the Civil Rights Act of 1964. Both cases were heard in federal court in Georgia and reviewed by the same three-panel core of judges who weighed evidence and simultaneously issued rulings involving each lawsuit. The *Heart of Atlanta* litigation traveled to the United States Supreme Court, and I listened to the audio transcript of arguments before the high court that October and reviewed the court's twenty-page ruling in December 1964.

From the Library of Congress, I obtained correspondence to the US Supreme Court involving the *Heart of Atlanta* case and Civil Rights Act of 1964. Multiple other documents, from Atlanta History Center archives on Lester Maddox's term as governor to Department of Justice reports on the civil rights killings of the era to senior essays written by the Atlanta ministers who challenged Maddox, proved crucial to my understanding and description of the events.

The narrative is enhanced by interviews with multiple voices, including the Reverends Albert Sampson and Woodrow T. Lewis, the two surviving ministers who tried to integrate the motel and restaurant, and Kay Willis, the widow of Pickrick plaintiff George Willis III. I interviewed the Reverend Jesse Jackson and Paula Young Shelton about events in Atlanta in the 1960s, and James Meredith about lawyer Constance Baker Motley. I interviewed experts in sociology and Black politics in Atlanta to understand the city's history of racial relations, and legal experts to more fully assess the significance of the US Supreme Court's *Heart of Atlanta v. USA* ruling. I interviewed Lester Maddox's biographer and former staff member, Bob Short, and interviewed Lester Maddox Jr. and Moreton Rolleston III, the sons of the restaurateur and motel owner, respectively.

My research was further aided by newspaper reports of the events as they occurred, as well as subsequent news stories describing the times and figures.

And my research was informed by twenty books that enhanced my understanding of the Civil Rights Act of 1964, the key players drawn into the legal sagas, the racial awakening in Atlanta and across the country, Georgia's civil rights struggles, and US Supreme Court rulings spanning the centuries:

At Canaan's Edge: America in the King Years 1965–68, by Taylor Branch

Atlanta Rising: The Invention of an International City 1946–1996, by Frederick Allen

Beyond Atlanta: The Struggle for Racial Equality in Georgia, 1940–1980, by Stephen G. N. Tuck

Chief Justice: A Biography of Earl Warren, by Ed Cray

Child of the Civil Rights Movement, by Paula Young Shelton

Equal Justice Under Law: An Autobiography, by Constance Baker Motley

Everything Is Pickrick: The Life of Lester Maddox, by Bob Short

An Idea Whose Time Has Come: Two Presidents, Two Parties, and the Battle for the Civil Rights Act of 1964, by Todd S. Purdum

The Legend of the Black Mecca: Politics and Class in the Making of Modern Atlanta, by Maurice J. Hobson

Master of the Senate: The Years of Lyndon Johnson, by Robert A. Caro

The Minister Who Wore Many Hats: The Life and Work of the Reverend-Doctor Charles E. Wells, Sr., by Barbara H. Wells

Parting the Waters: America in the King Years 1954–63, by Taylor Branch

The Passage of Power: The Years of Lyndon Johnson, by Robert A. Caro

Pillar of Fire: America in the King Years 1963–65, by Taylor Branch

Praying for Sheetrock, by Melissa Fay Greene

Race Against Time: A Reporter Reopens the Unsolved Murder Cases of the Civil Rights Era, by Jerry Mitchell

Race and the Shaping of Twentieth-Century Atlanta, by Ronald H. Bayor

Separate: The Story of Plessy v. Ferguson, and America's Journey from Slavery to Segregation, by Steve Luxenberg

Speaking Out: The Autobiography of Lester Garfield Maddox, by Lester Maddox

White Flight: Atlanta and the Making of Modern Conservatism, by Kevin M. Kruse

Here, chapter by chapter, I detail the source material for *Heart of Atlanta: Five Black Pastors and the Supreme Court Victory for Integration.* Where possible, I include links to relevant documents and websites.

Prologue: A Presidential Plea, a Legal Fight Alighted

This opening section is framed by President John F. Kennedy's address to the nation on June 11, 1963, when he delivered his most meaningful civil rights speech, a talk that laid the groundwork for the events that followed. Video footage is featured on the John F. Kennedy Presidential Library and Museum website at https://www.jfklibrary.org/learn/about-jfk/jfk-in-history/civil-rights-movement.

This section cites Alabama governor George Wallace's infamous "segregation forever!" refrain and his actions on the day the University of Alabama was integrated. The Universal News clip of the scene at the Tuscaloosa campus is found at https://unwritten-record.blogs.archives.gov/2014/06/09/this-week-in-universal-news-the-university-of-alabama-is-desegregated-1963/. Additional source material for Wallace's "segregation forever!" quotation can be found in a National Public Radio article, "Wallace in the Schoolhouse Door," found at https://www.npr.org /2003/06/11/1294680/wallace-in-the-schoolhouse-door. Details on Alabama's first Black student in 1956 come from reports including one by CNN at https://www.cnn.com/2019/05/09/us/alabama-first-black-student-trnd /index.html.

Details on Congress's history of defeating civil rights bills come from Robert A. Caro's Pulitzer Prize–winning biography, *Master of the Senate: The Years of Lyndon Johnson*, in, among other places, his introductory section, page xi.

Myriad sources describe civil rights protests and tragedies. For information on the Greensboro Four sit-in at the Woolworth's lunch counter, see "Greensboro Sit-In", by History.com editors, at https://www.history .com/topics/black-history/the-greensboro-sit-in; an NPR article, "The Woolworth Sit-In That Launched a Movement," at https://www.npr.org /templates/story/story.php?storyId=18615556; and a history of the event compiled by North Carolina A&T State University, at http://www.library .ncat.edu/resources/archives/four.html. Taylor Branch's Pulitzer Prize–winning *Parting the Waters: America in the King Years 1954–63* includes a detailed account of the sit-in movement, with Fred Shuttlesworth's quotation that the effort may "shake up the world" on page 273.

For information on James Meredith's quest to integrate the University of Mississippi, see archived footage at History.com, "James Meredith at Ole Miss", found at https://www.history.com/topics/black-history/ole-miss -integration, and a university summary of its integration battles, at https://50years.olemiss.edu/james-meredith/. For information on the violence against Freedom Riders, see "Freedom Rides (1961)" from the online reference center BlackPast, at https://www.blackpast.org/african-american -history/freedom-rides-1961/ and "How the Freedom Riders Movement Began," from the ThoughtCo. Reference site at www.thoughtco.com /the-freedom-riders-movement-2834894. The John F. Kennedy Presidential Library and Museum contains summaries on Meredith and the Freedom Riders, at https://www.jfklibrary.org/learn/about-jfk/jfk-in-history /civil-rights-movement. A BBC News article details the martial law ordered in Montgomery, Alabama, after assaults on Freedom Riders, published at http://news.bbc.co.uk/onthisday/hi/dates/stories/may/21

/newsid_4350000/4350591.stm. *Parting the Waters* describes the Freedom Rides in chapters 11 and 12, "Baptism on Wheels" and "The Summer of Freedom Rides," and devotes another chapter, 17, to Meredith: "The Fall of Ole Miss."

For information on Birmingham public safety commissioner Bull Connor's use of fire hoses and attack dogs, see an in-depth video report from the AL.com news site, "Bull Connor Used Fire Hoses, Police Dogs on Protestors (May 3, 1963)," published at https://www.al.com/birmingham-news-stories/2013/05/bull_connor_used_fire_hoses_po.html. *Pillar of Fire*, the second book of Taylor Branch's King trilogy, describes the national shock of Connor's offensive on page 77.

Books and magazine articles helped flesh out my understanding of President Kennedy's civil rights platform. One insightful book is Todd S. Purdum's *An Idea Whose Time Has Come*, which includes an eloquent description of Kennedy's speech on page 57 and the detail that Martin Luther King Jr. instantly dispatched a telegram praising the address on page 58. Page 40 tells how Kennedy was ushered into office with 70 percent of the Black vote. *Pillar of Fire*, on page 26, says that King had persistently pushed Kennedy to issue an executive order on segregation. A July 1963 *Atlantic* magazine article, "JFK's Civil-Rights Problem," reports that the president had vowed to take up civil rights "among the first orders of business" for Congress in 1961. The article is at https://www.theatlantic.com/magazine/archive/2013/08/jfks-civil-rights-problem/309481/.

A PDF of Martin Luther King Jr.'s "Letter from Birmingham Jail" is printed at the BlackPast online reference site, found at https://www.blackpast.org/african-american-history/1963-martin-luther-king-jr-letter-birmingham-jail/. *Parting the Waters* describes King's jailing and letter in chapter 19, "Greenwood and Birmingham Jail."

Details on the June 12, 1963, killing of Mississippi NAACP leader Medgar Evers come from multiple sources, including an FBI summary of "Famous Cases and Criminals" at https://www.fbi.gov/history/famous-cases/medgar-evers and a History.com profile at https://www.history.com/topics/black-history/medgar-evers. *Parting the Waters*, on page 825, details the night Evers was killed, including his daughter's plaintive plea, that he carried anti–Jim Crow T-shirts when he was gunned down, and his last words: "Turn me loose!"

For details describing each of the eleven provisions of the Civil Rights Act of 1964, see a Library of Congress summary, found at https://www .loc.gov/exhibits/civil-rights-act/epilogue.html. A Reuters story in 2020 describes the Supreme Court's landmark ruling barring discrimination against LGBT workers, citing the Civil Rights Act of 1964, found at https:// www.reuters.com/article/us-usa-court-lgbt/in-landmark-ruling-supreme -court-bars-discrimination-against-lgbt-workers-idUSKBN23M20N.

Video footage of President Lyndon B. Johnson signing the act into law can be viewed on Universal Newsreel, "President Signs Historic Bill," at https:// www.youtube.com/watch?v=ZaRUca7FyAc. The *New York Times* editorial "A National Victory," published July 3, 1964, can be read at https://www .nytimes.com/1964/07/03/archives/a-national-victory.html.

Interviews in the prologue were conducted on February 4, 2020, with legal scholar Rachel Moran and on June 17, 2019, with Albert Sampson.

1: An Awakening in Atlanta

Scores of sources and interviews helped me construct this chapter describing the growing influence of Black communities in Atlanta in the 1960s and further understand how racial tensions persisted in a locale that famously called itself the "City Too Busy to Hate."

The description of the Interdenominational Theological Center's history comes from its website, at https://www.itc.edu. Descriptions of Lester Maddox and his business come from sources including the Maddox autobiography, *Speaking Out*. Details describing the Heart of Atlanta's amenities come from a 1960 advertisement found in the archives of the *Atlanta Daily World* newspaper and from a feature story in Today in Georgia History at https://www.todayingeorgiahistory.org/content/heart -atlanta-motel.

I obtained multitudes of material involving Lester Maddox and his restaurant, including several copies of his "Pickrick Says" advertisements, from court filings and historical archives. The archives of the *Atlanta Daily World* included a June 26, 1963, story, headlined SEVERAL DOWN-TOWN ATLANTA RESTAURANTS DESEGREGATE, which notes how Maddox resigned from local, state, and national restaurant associations. Another *Atlanta Daily World* story, published January 16, 1963, describing the inauguration ceremonies for Georgia governor Carl Sanders, reports that a commercial plane flew overhead with a sign that said EAT SEGREGATED, GO PICKRICK.

I reviewed historical news accounts describing Moreton Rolleston's fight against integration; the Rolleston quotation "This is the end of the line" appears in a *Chicago Defender* story on December 16, 1964, headlined SOUTHERNERS GLOOMILY AGREE SEGREGATION IS A LOST CAUSE. I reviewed photos of Rolleston and his motel, including pictures of the proprietor in front of his resort's pool.

Chapter 1 cites civil rights killings in 1964, information I constructed from sources, including Department of Justice filings; the sources for these deaths are cited in subsequent chapters, when I describe each fatality in more detail.

Atlanta's history of racial politics, growth, and tension has been developed from myriad sources. The *Ebony* magazine story "ATLANTA Black Mecca of the South" is cited at sources including Wikipedia at https://en.wikipedia.org/wiki/Black_mecca. *Atlanta Rising* by Frederick Allen details on page 93 how the Atlanta of 1960 remained segregated in taxicabs, schools, and shops, and pages 94–96 describe the protest targeting the Rich's department store. Information about Martin Luther King's arrest at Rich's, and the subsequent letter he hand-scrawled, come from Stanford University's Martin Luther King, Jr. Research and Education Institute, found at https://kinginstitute.stanford.edu/king-papers /documents/draft-statement-judge-james-e-webb-after-arrest-richs -department-store.

Paula Young Shelton's children's book, *Child of the Civil Rights Movement*, describes how her family was turned away from a Whites-only restaurant decades before her father, Andrew Young, would become Atlanta mayor. I interviewed Shelton about the Atlanta of her youth on December 19, 2020.

Information about King's involvement at the Ebenezer Baptist Church comes from Stanford University's King Institute, at https:// kinginstitute.stanford.edu/encyclopedia/ebenezer-baptist-church-atlanta -georgia. The Stanford Institute further includes a section devoted to the

Southern Christian Leadership Conference, found at https://kinginstitute
.stanford.edu/encyclopedia/southern-christian-leadership-conference
-sclc. The BlackPast online website includes a summary of the SCLC's early
days, challenges, and ultimate growth, at https://www.blackpast.org/african
-american-history/southern-christian-leadership-conference-1957/. The
Atlanta Journal-Constitution produced a feature about Auburn Avenue
and its role in Black Atlanta's growth and prosperity, found at https://www
.ajc.com/lifestyles/reasons-celebrate-black-history-month-auburn-avenue
/TrzGacIFmh9Ktf58xVEGrN/.

The Atlanta History Center includes information and a video exploring Atlanta's school integration battle following the *Brown v. Board of Education* decision, found at https://www.atlantahistorycenter.com/explore
/online-exhibitions/atlanta-in-50-objects/school-integration. An Emory
University blog includes details about the school desegregation fight,
at https://scholarblogs.emory.edu/woodruff/news/naacp-and-school
-desegregation. The book *Race and the Shaping of Twentieth-Century
Atlanta* explores the desegregation fight in, among other places, pages 222
to 226. An *Atlanta Journal-Constitution* story describes the Black community's quest to integrate golf courses; "Atlanta Desegregation Began on
a Golf Course" can be found at https://www.ajc.com/news/local/atlanta
-desegregation-began-golf-course/RzVCZYtu21sB4hLuLorf1M/. *Atlanta*
magazine, CBS46, and others described the city's short-lived Berlin Wall,
at https://www.atlantamagazine.com/civilrights/atlantas-berlin-wall/ and
https://www.cbs46.com/news/atlantas-berlin-wall-built-to-keep-black
-residents-out-of-all-white-community/article_2bdee5d6-8bd4-5ef0
-bfc5-61ea542dd482.html.

To learn more about Atlanta's demographic, racial, and political
evolution, I sought the view of academics. I interviewed Andra Gillespie,
a professor of political science at Emory University, on April 3, 2020,
and Deirdre Oakley, a Georgia State University professor of sociology,
on April 8, 2020.

I interviewed the Reverend Jesse Jackson on May 19, 2020.

The *Atlanta Daily World* archive is the source for the arrests I cite
in 1960, in a story headlined TWENTY-TWO STUDENTS GIVEN TEN DAYS
EACH IN "DEMONSTRATIONS" and published on October 21, 1960. Details
about the violent protests at Leb's Restaurant come from a thorough

accounting of the unrest kept as part of Georgia Tech's Ivan Allen Jr. Digital Collection and found at https://ivanallen.iac.gatech.edu/artifacts /items/show/372.

The *Atlanta Inquirer* newspaper is the source of stories examining racial unrest in 1964. The *Inquirer* headlines I cite come from its news pages on July 11 and 18, and August 15 of 1964. The description of the newspaper as the "loud voice in Atlanta" comes from its website.

Census information allowed me to describe how Atlanta's Black population expanded. The report *Historical Census Statistics on Population Totals by Race, 1790 to 1990*, includes information on Atlanta in table 11.

Telling details on the disparities facing Atlanta's Black community, and on the strengthening power of its middle and upper classes, come from Maurice J. Hobson's *The Legend of the Black Mecca*. Hobson details the growing number of registered voters on page 26, the disparity in recreational amenities on page 30, and the lack of Black people in high positions on page 31. Hobson notes how Atlanta elected its first Black Board of Aldermen since Reconstruction on page 33 and describes Maynard Jackson's rise to become its first Black mayor on page 3 and elsewhere. Information about Mayor Jackson can be found in a profile at https://www.britannica.com/biography/Maynard-Jackson and in a 2003 *Atlanta Journal-Constitution* obituary at https://www.ajc.com /news/crime--law/maynard-jackson-1938-2003-lion-man/s5LIVTYs 5K3E87AOmDU3OJ/.

This chapter also benefits from *White Flight: Atlanta and the Making of Modern Conservatism* by Kevin M. Kruse. Chapter 5 details the behind-the-scenes racial troubles after Atlanta schools desegregated, and chapter 7 describes the college students' "Appeal for Human Rights" ad campaign.

Another insightful book is *Race and the Shaping of Twentieth-Century Atlanta* by Ronald H. Bayor. Page 40 cites the coalition of nine civil rights groups that demanded change in Atlanta, and page 83 notes how Atlanta's Black residents filled 44 percent of the population but half that percentage of city land. Page 18 features a chart listing the percentage of Black registered voters over time, and pages 22–23 include a copy of a handbill urging Black residents to vote and a photograph of hundreds of voters lining up to register.

Details about the Atlanta civil rights protests come from the *Atlanta Inquirer* and other sources. The *Inquirer*'s July 11, 1964, edition includes a photo summary of the protesters picketing the "fire trap" school. The July 18, 1964, front page included a story about the death of Jerry Maxey, headlined $100 REWARD POSTED IN HANGING CASE HERE. Further information about Maxey's death came in AP reports that July 2, headlined BOY, 14, FOUND HANGED, and on July 30, headlined NEGRO'S DEATH CALLED SUICIDE. The story about the Black man knifed by four White assailants appeared on the *Inquirer*'s front page, August 15, 1964.

Martin Luther King's speech, "On some positions, cowardice asks the question," is archived at the Stanford University King Institute, at https://kinginstitute.stanford.edu/king-papers/publications/knock-midnight-inspiration-great-sermons-reverend-martin-luther-king-jr-10.

Information about the ministry students' efforts to integrate the Pickrick and Heart of Atlanta comes from multiple sources, notably the federal court archives in the two legal cases. In both cases—for *Heart of Atlanta Motel v. USA and Robert F. Kennedy* and *Willis, Lewis, and Dunn v. The Pickrick and Lester G. Maddox*—I obtained the full case filings and transcripts at the National Archives at Atlanta during research in September 2019.

The audio of the subsequent legal arguments before the US Supreme Court in the *Heart of Atlanta* case can be found at https://www.oyez.org/cases/1964/515. I interviewed civil rights scholar Rachel Moran about the Supreme Court ruling's significance on February 2, 2020.

Summary profiles of the five ITC ministry students at the front lines of the integration battles come through multiple sources. I interviewed Woodrow T. Lewis multiple times, including on July 19, 2019, in Spartanburg, South Carolina, and over the phone on March 29, 2020. I interviewed Albert Sampson multiple times, including in Chicago on July 5, 2019. I interviewed Kay Willis, the widow of lead plaintiff George Willis III, in Texas on March 9, 2020. She shared newspaper clippings detailing her husband's experiences as an army boxer.

I learned about the Reverend Charles Wells Sr. from a book published by his wife, Barbara Wells, *The Minister Who Wore Many Hats*.

Details about Albert Dunn's earlier protest arrest come from an *Atlanta Daily World* story from February 16, 1961, "Eight Ministers Arrested at Terminal Station Here." Dunn's statement that Martin Luther King Sr. urged him not to confront Maddox is from an August 7, 1994, *Atlanta Journal-Constitution* story by Jim Auchmutey.

Many profile details about one of the ministers' lawyers, Constance Baker Motley, come from her book *Equal Justice Under Law*. I interviewed James Meredith about Motley on July 26, 2020, and Reverend Lewis about her on March 29, 2020. Motley's *New York Times* obituary was published September 29, 2005, found at https://www.nytimes .com/2005/09/29/nyregion/constance-baker-motley-civil-rights-trailblazer -dies-at-84.html. Other sources of information about Motley come from a Columbia University tribute, at http://c250.columbia.edu/c250_celebrates /remarkable_columbians/constance_motley.html, and a write-up in the National Women's Hall of Fame, at https://www.womenofthehall.org/inductee /constance-baker-motley/.

Quotations from Albert Sampson that end this chapter came on July 21, 2019, when he told me that "this is the most important story in Black history."

2: Lester Maddox: "Stand Up for America"

This chapter profiling Lester Garfield Maddox is built in part through the Pickrick operator's own words, in his autobiography, *Speaking Out*. I also obtained court transcripts in the ministry students' legal case against the future governor, in which Maddox testified under oath about his actions and motivations in precluding Black customers from his restaurant. Other source material includes interviews with the ministers and Maddox's son and biographer, video archives, the biography of him, books about Atlanta, and news accounts.

The chapter title comes from Maddox's autobiography, chapter 13. The opening pages of this chapter are built largely from the Maddox autobiography, in which he describes his poverty-stricken upbringing and entrepreneurial spirit throughout the book's chapter 1, in pages 1–11. *Speaking Out* chapters 2 and 3, pages 13–36, describe the courtship of his future wife and his ultimate opening of the Pickrick restaurant in 1947.

Another resource is *Atlanta Rising: The Invention of an International City 1946–1996*. Details about Maddox's mother's fundamentalist views appear on page 78 and the description of Maddox resembling "an angry chicken" on page 79.

Video footage of Maddox greeting customers at his restaurant can be found in the Civil Rights Digital Library. I also viewed footage from WSB-TV 2 in Atlanta, titled "Ga. Gov. Lester Maddox at His Segregated Cafeteria, 1965." Maddox's courtroom testimony on February 1, 1965, included details about the patriotic memorabilia he sold and about the "fight that I'm waging" for liberty. I obtained the transcript at the National Archives at Atlanta in 2019.

A *New York Times* profile, "Meet Lester Maddox of Georgia: 'Mr. White Backlash,'" was published November 6, 1966, and described Maddox as resembling "the man behind the prescription counter." Reese Cleghorn's profile cites one of the "Pickrick Says" ads I cite, beginning "A GREAT TRAGEDY of our time." Cleghorn also cites the Maddox leaflets I describe, one involving "One drop of Negro blood" and the other a cartoon of grandparents aghast to see interracial grandchildren. I obtained other "Pickrick Says" ads from court filings, including one from July 4, 1964, in which I measured the length and width of the advertisements, and another—while Maddox operated the Lester Maddox Cafeteria—that begins "AND IT IS A SAD DAY." Bob Short's *Everything Is Pickrick* includes a quotation on page 40 that "most people would get the Saturday paper."

Speaking Out, page 54, includes the Maddox quotation that begins "I am a segregationist." Pages 44–45 include quotations criticizing Atlanta newspapers.

The quotation from an Alabama Pickrick patron describing how he felt at ease eating with other White patrons comes from a courtroom deposition I obtained in the ministers' suit, given November 12, 1964. Multiple sources, including the book *White Flight*, detailed Maddox's role creating two groups, GUTS and PASS.

A *New York Times* analysis that Donald Trump was a millionaire by age eight is at https://www.nytimes.com/interactive/2018/10/02/us/politics /trump-family-wealth.html. A *Washington Post* column likening Trump to Maddox is at https://www.washingtonpost.com/opinions/2019/07/18

/trump-chooses-open-racism-what-does-his-party-choose/. I interviewed
Kay Willis, the widow of plaintiff George Willis, on August 29, 2019, about
her views that a Trump presidency had opened old racial wounds. Information about the "Unite the Right" rally in Charlottesville comes from sources,
including a Department of Justice court filing, found at https://www
.justice.gov/opa/press-release/file/1075091/download, and news reports,
including CNN, at https://www.cnn.com/2019/06/28/us/charlottesville
-car-attacker-sentencing/index.html. Politico produced a transcript of
Trump's post-rally comments, at https://www.politico.com/story/2017/08/15
/full-text-trump-comments-white-supremacists-alt-left-transcript-241662.

Maddox's depiction of his opponents as "the enemies of freedom"
appears in his book on page 172, and the picket sign I cite comes from
a photograph just after page 40. The photo of the Maddox and Wallace
couples appears after page 112. The WALLACE FOR PRESIDENT banner
plane is noted on page 168 in Bob Short's Maddox biography, *Everything
Is Pickrick*, and an *Atlanta Daily World* UPI article from May 30, 1964,
is the source for the Maddox quotation that the state governor "slapped
the faces" of patriotic Georgians by opposing Wallace's visit.

Speaking Out, page 34, includes Maddox quotations deriding the
Atlanta newspapers and the anecdote describing how he visited the
newspaper to see how many Black employees were on staff. I interviewed Lester Maddox Jr. outside his Georgia home on August 20, 2020.

Everything Is Pickrick is the source for the description of Maddox's
"childlike honesty" in the preface's page x, and the detail about the
governor singing gospel hymns with prisoners comes from page 109.
The preface includes the quotation from author Bob Short describing
Maddox as "the most honest politician I have ever known" on page
xiii. The same page notes that the Pickrick demonstrations would be
"an albatross" around Maddox. Short's book, on page 47, notes Ivan
Allen's margin of victory over Maddox in the 1961 mayoral race and
cites the accord between Black leaders and the Chamber of Commerce
on page 53. I interviewed Bob Short on May 20, 2020, and again on
November 10, 2020.

The Maddox quotation that he beat "everybody but Martin Luther
King" came from the *New York Times* 1966 profile. The detail that
Maddox lost the Black vote to Allen 31,000 to 125 is cited on page 33 of

The Legend of the Black Mecca. The similarly striking detail that William Hartsfield won 98 percent of the Black vote in the 1957 mayoral election appears on page 30 of *Race and the Shaping of Twentieth-Century Atlanta*; page 37 includes the quotation that, had Black citizens not voted, Maddox would have won the 1961 race.

Maddox's comments about chasing off Ivan Allen or Ralph McGill from his restaurant came in courtroom testimony he gave on February 1, 1965.

3: King's Lessons, and Bloodshed in the South

This chapter is built in part from two major sources: Martin Luther King's "I Have a Dream" speech in Washington August 28, 1963, and Department of Justice and other files describing the series of killings and assaults throughout the South. I interviewed Woodrow Lewis on December 10, 2020, and Albert Sampson on December 11, 2020, about these events.

The John F. Kennedy Presidential Library includes a summary of the March on Washington for Jobs and Freedom, at https://www.jfklibrary .org/learn/about-jfk/jfk-in-history/civil-rights-movement. A video of Joan Baez singing "We Shall Overcome" can be seen at https://www.youtube.com /watch?v=7akuOFp-ET8. Text of John Lewis's Washington march speech is at https://voicesofdemocracy.umd.edu/lewis-speech-at-the-march-on -washington-speech-text/. The Reverend King's speech can be found at https://www.youtube.com/watch?v=smEqnnklfYs. A transcript of his talk is at the Stanford University King Institute, at https://kinginstitute .stanford.edu/king-papers/documents/i-have-dream-address-delivered -march-washington-jobs-and-freedom.

Details on the killing of the four girls in Birmingham on September 15, 1963, are described in an FBI account, "Baptist Street Church Bombing," found at https://www.fbi.gov/history/famous-cases/baptist-street -church-bombing, and a History.com summary, at https://www.history.com /this-day-in-history/four-black-schoolgirls-killed-in-birmingham. Other sources are a *New York Times* article, at https://www.nytimes.com/2002/05/23 /us/38-years-later-last-of-suspects-is-convicted-in-church-bombing.html, and a CBS News report, at https://www.cbsnews.com/video/mlks-1963-eulogy -after-the-birmingham-church-bombing/.

Information about the killing of Mississippi's Louis Allen is detailed in a lengthy Department of Justice report, found at https://www.justice.gov/crt /case-document/herbert-lee, and in a case study compiled by the Student Nonviolent Coordinating Committee, found at https://snccdigital.org /events/louis-allen-murdered/.

The murder of Johnnie Mae Chappell in Florida is described in a lengthy DOJ report, found at https://www.justice.gov/crt/case-document /johnnie-m-chappell-notice-close-file. In addition, I read a *First Coast News* report that aired fifty-five years after her death, at https:// www.firstcoastnews.com/article/news/i-cant-forget-it-said-shelton -chappell-about-the-murder-of-his-mother/77-964eb889-a1dd-4dbc -a161-a4459a663b8d.

Details about the racial killings in Mississippi come from Justice Department filings, news accounts, and Jerry Mitchell's book *Race Against Time*. The murders of Henry Dee and Charles Moore are detailed in a DOJ cold-case overview, found at https://www.justice.gov/hatecrimes /spotlight/civil-rights-era-cold-cases. Details on the killings of James Chaney, Andrew Goodman, and Michael Schwerner come from a comprehensive Justice Department report, at https://www.justice.gov/crt/case -document/micheal-schwerner-james-chaney-andrew-goodman, and *Murder in Mississippi* from PBS, at https://www.pbs.org/wgbh/americanexperience /features/freedomsummer-murder/.

NPR produced an account of the Saint Augustine, Florida, motel proprietor who splashed acid in the swimming pool, found at https://www .npr.org/2014/06/13/321380585/remembering-a-civil-rights-swim-in-it -was-a-milestone. Stanford's King Research and Education Institute has a page devoted to the Saint Augustine movement, found at https:// kinginstitute.stanford.edu/encyclopedia/st-augustine-florida. *Pillar of Fire* devoted multiple sections to King's quest to integrate the Florida city.

4: A Revolt Hatched in a Seminary

This chapter is constructed largely through interviews with the ministers who tried to integrate the Pickrick and Heart of Atlanta.

Other sources include an FBI report on the killing of Medgar Evers by the White supremacist Byron De La Beckwith, at https://www.fbi

.gov/history/famous-cases/medgar-evers, and a *New York Times* story from January 23, 2001, upon Beckwith's death, found at https:// www.nytimes.com/2001/01/23/us/byron-de-la-beckwith-dies-killer -of-medgar-evers-was-80.html. Part II of Jerry Mitchell's book *Race Against Time* describes how the Mississippi journalist investigated Evers's death decades later. An Associated Press story detailed Beckwith's 1994 conviction, at https://apnews.com/c18776f9f3cd1b 5b312627ec5542dd84.

I interviewed the Reverend Woodrow T. Lewis several times to discuss the students' protest plans, including on July 19, 2019, in South Carolina, and over the telephone on July 30, 2019, and March 17, 29, and May 23, 2020.

I interviewed the Reverend Albert Sampson in Chicago on July 5, 2019, and over the phone on May 24, June 30, and July 19, 2020, two days after the death of C. T. Vivian. The *Washington Post* obituary of Vivian can be found at https://www.washingtonpost.com/local/obituaries /ct-vivian-king-aide-bloodied-on-the-front-lines-of-civil-rights-protest -dies-at-95/2020/07/17/a08e640c-c838-11ea-b037-f9711f89ee46_story .html. Emory University cited Vivian's Project Vision, at https://news .emory.edu/stories/2013/11/upress_rev_vivian_to_speak/campus.html. Another Sampson interview, about his battle with an Alabama sheriff, came September 5, 2020.

I interviewed Jesse Jackson on May 19, 2020, about his experience with Sampson starting while both were college students. An *Everett Herald Leader* profile of Sampson's youth can be found at https:// everettleader.com/2020/02/12/rev-dr-albert-r-sampson/. I interviewed Kay Willis in Texas on March 9, 2020, and on the phone on May 24, 2020.

The Interdenominational Theological Center website includes details of the school's founding and history: https://www.itc.edu/. An *Atlanta Journal-Constitution* anniversary story on August 7, 1994, is the source of the Reverend Albert Dunn quotation about "Daddy King" and Lester Maddox.

5: Filibuster, Politicking, and the Vote That Saved JFK's Plan

This chapter exploring the bumpy political journey to the passage of the Civil Rights Act of 1964 is built from sources including congressional reports, historical documents, and deep-dive books.

Audio of President Johnson's address to the nation five days after the assassination of President Kennedy, when LBJ pledged to uphold the civil rights measure, can be found at History.com, at https://www.history.com /speeches/lyndon-johnsons-address-to-congress-after-kennedy-assassination.

Author Robert A. Caro's account of Johnson's ruling of the Senate and his rise to the presidency featured scores of telling details. *The Passage of Power*, his exploration of Johnson's ascension to the Oval Office, includes the quotation "What the hell's the presidency for?" in the introduction on page xv. Page 564 cites the quotation from Johnson that Hubert Humphrey "drink with Dirksen!" Page 3 of *The Passage of Power* tells how Johnson worked on a road gang in Texas, and page 257 mentions how he taught in a "Mexican school" in a Texas town.

Caro's *Master of the Senate* describes Johnson's civil rights about-face. Page 714 details how LBJ used the word "boy" when talking with Black men, and page 886 tells how Johnson could change his mind "with absolute conviction." The introduction's page xxiii documents Johnson's "abrupt and total reversal" on civil rights, describing how he muscled through legislation in 1957, and page xv tells how Johnson for two decades opposed civil rights reform. Page 1002 describes the practical impact of the 1957 legislation, and page xi tells how hundreds of voting rights bills had been killed in Congress before then. A US House of Representatives summary of the Civil Rights Act of 1957 is at https://history.house.gov/Historical-Highlights/1951-2000/The-Civil -Rights-Act-of-1957/.

Taylor Branch's *Pillar of Fire*, page 180, includes the Johnson quotation telling Republicans they were "either the party of Lincoln or you ain't." A photograph after page 208 shows LBJ standing nose to nose with Georgia's Richard Russell and includes the quotation that Johnson would "run you down."

I reviewed notes of meetings involving the NAACP, President Johnson, and members of Congress as the Civil Rights Act of 1964 proceeded toward passage. They include reports written on January 21, March 5, March 16, and April 3, 1964.

I also reviewed multiple congressional reports during the bill's travails through the House and Senate, including Everett Dirksen's speech on June 10, 1964, urging his colleagues to approve. The text of the speech can be found at https://www.senate.gov/artandhistory/history/resources /pdf/DirksenCivilRights.pdf. Other sources include a post at the *Facetoface* Smithsonian blog, "Everett Dirksen: Forgotten Civil Rights Champion," at https://npg.si.edu/blog/everett-dirksen-forgotten-civil-rights-champion. For a vivid image of Dirksen in action, the chapter cites Todd Purdum's description from page 211 of *An Idea Whose Time Has Come.*

A US Senate report detailed how the filibuster was busted, found at https://www.senate.gov/about/powers-procedures/filibusters-cloture /civil-rights-filibuster-ended.htm#:~:text=At%209%3A51%20on%20 the,working%20days%2C%20including%20seven%20Saturdays. Details on Clair Engle's vote from his wheelchair come from that Senate report and another, at https://www.senate.gov/senators/FeaturedBios/Featured_Bio _EngleClair.htm.

A *Constitution Daily* blog post discussed key members seeking to kill the bill, found at https://constitutioncenter.org/blog/the-filibuster-that -almost-killed-the-civil-rights-act/. News reports profiling key filibusters, including a *New York Times* obituary of Strom Thurmond, are at https:// www.nytimes.com/2003/06/27/us/strom-thurmond-foe-of-integration -dies-at-100.html; the same 2003 obituary said Georgia's Richard Russell Jr. once likened the FBI's investigation of civil rights cases to Hitler's use of the Gestapo. An obituary on Arkansas's J. William Fulbright appeared in the *New York Times*, at https://www.nytimes.com/1995/02/10 /obituaries/j-william-fulbright-senate-giant-is-dead-at-89.html, and one appeared on North Carolina's Sam Ervin in the *Los Angeles Times*, at https:// www.latimes.com/archives/la-xpm-1985-04-24-mn-7139-story.html. For details on West Virginia's Robert Byrd, see "6 Choice Moments from Sen. Robert Byrd's 56 Years," from the *Atlantic*, at https://www.theatlantic .com/politics/archive/2009/11/6-choice-moments-from-sen-robert-byrd -s-56-years/347529/.

From the Library of Congress, I obtained Supreme Court correspondence that included the *Alabama Farmer* column. The Library of Congress posted a video of the CBS debate between Thurmond and Humphrey, found at https://www.loc.gov/exhibits/civil-rights-act/multimedia /hubert-humphrey-and-strom-thurmond.html. And the Library of Congress produced a summary of the bill's passage, at https://www.loc.gov/exhibits/civil -rights-act/civil-rights-act-of-1964.html.

The Universal Newsreel of LBJ's Civil Rights Act signing ceremony on July 2, 1964, can be viewed at https://www.youtube.com /watch?v=ZaRUca7FyAc. I interviewed Albert Sampson about the bill's signing on September 5, 2020.

Details describing the Georgia killing of Lieutenant Colonel Lemuel Penn come from sources including a Department of Justice annual report for 1966, at https://www.justice.gov/sites/default/files/ag /legacy/2011/08/23/01-10-1967.pdf. *New York Times* reports describing the suspects are at https://www.nytimes.com/1964/08/07/archives/suspects-in -penn-killing-identified-by-bureau-as-ku-klux-klansmen.html, and the confession of another man, at https://www.nytimes.com/1964/09/03/archives /confession-read-in-penns-slaying-klansman-describes-events-before. html. An examination of Penn's death is in the New Georgia Encyclopedia, at https://www.georgiaencyclopedia.org/articles/history-archaeology /lemuel-penn-murder.

Information on the Rochester race riot of 1964 comes from the *Democrat and Chronicle* newspaper, at https://www.democratandchronicle.com /story/news/2014/07/19/roberta-abbott-buckle-rochester-riots/12855941/ and the Harlem rioting from Britannica, at https://www.britannica.com/event /Harlem-race-riot-of-1964.

A United Press International story published July 7, 1964, in the *Chicago Defender* described the racial fracas at a swim-in in Atlanta, Texas, and a *New York Times* story published the same day detailed events in Jackson, Mississippi, where the Robert E. Lee Hotel shut its doors. The *Times* story can be read at https://www.nytimes.com/1964/07/07 /jackson-hotel-closes.html.

Lester Maddox's criticism describing how Lyndon Johnson "deserted" the cause comes from Maddox testimony in the civil suit against him, given February 1, 1965. A "Pickrick Says" ad placed July 4, 1964, also obtained in my research, features Maddox railing against "race mixing" in the city.

6: *Heart of Atlanta v. USA*:
The First Legal Challenge Arrives

This chapter more fully introduces Moreton Rolleston Jr., the motel proprietor who filed suit against the Civil Rights Act of 1964 on the evening Lyndon Johnson signed the bill into law. One key resource is a video interview the Atlanta History Center conducted with Rolleston as part of its Veterans History Project, found at https://www.youtube.com /watch?v=0yn5jiYWuBU. The eighty-four-minute interview produced several quotations that help open the chapter. I reviewed historical ads and photos of Rolleston in front of the Heart of Atlanta from news archives. And the Atlanta History Center archives detailed construction and expansion of the motel, the first of its kind downtown.

Kevin Kruse's *White Flight*, chapter 6, cites Rolleston's work pushing for segregated schools in 1959. Chapter 8 cites a letter Rolleston wrote to patrons saying he would not accept Black lodgers during an NAACP 1962 convention, and how he filed his civil rights act lawsuit by driving to the clerk's house.

I interviewed Moreton Rolleston III in Georgia on August 20, 2020. Other sources about his father include *Atlanta Daily World* stories on January 12 and 29, 1964, describing how he rejected integrators, including future Georgia congressman John Lewis, while armed with a tear gas pistol. Rolleston's comment about the "eventual dictatorship" he envisioned coming from Washington comes in news interviews after he lost his lawsuit, kept by the Civil Rights Digital Library.

Rolleston's lawsuit against the United States provides further information. The court filing of *Heart of Atlanta Motel v. USA and Robert F. Kennedy* is at the National Archives at Atlanta. The file includes the government's rebuttal to Rolleston's allegations. The *New York Times* noted how Rolleston brought his lawsuit two hours and ten minutes after Lyndon Johnson signed the law, at https://www.nytimes.com/1964/07/07 /atlanta-motel-sues-in-major-test-of-rights-act.html.

This chapter describes how Albert Sampson and Charles Wells were rebuffed when they tried to rent rooms at the Heart of Atlanta. When the case went to a crucial court hearing later in July 1964, Sampson and Wells were the sole government witnesses. Transcripts of their courtroom testimony, on July 17, 1964, are from the archives in Atlanta. This chapter includes profile material on the two reverends, built from interviews and other sources.

I interviewed Sampson in Chicago on July 5, 2019, and over the phone on March 23 and May 24, 2020. Sampson sent to me three editions of the *Atlanta Inquirer*, where he was associate editor. The July 11, 1964, issue included his column "NAACP Battlefront." Information on a politician Sampson supported, John Winters, is from the North Carolina History Project, at https://northcarolinahistory.org/encyclopedia/john-w-winters-sr-1920-2004/. Profile information on Charles Wells was gleaned in part from an interview with Sampson on May 24, 2020, and largely from a book his wife Barbara wrote about him, *The Minister Who Wore Many Hats*. The book included news clippings of his integration battles in Georgia.

7: Pickrick Showdown: Axe Handles, Guns, and Fists

This chapter, describing the ministers' first attempt to integrate the Pickrick one day after the civil rights law took effect, is built from interviews with key participants, court filings, books, news accounts, and other information.

I interviewed the Reverend Woodrow Lewis on several occasions about the integration efforts, including in South Carolina on July 19, 2019, and over the phone on March 17, 29, and May 27, 2020. I interviewed the Reverend Albert Sampson about the impact of lawyer Constance Baker Motley on the case on March 23, 2020, and interviewed Kay Willis, widow of lead plaintiff George Willis, in Texas on March 9, 2020.

The ministry students' lawsuit, *Willis, Lewis and Dunn v. Pickrick and Maddox*, is the source of much of the material about their court case. George Willis's seminary school essay, in which he recounted that evening's altercation, came from the archives of the ITC.

Kevin Kruse's *White Flight*, chapter 8, describes the Lester Maddox July 4 rally in which the segregationist uttered, "Never! Never! Never!" Another source is a WSB-TV 2 Atlanta report, "A Look Back: WSB-TV and the Civil Rights Movement," at https://www.wsbtv.com/news/local/a-look-back-wsb-tv-and-the-civil-rights-movement/840686900/.

Department of Justice memos to the FBI about the Pickrick are from the Atlanta History Center, which I obtained during a research visit on August 19, 2020. Books by Maddox and his biographer, and the autobiography of Constance Baker Motley, also provide information. Maddox explains the purchase of his first gun on pages 53–54 of *Speaking Out* and details his reaction to the violence at Leb's Restaurant on page 52. *Everything Is Pickrick* recounts earlier integration attempts at the restaurant on pages 54 and 56. The quotation "he was hailed by segregationists" comes from the book's page 58.

Motley's *Equal Justice Under Law* autobiography is the source for some of the profile information about her, with material drawn from pages 24, 26, 41, 47, 48, 55, 56, and 59. Details of her work with James Meredith come from the chapter "James Meredith and the University of Mississippi." In addition, photos in her book helped me describe her place in the legal world. NPR produced an informative story about Meredith, "Integrating Ole Miss: A Transformative, Deadly Riot," at https://www.npr.org/2012/10/01/161573289/integrating-ole-miss-a-transformative-deadly-riot. I interviewed Meredith on July 26, 2020.

Other information about Motley comes from a National Women's Hall of Fame profile, at https://www.womenofthehall.org/inductee/constance-baker-motley/. I viewed video of Motley addressing the press after filing the Maddox lawsuit from the Civil Rights Digital Library and read a 2005 *New York Times* obituary, at https://www.nytimes.com/2005/09/29/nyregion/constance-baker-motley-civil-rights-trailblazer-dies-at-84.html. The NAACP Legal Defense and Educational Fund detailed Motley's role at the University of Alabama, at https://www.naacpldf.org/press/fifty-years-ago-the-stand-in-the-schoolhouse-door/, and a US Courts profile cited her work in other cases, including integration of the University of Georgia, at https://www.uscourts.gov/news/2020/02/20/constance-baker-motley-judiciarys-unsung-rights-hero. I interviewed Motley's former legal colleague,

Michael Meltsner, on July 5, 2020. His book *With Passion: An Activist Lawyer's Life* includes the anecdote about Motley challenging a school official in South Carolina, in a chapter called "Charleston and Beyond."

A 2003 *Atlanta Journal-Constitution* obituary of plaintiffs' lawyer William Alexander, https://www.legacy.com/amp/obituaries/atlanta/1337099, provided other profile information.

Contemporaneous news accounts aided my research. The photo of Maddox leading Albert Dunn away from the Pickrick by pistol appeared on page 10 of the *Atlanta Journal* and *Constitution* on July 4, 1964, and was included as "Exhibit A" in the students' lawsuit. A July 1964 *New York Times* story included the "I'll use axe handles" quotation and can be found at https://www.nytimes.com/1964/07/18/archives/2-rights-act-suits-argued-in-court-in-atlanta-us-judges-heat-first.html. An *Atlanta Times* story on July 11, 1964, reported on Maddox's press conference in which he vowed to go to jail rather than comply with the new civil rights law. The *Atlanta Inquirer* of July 11, 1964, included an editorial about Maddox's court appearance on his gun charge; Atlanta news accounts reported on the hearing.

Details about the protests at Leb's were gleaned from sources including a thorough Georgia Tech digital collection account, found at https://ivanallen.iac.gatech.edu/artifacts/items/show/372. Another source is *Atlanta Rising: The Invention of an International City 1946–1996*; a snapshot of the weekend disruption appears in pages 131–35. Details about the Leb's protests led by White students come from an Associated Press story, at https://www.nytimes.com/1964/02/03/archives/atlanta-whites-ask-end-of-segregation.html.

8: The Courtroom Showdowns

This chapter is constructed in large part from the court transcript of the July 17, 1964, hearing in which three federal judges heard evidence in both legal cases—the *Heart of Atlanta* case against the government, and the ministry students' case against Lester Maddox.

News accounts and books provided other information. A 1985 UPI obituary of Judge Frank Arthur Hooper Jr. included profile details. *White Flight* includes the detail in its chapter 8 that

Maddox drove to court with an American flag attached to his car's antenna. An *Atlanta Daily World* story from July 18, 1964, described the courtroom scene, headlined FEDERAL COURTS HEAR ATLANTA MOTEL, RESTAURANT CASES IN FIRST TESTS OF CIVIL RIGHTS ACT. A 2003 *New York Times* obituary profiled Justice Department civil rights lawyer Burke Marshall, found at https:// www.nytimes.com/2003/06/03/us/burke-marshall-a-key-strategist-of -civil-rights-policy-dies-at-80.html.

Steve Luxenberg's book *Separate: The Story of Plessy v. Ferguson, and America's Journey from Slavery to Segregation* on page 348 details the death of the Civil Rights Act of 1875 through the US Supreme Court ruling of 1883. Further information about the Civil Rights Act of 1875 was gleaned from Britannica, at https://www.britannica.com/topic /Civil-Rights-Act-United-States-1875 and https://www.britannica.com/topic /Civil-Rights-Cases.

A "Pickrick Says" ad from July 1964 included Maddox's view of the federal government scrutiny of his operations.

9: Two Major Rulings, and a Backlash Against the Supreme Court

Copies of the federal court's July 22 and July 23 rulings were obtained from archives in Atlanta. An *Atlanta Constitution* story published July 23, 1964, "Federal Court Orders Maddox and Motel to Serve Negroes," chronicled the initial ruling. Other court filings include the Supreme Court's refusal to stay the federal court's ruling against Rolleston and Maddox.

Correspondence sent to Justice Hugo Black, including letters from citizens enraged by his ruling denying the stay requests of the Pickrick and Heart of Atlanta, are from the Library of Congress. Black's handcrafted ruling was among the Library of Congress files. Video footage of Maddox discussing Black's ruling is from the Civil Rights Digital Library, found at http://crdl.usg.edu/cgi/crdl?format=_video&query=id%3Augabma _wsbn_wsbn31716&_cc=1&Welcome. Maddox's autobiography on page 62 notes his support from well-wishers and his use of a manikin to express his views.

10: The Ministers and Pickrick: Back for Seconds, Thirds

This chapter detailing the ministry students' second and third attempts to enter through the front door of the Pickrick is based upon interviews with the two surviving ministers, court records, and news accounts describing the integration attempts on August 11 and September 28, 1964.

I interviewed Albert Sampson, who joined the August 11 attempt, in Chicago on July 5, 2019, and then again over the phone on May 4 and May 27, 2020. I interviewed Woodrow T. Lewis, who took part in the September attempt, in South Carolina on July 19, 2019, and also over the phone on July 30, 2019, and March 29, 2020. The court records in the ministers' suit against Maddox included affidavits filed by Sampson and Charles Wells on August 12, 1964. Wells, who took part in both attempts to eat at the restaurant, filed another affidavit September 28, and lead plaintiff George Willis filed one on September 29. The chapter includes testimony from the fifth integrating minister, Albert Dunn, given during a court hearing on February 1, 1965. Court documents included briefs filed by counsel for the government and the ministers.

Cook Ozell Rogers's comments come from an Associated Press story, "'Not Hurting My Race,' Pickrick Negro Asserts," published on August 12, 1964.

Descriptions of the two integration attempts come from newspapers, including stories in the *New York Times* describing both encounters, first on August 12, 1964, found at https://www.nytimes.com/1964/08/12/archives /atlanta-restaurant-defies-high-court-again-bars-negroes.html, and the second on September 29, found at https://www.nytimes.com/1964/09/29 /archives/negroes-barred-again-by-maddox-cafe-in-atlanta.html. Further details are from a UPI story published August 12, 1964, and an *Atlanta Journal* account from August 11, 1964, "Angry Whites Repulse Negroes Trying to Integrate Pickrick." A UPI photo published in the *Chicago Defender* on August 15, 1964, showed Maddox wiping tears as he closed his restaurant and weeping for the "southern way of life." The *Atlanta Journal* covered the second fracas in a story published September 28, 1964, and headlined MADDOX BARS FOUR NEGROES.

An *Atlanta Journal* story published August 26, 1964, "Maddox Gets a Heckling at Atlantic City," described his protest at the Democratic National Convention. Lester Maddox's autobiography, page 62 is the source for the "Nikita Khrushchev!" quotation. Page 65 includes the quotation "Now get out of here!" and his description of more "agitators" trying to eat at his restaurant. I obtained the "Lester Maddox Says" ad from the Atlanta court archives.

11: "The People's Court" and the Heart of Atlanta Motel

This chapter is constructed in part from a review of signature Supreme Court rulings under Earl Warren and a book and news accounts about his career.

I gleaned profile information on Warren from a 1974 AP obituary published in the *Los Angeles Times*, at https://www.latimes.com /local/obituaries/archives/la-me-earl-warren-19740710-story.html, and *New York Times* coverage of his funeral, at https://www.nytimes .com/1974/07/13/archives/earl-warren-is-buried-in-army-rites-at -arlington-references-to.html. Biographies of Warren are from Britannica.com, at https://www.britannica.com/biography/Earl-Warren and at the Oyez website, at https://www.oyez.org/justices/earl_warren.

Information about Warren's life comes from *Chief Justice: A Biography of Earl Warren* by Ed Cray. Page 22 includes the Warren quotation assessing the hardships he viewed while working at the Southern Pacific railroad company. Page 452 cites the Virginia judge's language in the *Loving* case, when the judge said God "did not intend for the races to mix." Page 459 includes Warren's comment that the *Miranda* case "will be one of the most important opinions of our time." Page 460 cites the law enforcement reaction to the *Miranda* ruling.

This chapter includes information about five seminal Supreme Court rulings under the Warren court beyond *Heart of Atlanta: Mapp v. Ohio, Engel v. Vitale, Gideon v. Wainwright, Miranda v. Arizona,* and *Loving v. Virginia.* The court's opinions in each case are at the following:

Mapp: https://www.law.cornell.edu/supremecourt/text/367/643

Engel: https://supreme.justia.com/cases/federal/us/370/421/

Gideon: https://www.law.cornell.edu/supremecourt/text/372/335

Miranda: https://supreme.justia.com/cases/federal/us/384/436/

Loving: https://www.law.cornell.edu/supremecourt/text/388/1%26amp

I reviewed the entire federal court archive of the *Heart of Atlanta* case at the National Archives at Atlanta, including briefs filed by Rolleston and rebuttals by the US government.

12: Arguments Before the High Court

This chapter is built largely from oral arguments in the *Heart of Atlanta v. USA* Supreme Court case. The full oral arguments before the high court on October 5, 1964, can be heard at https://www.oyez.org/cases/1964/515.

This chapter also profiles Justice Hugo Black, including reference to his earlier ties to the KKK. Sources on Black include a 1971 *New York Times* obituary, at https://www.nytimes.com/1971/09/25/archives/justice -black-dies-at-85-served-on-court-34-years-civil-liberties-a.html; a 2017 *Smithsonian* magazine story, "This Supreme Court Justice Was a KKK Member," at https://www.smithsonianmag.com/smart-news/supreme-court -justice-was-kkk-member-180962254/; a Britannica.com profile, at https://www.britannica.com/biography/Hugo-L-Black; and an NPR *All Things Considered* report: https://www.npr.org/2005/09/11/4828849/a -life-of-justice-hugo-black-of-alabama. Another source on Black is *Chief Justice*. Page 263 cites Black's former KKK membership and notes the justice's competitive streak outside the judicial chambers and his propensity to carry the US Constitution in his pocket.

Profile information on US solicitor general Archibald Cox comes from, among other sources, a *Washington Post* recap of its Watergate coverage: https://www.washingtonpost.com/wp-srv/politics/special/watergate /cox.html.

13: Judgment Day: The US Supreme Court Rules

This chapter is built largely from the US Supreme Court's ruling on December 14, 1964, dismissing Moreton Rolleston's case and affirming Title II of the Civil Rights Act of 1964. The court's ruling is part of the *Heart of Atlanta v. USA* archive. The *New York Times* published the ruling in full, at https://www.nytimes.com/1964/12/15/archives/text-of-high-court -ruling-upholding-public-accommodations-title-of.html.

The justices also ruled against an Alabama barbecue eatery, Ollie's, that sued the government. A synopsis of *Katzenbach v. McClung* is at https://www.law.cornell.edu/supremecourt/text/379/294, and a story about Ollie's is found at https://www.al.com/living/2014/12/50_years_ago_the _supreme_court.html.

Other sources include interviews I conducted with law professors Rachel Moran on February 4, 2020, and December 14, 2020, and Michael Meltsner on July 5, 2020. I read a 2001 book studying the court's two rulings, *Civil Rights and Public Accommodations*, by professor Richard C. Cortner.

I visited the National Museum of African American History and Culture in January 2020, where I looked for, but did not find, any mention of the *Heart of Atlanta* case. That July, museum staff provided me a listing of all the Supreme Court cases it has showcased; *Heart of Atlanta v. USA* was not among them.

The various top Supreme Court listings can be read at https:// www.americanbar.org/groups/public_education/programs/constitution _day/landmark-6cases/, https://www.usatoday.com/story/news/politics /2015/06/26/supreme-court-cases-history/29185891/, https://www.uscourts .gov/about-federal-courts/educational-resources/supreme-court-landmarks, https://www.cnn.com/2013/06/21/us/top-u-s-supreme-court-decisions -fast-facts/index.html, and https://time.com/4055934/best-supreme-court -decisions/.

Contemporaneous reaction to the high court's opinion is cited in the *Chicago Defender* published on December 15 and 17, 1964, including a column by editor John H. Sengstacke.

I interviewed Reverend Albert Sampson on March 23, 2020, to hear his perspective of the ruling, and interviewed Jesse Jackson May 19, 2020.

Information on the Bloody Sunday march in Selma comes from sources including federal judge Frank Johnson's March 17, 1965, court ruling, obtained from the Library of Congress. A National Archives summary of the 1965 Voting Rights Act is at https://www.archives.gov/legislative /features/voting-rights-1965. Taylor Branch's *At Canaan's Edge* includes a recounting of the Selma march in, among other places, chapter 5, "Over the Bridge."

Information on the Watts riots in Los Angeles was gleaned from sources including Stanford's Martin Luther King, Jr. Research and Education Institute at https://kinginstitute.stanford.edu/encyclopedia /watts-rebellion-los-angeles, and the BlackPast website at https://www .blackpast.org/african-american-history/watts-rebellion-august-1965/. *At Canaan's Edge* includes accounts of the Watts rebellion and its impact on Lyndon Johnson and subsequent federal policy, including in the book's chapters 20 and 21.

Moreton Rolleston's reaction was captured by news reporters just after the ruling and archived at the Civil Rights Digital Library. I interviewed his son, Moreton Rolleston III, on August 20, 2020. Lester Maddox expressed his view of the Warren court in his book's page 61. Warren's attaboy to Justice Clark, "Bueno," comes from *Chief Justice*, page 442.

14: More Shoves, Venom, and Axe Handles

This chapter is constructed largely from viewing a soundless video capturing Lester Maddox shoving the ministry students who showed up at his diner on January 29, 1965. The Civil Rights Digital Library video can be found at http://crdl.usg.edu/export/html/ugabma/wsbn/crdl_ugabma _wsbn_47697.html.

I interviewed the lone surviving minister from this attack, Reverend Woodrow T. Lewis, in South Carolina on July 19 and 20, 2019, and also Kay Willis, the widow of the lead plaintiff, on the phone on August 29, 2019, and in Texas on March 9, 2020. After I contacted them, Lewis and Willis viewed the footage for the first time. I also reviewed an *Atlanta Journal* story published January 30, 1965, "Maddox Bars Negroes with 'Body Force.'"

15: Closing Time at the Pickrick and Lester Maddox Cafeteria

The heart of this chapter describes a court hearing February 1, 1965, to adjudge whether Lester Maddox was once again in contempt of court for refusing to serve Black patrons. This transcript, which runs some 360 pages long, was obtained from the National Archives at Atlanta, and it includes testimony from Maddox, the ministry students, and other witnesses. The transcript includes the cross-examinations from lawyers for both sides, plus federal judge Hooper's probing questioning of Maddox's actions. The chapter also cites Hooper's ruling four days later holding Maddox in contempt.

I interviewed Lester Maddox Jr. in Georgia on August 20, 2020.

I reviewed news archives detailing Maddox's restaurant closing. "Maddox to Comply with U.S. Court Order" was published in the *Atlanta Journal-Constitution* on February 7, 1965, and "Maddox Changes His Mind, Puts Cafeteria Up for Sale," in the *Atlanta Journal* on February 8, 1965. "Ex-Employees Lease Maddox's Cafeteria" was published in the *Atlanta Journal* on February 18, 1965.

The PUT TO DEATH sign Maddox fashioned appeared after page 40 in his autobiography, and page 67 includes his view that it was a "sad and tragic moment" when he closed his business. Video footage from the Civil Rights Digital Library showing Maddox giving a press conference after the restaurant closing can be seen at http://crdl.usg.edu/cgi /crdl?format=_video;query=id:ugabma_wsbn_wsbn42636.

Court files I reviewed from the Pickrick case include the high court's refusal to hear Maddox's contempt appeal. The chapter includes an interview with Woodrow Lewis on March 29, 2020.

Bob Short's Maddox biography describes the court hearing over the pending gun charge on page 65; I also read a UPI story published in the *Chicago Defender* on April 14, 1965, that provided further hearing details, headlined GA. NEGRO TO JURY: HE POINTED PISTOL AT ME. A *New York Times* obituary of Judge Dan Duke is published at https://www .nytimes.com/1999/04/01/us/lawrence-d-duke-sr-86-fought-the-klan -in-georgia.html. *Everything Is Pickrick* notes, on page 68, how Maddox announced his bid for governor in September 1965. His friend's encouragement that "this thing will make you governor" appears on his autobiography's page 69.

16: A New Governor in Georgia

The chapter describing Maddox's surprising rise to become governor is built from sources including Georgia election result records, interviews, newspaper stories, and books by Maddox, his biographer, and veteran Atlanta writers.

Maddox's 1966 campaign diary is among the holdings I reviewed at the Atlanta History Center on August 19, 2020. I viewed Maddox's campaign platform brochures and gubernatorial correspondence, as well as the boxes of cards sent to him while in the hospital, during the same trip.

Bob Short's *Everything Is Pickrick* includes revealing details about Maddox's gubernatorial campaign, the path that took him to office, and his actions as governor. Details were gleaned from the preface's pages x and xi, along with pages 104, 108–9, 123–24, and 170. Maddox quotes George Wallace endorsing him on page 84 of *Speaking Out* and discusses his view of early release of state inmates on page 112.

A November 6, 1966, *New York Times* story, "Meet Lester Maddox of Georgia: 'Mr. White Backlash,'" includes the analysis describing how Maddox surprised both political parties and the detail that the Georgia KKK sent out an alert supporting his candidacy. A 2003 *New York Times* Maddox obituary included the details that God had been his campaign manager and that his election made Martin Luther King Jr. "ashamed" to be a Georgian, found at https://www.nytimes.com/2003/06/25/us /lester-maddox-whites-only-restaurateur-and-georgia-governor -dies-at-87.html. Other Maddox obituaries were published in the *Los Angeles Times*, at https://www.latimes.com/archives/la-xpm-2003-jun-26-me -maddox26-story.html, and the *Atlanta Journal-Constitution*, headlined Last Segregationist Governor Dies; Contradictory Character Defied Change, Labels, by Jim Tharpe. The Atlanta obituary cited Maddox's record hiring Black Georgians as governor, while noting that few were appointed to high-level slots.

I examined election result records to describe the razor-thin vote that catapulted Maddox to office even though his Republican opponent, Bo Callaway, garnered more votes. The results can be found at https://www.ourcampaigns.com/RaceDetail.html?RaceID=40398. *Beyond Atlanta: The Struggle for Racial Equality in Georgia, 1940–1980* reports that Maddox won 4 percent of the Black vote, on page 194, and that Black write-in votes may have hindered his opponent's ability to take office, on page 219. I learned about Callaway from the New Georgia Encyclopedia, at https://www.georgiaencyclopedia.org/articles/government-politics/howard-hollis-bo-callaway-1927-2014, and from the *New York Times* story about the election published November 6, 1966. A *Ledger-Enquirer* obituary of Callaway is at https://www.ledger-enquirer.com/news/local/article29324335.html.

An Emory University Cold Cases Project described the city's 1966 rioting, at https://coldcases.emory.edu/hulet-m-varner-jr/#:~:text=On%20September%206%2C%201966%2C%20hours,baseball%20team%20to%20the%20city.

King's 1967 sermon is archived at Stanford University's King Institute, found at https://kinginstitute.stanford.edu/king-papers/documents/three-dimensions-complete-life-sermon-delivered-new-covenant-baptist-church.

I interviewed Reverend Woodrow Lewis on July 30, 2019, and March 29, 2020, to gauge his reaction to Maddox's election. Albert Dunn's quotation on the same topic is from an *Atlanta Journal-Constitution* story published August 7, 1994. I interviewed Reverend Albert Sampson on May 4 and May 27, 2020, to hear his view of Maddox's rise to the governor's mansion. King Sr. profile material was found at Stanford University's King archive, at https://kinginstitute.stanford.edu/encyclopedia/king-martin-luther-sr.

I interviewed Bob Short about his views of Maddox on May 20 and November 10, 2020. An NAACP profile of civil rights leader and Georgia House member Julian Bond is at https://naacp.org/find-resources/history-explained/civil-rights-leaders/julian-bond.

The quotation describing Lester Maddox as "a decent and honest governor" comes from page 61 of *Praying for Sheetrock*, by Melissa Fay Greene.

News accounts helped describe some of Maddox's controversial actions as governor, including two *Atlanta Daily World* stories published January 10, 1968, detailing his proposed rioting bill, one headlined Gov. Maddox's State of State Speech Gets "Cool" Reaction. A February 26, 1970, story in the *Chicago Daily Defender* reported how

US Speaker John W. McCormack chided Maddox for passing out axe handles in the House of Representatives restaurant. The *AJC* recounted Maddox's bid to ban the sale of newspapers on state grounds: https://www.ajc.com/news/local/deja-news-georgia-governor-bans-ajc-from -state-office-grounds-1970/xOfOkzHXbBSyrVF6DHjmrL/.

Frederick Allen's *Atlanta Rising* recounts striking details about Maddox's stand during King's funeral. Page 160 notes that Maddox told troopers to "shoot them down and stack them up" if mourners tried to enter the capitol. Page 156 reported how Maddox told fellow White people to "flatten the tires" of integrating school buses and had the state lower the flag after a US Supreme Court ruling over civil rights. Page 149 cites Atlanta mayor Ivan Allen saying the state seal "lies tarnished" after Maddox won the Democratic gubernatorial runoff.

The *Atlanta Journal-Constitution* story "The Governor's Fortress" helped describe Maddox's actions on the day of King's funeral, found at https://www.ajc.com/news/local/lester-maddox-turned-the-capitol-into-fortress -during-mlk-funeral/EVWyS3G6oyFdujb3z84ptL/. Footage of King's funeral can be found at C-SPAN, at https://www.c-span.org/video/?443156-1 /martin-luther-king-jr-funeral-coverage-1968. Maddox's explanation for why he skipped King's funeral appears on his book's page 129.

Everything Is Pickrick, page 66, included the anecdote describing how Maddox refused to step back inside the site of his former restaurant as governor.

Epilogue: Legacy

For details on George Floyd's killing, I relied on video footage, news accounts, and interviews. I spoke with the Reverend Albert Sampson about Floyd on May 27, 2020. News accounts and photos I relied upon came from Reuters, at https://www.reuters.com/article/us-minneapolis-police -military/perils-for-pentagon-as-trump-threatens-to-militarize-response -to-civil-unrest-idUSKBN239324, at https://www.reuters.com/article /us-minneapolis-protest-police/black-lives-matter-protests-for-u-s-racial -justice-reach-new-dimension-idUSKBN23C1A7, and at https://www .reuters.com/news/picture/outrage-across-america-over-george-floyd -idUSRTS39ZYJ. The *New York Times* produced a harrowing video account of Floyd's killing, headlined How George Floyd Was Killed in Police Custody, at https://www.nytimes.com/2020/05/31/us /george-floyd-investigation.html. An NPR report, "Peaceful Protesters Tear-Gassed to Clear Way for Trump Church Photo-Op," is at https://www .npr.org/2020/06/01/867532070/trumps-unannounced-church-visit -angers-church-officials. Video of the tear gas in DC is from *The Telegraph*, at https://www.youtube.com/watch?v=AzBhYhu7NYI. Another source is a 2021 USA Today report, https://www.usatoday.com/story/news /politics/2021/06/09/lafayette-park-not-cleared-donald-trump-photo-opp -report-says/7622478002/. Sources on the reaction to Jacob Blake's shooting include ESPN, at https://www.espn.com/tennis/story/_/id/29749495/naomi -osaka-play-ws-semi-protest-jacob-blake-shooting-tourney-pauses-play.

The Fulton County, Georgia, 2020 presidential election results are at https://results.enr.clarityelections.com/GA/Fulton/105430/web.264614/# /summary. A *Washington Post* report on the militant groups wreaking havoc one month after Trump's loss is at https://www.washingtonpost.com/local /trump-dc-rally-maga/2020/12/11/8b5af818-3bdb-11eb-bc68-96af0daae728 _story.html. The *Post* expose of Trump's hour-long call pressing Georgia's secretary of state to "find" him votes is at https://www.washingtonpost .com/politics/trump-raffensperger-call-georgia-vote/2021/01/03/d45acb92 -4dc4-11eb-bda4-615aaefd0555_story.html, and a *New York Times* account of Trump's plot with a justice official is at https://www.nytimes.com/2021/01/22 /us/politics/jeffrey-clark-trump-justice-department-election.html?action =click&module=Top%20Stories&pgtype=Homepage. I watched the insurrection of Congress unfold live on CNN.

CNN's Van Jones's postelection comments are at https://www.cnn.com /videos/politics/2020/11/07/van-jones-reaction-2020-election-result -elexnight-vpx.cnn/video/playlists/presidential-election-2020/.

The Library of Congress summary of the Civil Rights Act of 1964 is at https://www.loc.gov/exhibits/civil-rights-act/epilogue.html.

Source material for the case figure updates includes the following:

Lester Maddox

Obituaries are in the *Los Angeles Times*, at https://www.latimes.com /archives/la-xpm-2003-jun-26-me-maddox26-story.html, and *New*

York Times, at https://www.nytimes.com/2003/06/25/us/lester-maddox
-whites-only-restaurateur-and-georgia-governor-dies-at-87.html. The family's four-thousand-word obituary is at https://www.legacy.com/obituaries
/atlanta/obituary.aspx?n=lester-g-maddox&pid=1115933&fhid=4905.
A 1977 *Washington Post* story, "Hard Times for Lester Maddox," is
at https://www.washingtonpost.com/archive/lifestyle/1977/06/23/hard
-times-for-lester-maddox/755191cb-f835-4c2f-b06a-8ebc591db5fb/.

Moreton Rolleston Jr.

The Georgia Supreme Court debarment order is at https://www.gabar.org
/publicdiscipline/pdf/S07Y0645Rolleston_D.pdf. The *Journal-Constitution*
chronicled the Rolleston–Tyler Perry dispute, as did the Forbes website: https://www.forbes.com/sites/amydobson/2020/06/24/the-full-circle
-moment-behind-the-record-breaking-sale-of-tyler-perrys-former
-mansion-now-owned-by-steve-harvey/#5b603c00787d. A court order
dismissing the case is at https://law.justia.com/cases/federal/appellate
-courts/ca11/06-13620/200613620-2011-02-28.html.

Constance Baker Motley

Sources include a *New York Times* obituary, at https://www.nytimes
.com/2005/09/29/nyregion/constance-baker-motley-civil-rights-trailblazer
-dies-at-84.html, National Women's Hall of Fame tribute, at https://www
.womenofthehall.org/inductee/constance-baker-motley/, and US Courts
profile: https://www.uscourts.gov/news/2020/02/20/constance-baker
-motley-judiciarys-unsung-rights-hero.

Albert Dunn

One source is a 1994 article in the *Lantern*, an ITC publication, "'Pickrick:'
Thirty Years Later." Another is the Civil Rights Digital Library, at http://
crdl.usg.edu/people/d/dunn_albert_lee_1935_2005/?Welcome.

Woodrow T. Lewis

Interviews with the author from 2019 through 2021 are used. I interviewed Lewis's former CORE colleague, the Reverend Waverly Yates, on

August 9, 2020. I interviewed Lewis about his bingo charities on January 9, 2021, and reviewed South Carolina news clippings and court papers from the 1990s about the charity license dispute, plus state filings listing the nonprofits in good standing.

Albert Sampson

Interviews with the author from 2019 through 2021 are used. The Illinois House of Representatives resolution honoring Sampson's Chicago church is at https://www.ilga.gov/legislation/fulltext.asp?DocName=09300HR0490lv&SessionID=3&GA=93&DocTypeID=HR&DocNum=0490&print=true. The *Chicago Reader* profiled Sampson's Black farmers market mission at https://www.chicagoreader.com/chicago/chicago-food-deserts-hopkins-park-black-farmers/Content?oid=2272825.

George Willis III

Information comes from interviews with Kay Willis in 2019 and 2020. Willis shared with me the booklet at his 2012 funeral, "The Lord Is My Shepherd," and a copy of her husband's resume.

Charles Wells Sr.

Sources include his wife's book, *The Minister Who Wore Many Hats*, and an obituary: https://www.legacy.com/obituaries/atlanta/obituary.aspx?n=charles-e-wells&pid=1961925.

INDEX

Page numbers in italics indicate caption or photograph.

ABOUT THE AUTHOR

RONNIE GREENE IS AN INVESTIGATIVE JOURNALIST who edits in-depth stories for Reuters and teaches graduate writing at Johns Hopkins University. Greene is the author of two critically acclaimed nonfiction books in addition to *Heart of Atlanta*. One is *Shots on the Bridge: Police Violence and Cover-Up in the Wake of Katrina*, published in 2015 and awarded the Investigative Reporters and Editors Book Award. His first book, *Night Fire: Big Oil, Poison Air, and Margie Richard's Fight to Save Her Town*, was published in 2008.

Greene's journalism has been honored with an Emmy Award, the Harvard Goldsmith Prize for Investigative Reporting, and the IRE Medal. A project he edited at the nonprofit Center for Public Integrity, Breathless and Burdened, earned the 2014 Pulitzer Prize for Investigative Reporting. Greene spent much of his career at the *Miami Herald* before moving near Washington in 2011. A *Miami Herald* project he coedited, Neglected to Death, was named a 2012 Pulitzer Prize Finalist in Public Service reporting.

Greene earned a journalism degree from Virginia Commonwealth University and a master's degree in nonfiction writing from Johns Hopkins University.